**Unlawful Violence**

**CRITICAL MEXICAN STUDIES**
*Series editor: Ignacio M. Sánchez Prado*

Critical Mexican Studies is the first English-language, humanities-based, theoretically focused academic series devoted to the study of Mexico. The series is a space for innovative works in the humanities that focus on theoretical analysis, transdisciplinary interventions, and original conceptual framing.

Other titles in the series:
    *The Restless Dead: Necrowriting and Disappropriation,*
        by Cristina Rivera Garza
    *History and Modern Media: A Personal Journey,* by John Mraz
    *Toxic Loves, Impossible Futures: Feminist Living as Resistance,*
        by Irmgard Emmelhainz
    *Drug Cartels Do Not Exist: Narcotrafficking in US and Mexican Culture,*
        by Oswaldo Zavala

# Unlawful Violence
Mexican Law
and Cultural Production

**Rebecca Janzen**

Vanderbilt University Press
*Nashville, Tennessee*

Copyright 2022 Vanderbilt University Press
All rights reserved
First printing 2022

Library of Congress Cataloging-in-Publication Data
Names: Janzen, Rebecca, 1985– author.
Title: Unlawful violence : Mexican Law and cultural production
   / Rebecca Janzen.
Description: Nashville : Vanderbilt University Press, [2022] | Series:
   Critical Mexican studies ; [volume 4] | Includes bibliographical
   references and index.
Identifiers: LCCN 2021049369 (print) | LCCN 2021049370 (ebook) | ISBN
   9780826504449 (paperback) | ISBN 9780826504456 (hardcover) | ISBN
   9780826504463 (epub) | ISBN 9780826504470 (pdf)
Subjects: LCSH: Violence—Mexico—History—21st century. | Criminal
   justice, Administration of—Mexico—History—21st century. |
   Mexico—Politics and government—21st century.
Classification: LCC HN120.Z9.V5 J36 2020  (print) | LCC HN120.Z9.V5
   (ebook) | DDC 303.60973/0905—dc23/eng/20211027
LC record available at https://lccn.loc.gov/2021049369
LC ebook record available at https://lccn.loc.gov/2021049370

# Contents

Acknowledgments                            vii

**Introduction**                                    1

1  Justice Breaks Down in *Una novela criminal*              13

2  Women Dream in *¡Basta!* and in Antiviolence Laws        47

3  Children's Rights and Dreams
    in *Historias de niñas extraordinarias*                        94

4  From Tapachula to Juárez: Migration and Violence       139

   Conclusion                                        165

Notes                           169
References                    201
Index                           223

# Acknowledgments

Thanks to my friends and family for supporting this research endeavor: my parents, Marlene Toews Janzen and Bill Janzen, and my brother and sister-in-law, Phil Janzen and Rachel Powers (and our pandemic Christmas). I would also like to thank extended family and friends, including Ghenette Houston and Brian Ladd, Steve and Gloria Houston, Jane Willms, Ben Willms, Paul Siebert and Moira Toomey, Dave Siebert and Dana Murray, Ally Siebert and Tyler Good, and relatives who have taken a special interest in this project: Clara Toews, Ed and Bev Toews, and Sol Janzen. Many thanks to my coven, Becky, Christy, Emily, Erin, Lindsay, Jenny, Carly, Laura, Liz, Mary, Allie, Rachel, Kristin, and Lauren.

My lady locusts, Amanda L. Petersen, Cheyla Samuelson, Ilana Luna, Sara Potter, and Rebecca Ingram, and my writing group, John Waldron, Emily Hind, Carolyn Fornoff, Carmen Serrano, Sophie Esch, and Rebeca Hey-Colón. My on-campus Zoom writing group, facilitated by Kunio Hara, and others, especially Alex Carrico and Danny Jenkins.

Thanks also to Ashley Byock for organizing an American Comparative Literature Association seminar with me about related issues in the spring of 2018, a conversation with Stephanie Kirk during the Mid-America Conference on Hispanic Literatures in 2017 about secular and religious law in colonial Mexico, a conversation with Laura Podalsky about the organization of this project at the Latin American Studies Association in 2018, and to other colleagues for engaging with me about issues of Mexican literature, legal studies, and form, at the Association for the Study of the Arts of the Present, Modern Language Association, and Latin American Studies Association conferences. Thanks to Carlos Amador, O. Darwin Tsen, and

D. Lee Jackson for organizing a seminar at the Association for the Study of the Arts of the Present in New Orleans in the fall of 2018, with collaboration from Robin Blyn, James Arnett, Brantley Nicholson, Victoria Lupascu, and others. Thanks also to Robin Blyn and Maria Bose for organizing a rich discussion in an American Comparative Literature Association seminar (with Darwin Tsen and Victoria Lupascu) in the spring of 2021, when I returned to these issues.

I wrote and revised most of this book during the summer of 2020 and during a junior teaching leave in the fall semester of 2020. During that time, I went on walks and hikes in many parks in South Carolina with Sarah and Jon Carroll (and their dogs), Grace Yan and Nick Watanabe (and their dog), and other friends. Alanna Breen, TJ Kimel, and Casey Carroll introduced me to fine whiskey, and I now appreciate some of it.

The University of South Carolina was also particularly important for this research. I mentioned the subject of law and literature to my colleague Andy Rajca a few weeks after I started working at U of SC and he immediately introduced me to a colleague in English, Anne Gulick, who gave me an excellent introductory bibliography on the subject and helpful tips for life in South Carolina. Eve Ross in the School of Law explained how law journals work and how lawyers and legal scholars conduct research. Eve also gave me a bibliography that forms the foundation of how I understand civil law in Mexico. Steve Austermiller at the Rule of Law Collaborative helped me understand US Agency for International Development projects that encourage civil law countries to adopt common law practices.

Thanks also to my friends in the Richland County Public Defender's Office whose anecdotes from the courts and jail in Columbia, South Carolina, were crucial to developing an abolitionist perspective. Special thanks to Kieley Sutton, who invited me to watch her in City Court, and to Nathan Rouse, for explaining how lawyers understand US laws and the US Constitution, and for giving me comparable examples to some particularities of Mexican law (such as the right to *amparo*).

The Midwest Modern Language Association provided me with a scholarship to conduct research at the Newberry Library in Chicago, which provided a historical understanding of the development of the law in Mexico. The College of Arts and Sciences supported this research with two faculty research grants. The first one allowed me to travel to Mexico and visit archives and museums in Torreón, Veracruz, Xalapa, and Mexico City. Yadira Hidalgo González, Elissa Rashkin, and Rob Kruger in Xalapa provided crucial insights for Chapters 2 and 3 of this book. The second research grant was meant to fund further travel to Mexico, and since that was not possible, it allowed for purchasing relevant books and for Sean Grattan's excellent developmental editing prior to submitting the manuscript. Very special thanks to Julie Ann Ward for sending a prepublication translation of Nadia Villafuerte's *Barcos en Houston* (*Ships in Houston*) for translations in Chapter 4.

Thanks to Vanderbilt University Press—to editor Zachary Gresham for offering feedback on draft materials and to series editor Ignacio M. Sánchez Prado. Thanks also to Zack for finding such excellent peer reviewers who turned in their reviews so quickly during a pandemic.

# Introduction

This book—*Unlawful Violence*—tells a story about life in Mexico in the twenty-first century that has been reorganized by a particular nexus of economic development and violence (2000–2020). Although it is cognizant of the broader context of widespread murder, it focuses on the experiences of Mexican people whose lived experiences include many examples of systemic violence and are closely tied to the twenty-first-century expansion of capitalism in Mexico. This book portrays those personal experiences of people in Mexico in congressional debates, materials that explain concepts of human rights, and ordinary people's letters to Mexican presidents. The violence in people's lives in Mexico, then, is "unlawful" because the very laws that have been passed in this same time period state that violence is a crime and, as such, should not be happening. As *Unlawful Violence* is a work of cultural and literary studies, not of philosophical ethics, it focuses on those laws as cultural products from the first two decades of the twenty-first century in Mexico.

*Unlawful Violence* approaches the first two decades of the twenty-first century (2000–2020) by comparing legal and literary texts, including the Mexican Constitution, human rights laws, novels, and short stories.[1] That is, the monograph compares the laws that outline lawful and unlawful violence with the literary texts that help us imagine the consequences of the epidemic of violence and that interrogate whether there is lawful violence in situations so dire that there is no other response possible. The politicians who author the laws and constitutional amendments, and the authors of novels and short stories describe violence experienced by alleged criminals in Mexico's criminal justice system, by women, by children, and by migrants.² These same legal and literary texts articulate hopes for a better future—the legal texts, for example, outline ways a society should be and the ways that the government and population should interact. Letters Mexican people have written to the president about violence in women's and children's lives (and now housed in archives) complement the legal texts that portray those experiences of violence. The literary texts, for their part, imagine relationships between characters in fictionalized Mexicos and fantastical universes—and in most cases, alternative paths for people in the Mexico of the twenty-first century.

Jorge Volpi's 2018 *Una novela criminal* (*A Novel Crime*)—which I examine in the first chapter—is one such novel. Volpi fictionalizes the experiences of Israel Vallarta, a middle-aged Mexican man who was accused of kidnapping and murder as part of his role in the Zodiac drug cartel.³ The novel intersperses its recounting of Israel's life with the first-person narrator's assertions of the author's experiences trying to find out what really happened. Volpi's novel includes insights into Mexico's declaration of a war on drugs and addresses the federal government's reformation of the Mexican Constitution and criminal justice procedures, purportedly to better deal with organized crime, drug trafficking, kidnapping, and murder. The government also passed a series of human rights laws that purport to protect vulnerable Mexicans. Thus, the Mexican government passed comprehensive constitutional reforms and human rights laws, claiming to secure people's lives. This has not happened. People's lives are not secure. Instead, there is an extremely high level of violence in the country.

On December 1, 2006, Felipe Calderón was sworn in as Mexico's fifty-sixth president. On December 11, he declared a war on drugs, which rhetorically aligned Mexico with US antinarcotics strategies and encouraged further cooperation in that vein. A year later, Calderón and US president George W. Bush signed the Mérida Initiative for hemispheric security.⁴ The initiative officially emphasized dismantling criminal organizations, strengthening all border controls, reforming the justice system, and decreasing the demand for drugs.⁵ In 2011, it was reframed under four pillars: Combating Transnational Criminal Organizations, Institutionalizing the Rule of Law While Protecting Human Rights, Creating a Twenty-First Century US-Mexico Border, and Building Strong and Resilient Communities.⁶ The majority of US aid to Mexico since Calderón's election has been under the umbrella of the Mérida Initiative. Since 2008, the US has committed approximately $3.1 billion in aid to Mexico, and $1.5 billion in US foreign aid channeled through the Mérida Initiative is arms exports.⁷ The portion of Mérida Initiative funding dedicated to arms exports dwarfs any of the initiative's policy commitments. That massive influx of firearms and other military technology does not even include amounts the US has given to train Mexican police officers or to secure Mexico's southern border. In effect, Mexico has experienced significant militarization and paramilitarization as a result of the Mérida Initiative.[8] Massive amounts of arms and military technology have caused, and then exacerbated, the epidemic of violence in Mexico. The literary and cultural critic Oswaldo Zavala goes so far as to state that cartels are a fiction, created to benefit those in power in Mexico and in the United States.[9] Armed groups aligned with cartels, both of which could have been paid by some part of the government, combat federal and state police forces, as well as the Mexican military. The so-called war on drugs has reorganized life in Mexico in significant ways: there are more police forces and branches of the military, and they are all more visible. There are also more unexplained deaths. The presence of military and police in daily life means that there are new iterations of old fears and also new fears entirely. Those already at society's margins experience the most acute consequences of violence, as their lives are the ones most at risk.

Since Calderón's official declaration of a war on drugs and signing of the Mérida Initiative, life in Mexico has been characterized by a rapid uptick in violence. US-manufactured arms that entered the country through Mérida Initiative aid, private purchases, and other forms of trade, undoubtedly made these numbers possible. So too did US-style training, or "professionalization," of police and armed forces.[10] The *Washington Post* estimates that more than one hundred thousand people were murdered in Mexico between 2006 and 2012.[11] The numbers decreased between 2013 and 2015, but then the situation worsened. Between 2016 and 2019, Mexico's official statistics show that 129,984 people were murdered in Mexico; the murder rate effectively tripled.[12] There has been a significant increase in state-sponsored violence, meaning that state actors, such as police and military, have effected violence on the Mexican people.[13] During the same period, the numbers of men working in private security as well as militias and criminal groups who had access to arms also increased. The state deflected blame for the increased numbers of homicides to members of these groups.[14] It did not prosecute these people with any type of regularity. A deadly combination of militias, paramilitary groups, and forces allied with specific regional powers, usually called cartels, were responsible for the unstoppable death march.

Crime has become background noise in Mexico.[15] Nevertheless, the horrifying numbers still do not take into account the quotidian violence that devastates human life even if it does not end in death. In some cases, a crime may fade from interest because the alleged perpetrators are from a group without much public sympathy, as in the case of criminal defendants or incarcerated people. In other cases, the victims may belong to a vulnerable group, such as women, children, or migrants, who live with a high level of socially acceptable violence, so their deaths must be exceptionally gruesome in order to make any type of headline.[16] Their deaths, though, are no less significant.

Violence in Mexico occurs in a context marked by the Mérida Initiative's military aid, which itself occurs within the broader expansion of capitalism in the twenty-first century. Sayak Valencia's characterization of this period as gore capitalism in her 2010 work of the same name is particularly appropriate. Valencia notes that Third World countries experience significant bloodshed in order to be able to participate in the logic of capitalism.[17] Bloody, violent capitalism leads to a spectacle of violence, which she calls the *régimen live*.[18] It is clear that violence in Mexico is a consequence of such forces. The cultural critic Jasbir K. Puar develops a similar idea in *The Right to Maim* (2017), in which she explains that the right to maim is a system that profits off the slow development of disability among increasing numbers of the population.[19] She observes that the US government deliberately debilitates its own population and supports other governments, most notably in Israel, that do the same.[20] And yet gory violence is not the only type that is part of people's lived experiences. Slavoj Žižek's terminology is useful here, particularly his explanation of how violence is subjective and objective. Subjective violence, which is understood as something that disturbs the normal order, is perhaps the most obvious to people in society. And yet as he reminds us, objective violence is more prevalent. For Žižek, objective violence is a category that encompasses both violence within language and systemic violence.[21] Systemic violence is particularly nefarious. As Žižek states in the introduction to his book on violence, it is crucial to the "functioning of our economic and political systems" and, as he goes on to develop, is tied to capitalist expansion.[22] These forms of violence are a way that those in power accumulate even more power through the dispossession of those with less power. This is similar to how things have occurred in other moments of violence in the expansion of capital, accelerated and more obviously violent given the evolution of military technologies.

Violence, then, is a result of broad social forces, and it is most often experienced by those who give the most and gain the least from the capitalist economic expansion that has marked life in the first two decades of the twenty-first century. Over the course of the two decades I examine in this book, from 2000 to 2020, Mexican politicians passed a series of federal laws and constitutional reforms. A seeming recognition of what the political scientist David A. Shirk calls exceptionally "high levels of criminal impunity and weak protections for the rights of accused criminals," the country's constitutional and federal penal code changed in important ways.[23] Through changes to its constitution and new laws, the Mexican government created a vision to regulate life for Mexicans in the twenty-first century.[24] This book examines those legal reforms with the understanding that they express, in the words of the Argentine feminist anthropologist Rita Laura Segato, "la acogida y el reconocimiento de la existencia de cada comunidad de intereses" (welcoming and acknowledging the existence of each special interest group).[25] That is, in the twenty-first century, the Mexican state has recognized specific interests via a number of new laws. In 2008, the Mexican government passed a series of constitutional reforms that shifted Mexico's criminal justice system, based on the civil law, to an accusatorial model modeled after the common law, with oral arguments in court and jury trials, among other reforms.[26] The federal government also passed laws that recognized women's right to a life free of violence, the 2007 Ley General de Acceso de las Mujeres a una Vida Libre de Violencia (General Law for Women to Access a Life Free of Violence) and the 2014 Ley General de los Derechos de Niñas, Niños y Adolescentes (General Law on Girls', Boys' and Adolescents' Rights).[27] In 2008, it decriminalized undocumented immigration and in 2011 passed a law guaranteeing certain forms of safety for migrants through the Ley de Migración (Migration Law).[28] Some legal scholars believe that the system has not been able to absorb so many changes, particularly as it lacks basic social support.[29] In spite of these valid criticisms, the fact that so many new laws were passed shows that many in Mexico's Chamber of Deputies and Senate responded to the protests of the Mexican people. Mexican legislators, then, attempted to address people's needs, in particular through laws that protect vulnerable groups.

I compare these legal texts with novels and short stories that deal with the experience of pretrial detention, women's lived experiences of violence, children's experiences of violence, and migrants' experiences as they cross Mexico's southern border and attempt to travel north to enter the United States. Some of them, like Volpi's *Una novela criminal*, comment on constitutional reforms or, as in the edited collection *¡Basta! Cien mujeres contra la violencia de género* (*Enough! 100 Women against Gender-Based Violence*), comment on the new laws, in this case, laws that protect women.[30] Others, like Nadia Villafuerte's *Barcos en Houston* (*Ships in Houston*; 2005) refer to a general climate of poor law enforcement and the lack of rule of law, and to the lived experiences of Central American migrants in Mexico.[31] These works envision a different future, but one that remains anchored in their portrayal of the lived experiences of violence in Mexico.

Legal and literary texts tell us about Mexico. They document reality and strive for a better future. Texts like Volpi's novel and Villafuerte's short stories describe the reality of Mexico in the period of their production; others, like the short stories in ¡Basta! also include dreams about a better future.[32] Literature may be thought of as more imaginative than law, and as offering a better future, but imagination and aspirations for a better future are not its exclusive domain. Law, too, can be imaginative and creative. As Guyora Binder and Richard Weisberg, experts in the study of law and literature, observe, both types of texts reflect their context in different ways, and law and literature appropriate, reproduce, and reshape a culture.[33] Their understanding of culture is similar to society, that is, a set of social norms, roles, and conventions that shape the law; the law, in turn, shapes what a culture produces, that is, its works of art, literature, and philosophy. Following Binder and Weisberg, both law and literature reflect their context, particularly its ideas of authority.[34] In line with their work, *Unlawful Violence* analyzes the form and content of legal and literary texts to offer a better understanding of the violence embedded in social structures in twenty-first century Mexico.

*Unlawful Violence* observes that constitutional reforms and human rights laws, as well as novels and short stories, share some commonalities in terms of form and genre that offer insight into twenty-first-century Mexico. They are both a type of fiction, told in a fragmentary or nonlinear way. As the literary critic Anna Kornbluh has shown in *Order of Forms: Realism, Formalism, and Social Space*, forms are "at root the analysis of how language furnishes a medium for composing sustained repetitions, delimited contours, performative conjurings, and synthetic abstractions" and "engineer parallel formations in the phenomenal realm of everyday life."[35] As Kornbluh's analysis goes on to explore, nineteenth-century realist novels are realist because of the way their structure relates to nineteenth-century social life, and whatever realistic thing they represent within that structure is realistic only because of the structure. In the case of both the laws and the literature that I analyze here, form relates to context, and the content makes sense only within the legal or literary form. The legal texts, novel, and short-story collections I examine are—like the novels Kornbluh analyzes—also realistic because of their forms. The structure of each text relates to dominant social structures, as each presents significant tension between forms that impose social order and the rhetorical devices and literary strategies that contest the violent social order. Volpi's *Una novela criminal*, for instance, reflects the devastating effects of a punitive criminal justice system and the way that television news media promoted a false version of events lauding that same system. Its narrator challenges the official version of events by acting as a detective and employing metafictional techniques that include inserting other texts into the narrative. This means that the text is less orderly in that it does not follow a chronological timeline or a single character. Nevertheless, the ways that *Una novela criminal* reproduces the disorder in the world outside the novel challenges the order imposed by punitive systems.

In the context of twenty-first-century Mexico, legal and literary texts also explicitly and deliberately relate to the lived experiences of the Mexican people. For this reason, my analysis of these texts builds on analyses of literary nonfiction in Latin America, in addition to engaging in dialogue with Kornbluh's understanding of form and genre. I dialogue with work on the important *crónica*, which, as the critics Ignacio Corona and Beth Jörgensen state, is closely related to journalistic human-interest pieces and literature's short story and essay.[36] The *crónica* blends literature and history and is an important genre in relating the experiences of twenty-first-century Mexicans. The critic Gabriela Polit Dueñas, for instance, has explored the ways contemporary journalists have used the *crónica* genre to relate what she calls "social suffering," or the challenges of living with the effects of neoliberalism.[37] While her work analyzes journalistic production, I extend it to analyze literary fiction. Each text I examine, such as the collection of women's experiences of violence in *¡Basta! Cien mujeres contra la violencia de género*, employs a nonfiction approach or is fiction rooted to its context in form and content. The relationship between nonfiction and neoliberalism is also in keeping with the critic Daniel Worden's *Neoliberal Nonfictions*. Worden observes that literature, art, and photography from the 1960s onward in the United States, as symptoms of neoliberal economic and social policy in place since the 1960s, adopt a nonfictional approach.[38] Mexican literature also exhibits these, such as the work of the celebrated author Cristina Rivera Garza, who was awarded a MacArthur "Genius" Grant in 2020. While I do not analyze Rivera Garza's work here, her work has certainly influenced the texts that I do analyze. Volpi's *Una novela criminal*'s uncertainty, for instance, evokes Rivera Garza's controversial work on Juan Rulfo, *Había mucha neblina o humo o no sé qué: Caminar con Juan Rulfo* (*There Was a Lot of Fog, or Smoke, or I'm Not Sure What: Walking with Juan Rulfo*), based on extensive research and on Rivera Garza's own long-standing participation in the Mexican literary realm.[39] Other earlier examples of Rivera Garza's oeuvre integrate the archival within a more clearly defined novelistic form, such as *Nadie me verá llorar (No One Will See Me Cry)*.⁴⁰ This work brings archival documents into an imagined history of the La Castañeda mental health facility, pejoratively termed a *manicomio*, or insane asylum, and fictionalizes her historical research. She re-creates versions of documents that would have been used in the mental health facility, such as intake forms, and photographs of the people who purportedly lived there.⁴¹ In Rivera Garza's novel, fictionalized documents become history and historical documents become fiction.

I compare the genres of law and literature in order to better understand both types of texts, in part by building on the work of other critics of law and literature. One of these is the foremost literary critic of human rights, Joseph R. Slaughter. He has compared the rise of human rights with the bildungsroman, or coming-of-age novel.⁴² In so doing, he observes that when it comes to the question of laws that deal with human rights, there are often "triumphalist narratives about the virtue of human rights" that coexist with extensive human rights violations, which are often "cloaked in the palliative rhetoric of humanitarian intervention [and] the chivalric defense of women and children."⁴³ Slaughter's work reminds us that the emphasis on human rights is coupled with other troubling impositions of colonialist and patriarchal forms of social order. Sarah Brouillette's *UNESCO and the Fate of the Literary* chronicles in significant detail the relationship between colonialism and the development of so-called world literature.⁴⁴ Anne W. Gulick's *Literature, Law, and Rhetorical Performance in the Anticolonial Atlantic* shows how African and Caribbean writers envision new postemancipation worlds through a genre broadly understood as romance, as in a narrative of overcoming, salvation, and redemption.⁴⁵ Slaughter and Gulick both focus on the notion of development and overcoming and a parallel to human rights and anticolonial thinking, beginning with novels such as *Robinson Crusoe* and the Haitian Constitution in the eighteenth centuries, which resonated with writers in the twentieth.⁴⁶ Twentieth-century Mexican literature, influenced by these examples of world literature and political movements, also examines its context. I argue that Mexican literature is concerned with the ideal future and with describing this context in as truthful a way as possible. The tension between ideals of a better future and realistic representation is a hallmark of the period under study here. The literary text analyzed in *Unlawful Violence* exhibit a formal tension between constraint and disorder, as they represent characters who allude to the lived experiences of incarcerated people, women, children, and migrants in Mexico and also imagine better futures for all vulnerable people.

The forms used in literature and the law to bring to life the tension between description and aspiration share other similarities as well. As Caroline Levine explains, a form is an arrangement, an ordering, a patterning, and a shaping.[47] Forms, like politics, constrain, differ, overlap, intersect, and travel.[48] They may respond to a given set of social conditions, but some forms endure over time.[49] Legal texts are written in a form that is relatively consistent over time. Laws are nonlinear, divided, as most are, into sections and subsections, and written by multiple authors without attribution. *Unlawful Violence* imagines laws almost as a series of short stories that are the lawmakers' representation of reality. It is easier to compare novels and short stories with legal texts by considering laws almost as a type of flash fiction. The short stories I analyze—and most short stories in edited volumes—are collected and organized into a whole. These short stories, as well as the novels that I analyze, are told in nonlinear ways. There are multiple narrative voices in a single text. The literary texts differentiate between these voices, whereas the laws, which are also the product of multiple voices, do not point the reader to the multiple possible authors involved in their production. Moreover, in line with Levine's explanation, these formal elements are not unique to twenty-first-century Mexico. Novels in Spanish have presented metafictional narrative strategies, such as a narrator with an authorial voice, stories within a story, and intertextuality, since the first portion of Miguel de Cervantes's *Don Quixote* was published in 1605.[50] Yet the way these literary and legal texts employ established forms—particularly the way the texts exhibit certain forms that mirror the constraints of a punitive social order—and the ways narrators employ established techniques to contest the violent order relate to the Mexican context in the twenty-first century.

The potential in fragmentary and nonlinear stories is in line with what the critic David Palumbo-Liu has shown about interpreting social media dealing with human rights abuses and the 2012 Arab Spring. For Palumbo-Liu, the nonlinear nature of social media, with "multiple and possibly conflictual assertions of truth, value, and meaning," leads us to new ways of seeing rights that "would have been invisible otherwise, simply because they did not fit neatly into (or at least did not fit in *well*) a properly recognized and purposeful 'story.'"[51] Stories presented on social media and in print may be truthful and relate to their context in significant ways, but they may not always be rational. Twenty-first-century literature in Mexico is indebted, for example, to the absurdist and irrational traditions. The legal texts and works of literature analyzed in *Unlawful Violence* present stories with a clearer relationship to people's lived experiences, and some elements are not logical or linear. The short stories written by children in *Historias de niñas extraordinarias* (*Stories of Extraordinary Girls*; 2016) and *Historias de niñas extraordinarias 2* (*Stories of Extraordinary Girls 2*; 2017), for instance, include vampires and evil queens.[52] These stories jump around in time and space. In these texts, and in others, I return to Palumbo-Liu's observations and suggest a similar potential for understanding the Mexican context by reading nonlinear and not-always-logical stories.

At the same time, certain characteristics of legal and literary texts ground us in the twenty-first-century security apparatus. Forces of order interfere with the ways that legal and literary texts meander nonlinearly, as they represent people's lived experiences. I understand these forces in a formal sense, through the ways that laws are divided into sections, articles, and fragments, or the way a narrator takes authority in a short story to connect the ending to the beginning. The interruptions may also be in terms of content, where a discussion of various types of violence immediately follows a discussion of women's rights in the law that guarantees women a right to a life free of violence.[53] Similarly, chapters that deal with short stories in edited anthologies explore the question of ordering the stories. In the collection *¡Basta!*, for instance, stories are organized to offer multiple perspectives on the same issue. Toward the end of *¡Basta!*, a story called "La delegación," which appears on one side of the book, deals with a police officer retraumatizing a female character who reports sexual violence. On the facing page, in "SOS ¿Nos ayudamos?," a first-person narrator describes how her boss quashed her efforts to better the lives of women experiencing violence. Authority interrupts the female protagonists in both stories, and the stories' ordering shows that the public and bureaucrats are equally vulnerable to imposition of further authority.[54]

*Unlawful Violence*, then, analyzes texts that illustrate the many social sectors in Mexico attempting to create a better future. The literary and legal genres, as well as the forms they employ, allude to these extensive efforts to reorder society in order to make it better for all people. And yet the efforts are sometimes at cross-purposes. I focus on the ways these seemingly contradictory efforts interact and collide, and following Caroline Levine's observations about conflicting forms, I also aim to develop a "careful, nuanced understanding of the many different and often disconnected arrangements that govern social experience."[55] I hope that my reading of laws and literature as representations of violence and as dreams of a better future pushes me—and my readers—toward a better (and necessary) future.

The first chapter, "Justice Breaks Down in *Una novela criminal*," analyzes Jorge Volpi's *Una novela criminal*, about a bungled criminal case, alongside the constitutional reforms that significantly changed Mexico's criminal justice system.[56] The novel is told largely from the perspective of a narrator with Volpi's authorial voice, in the style of Latin American detective fiction. The narrator situates himself as a detective uncovering the truth about a criminal case, and the resulting novel is nonlinear, with shifting plotlines. I compare the organizing strategies in the novel and in the constitutional reforms to show that security forces enter both the constitution and the novel, interrupting the flow of the legal and the literary texts. By examining these organizing strategies, I show that while the constitutional reforms did not improve the lives of people in Mexico, the idea of reorganization has potential—if that reorganization is substantial enough to eliminate the often-unnoticed structural violence experienced by people such as the characters in the literary text.

The second chapter, "Women Dream in ¡Basta! and in Antiviolence Laws," engages with the violence that women experience in Mexico. It compares the Ley General de Acceso de las Mujeres a una Vida Libre de Violencia and a collection of very short stories, *¡Basta! Cien mujeres contra la violencia de género*. It contextualizes the stories and the law with women's own letters to the Mexican president about women's experiences of violence. These letters and the stories make reference to intimate partner violence, the genocide levels of violence against women, and the social forces that lead to these situations. The chapter shows that the law aims to protect women from experiencing any type of violence, whether in their homes or the courtrooms, and the stories' poignant illustrations prove that the goal of a fair criminal justice system has not yet been achieved. In both types of texts, patriarchal forces—often male partners or police—enforce a violent order and interrupt paragraphs that seem out of sequence or streams-of-consciousness reflections that appear disjointed. Examining the structure of the texts and these interruptions offers insight into how the seeming disorder of structural violence can lead to change.

The third chapter, "Children's Rights and Dreams in *Historias de niñas extraordinarias*," posits that children's rights are more nuanced than the perceived need of children to be protected from danger. To explore these issues, I examine the law Ley General de los Derechos de Niñas, Niños y Adolescentes, passed in 2014. The chapter then contextualizes this law with letters written to the president by or about children's experiences of violence. I bring this historical context to bear on my analysis of fiction written by girls about their lives, published in the same period as the laws and the letters to the president. The girls' stories chart fictionalized versions of their lived experiences and their hopes for the future in two edited collections, *Historias de niñas extraordinarias* and *Historias de niñas extraordinarias 2*. The chapter examines these different approaches to describing the lived experiences of children in Mexico. It shows that figures like parents, teachers, and other adults maintain the status quo in both types of texts, and it explores how the short stories' portrayals of girls' fantastical dreams of the future might counter the violent social order.

The fourth chapter, "From Tapachula to Juárez: Migration and Violence," deals with short stories that portray the Guatemala-Mexico border and the experiences of Central American migrants in Mexico. To do so, it compares the Ley de Migración (2011) with Nadia Villafuerte's collection of short stories about life at the border, *Barcos en Houston*. In both texts, forces of order, police officers, migration officials, and detention centers interrupt discussions of the free movement of people and, in the case of Villafuerte's collection, polyphonic stream-of-consciousness stories. The structure—and content—of *Barcos en Houston* captures the experience of migration and the interruptions encourage us as critics to consider how to reorganize structures to allow all people to flourish.

CHAPTER 1
# Justice Breaks Down in *Una novela criminal*

On December 8, 2005, the Mexican Federal Police arrested Israel Vallarta and Florence Cassez for kidnapping three victims, as part of their role in the gang Los Zodiacos, of which they were allegedly members. They were alleged to have held Cristina Ríos and her ten-year-old son Christian for fifty days and Ezequiel Elizalde for sixty-five.[1] The police alleged that as gang members, Vallarta and Cassez had kidnapped a woman called Valeria Cheja and then went on to kidnap three more people.[2] The day after police arrested Vallarta and Cassez, the television channel Televisa re-created and broadcast their staged arrest, as if the events were being recorded live. Israel and Florence were then detained. Cassez, a French citizen, was tried in Mexico, where initially a judge denied her appeal for extradition to France or to be tried by French law.[3] Eventually, after extensive negotiations between the French president Nicolas Sarkozy and the Mexican president Felipe Calderón, her case was retried. The Mexican Supreme Court tried the case under an *amparo* provision and, as a result of a Mexican constitutional provision for foreigners who have been alleged to have committed a crime, Florence Cassez was released to French custody in 2013.[4] In 2020, Vallarta had not yet had his trial.[5] He remains "more than anything a victim of this power that tortures him and that denied him due process" (*ante todo una víctima de ese poder que lo torture y le negó un proceso equitativo y justo*).[6]

Jorge Volpi's award-winning novel *Una novela criminal* situates Israel Vallarta's arrest and detention in the context of capitalist expansion and violence in Mexico. Volpi's self-proclaimed "nonfiction novel" explains how the Mexican government's interest in curbing drug trafficking led to the arrests of Vallarta and Cassez. Moreover, as *Una novela criminal* portrays the events that surround Vallarta's case it relates them to the context of sweeping constitutional reforms—part of programs related to the Mérida Initiative.[7] Volpi's work is based on interviews and rigorous archival research. As the reviewer Edward Waters Hood states, "Volpi, an accomplished writer interested in ethical issues, skillfully re-creates the events of this egregious violation of civil and human rights."[8] *Una novela criminal* reconstructs the events around the case, including the kidnapping, the arrest of Vallarta and Cassez, and the release of their victims, and it shows that the Mérida Initiative's goal of guaranteeing security in Mexico was, at best, a pipedream.

Volpi's fictionalized history explicitly comments on how the constitutional reforms—which adopted a model of criminal justice common in the United States, enshrining the presumption of innocence for people accused of crimes and implementing what is typically called the accusatorial model, in which lawyers make oral rather than written arguments in court and in which jury trials are allowed—did not protect the rights of incarcerated people such as the novel's character and the historical figure of Israel Vallarta. As I show how the literary and constitutional texts relate to one another, I focus on the ways that both texts include strategies that represent order, or accept the status quo, and strategies of disorder, which challenge the status quo. I also explore the question of truthfulness. Both types of text are truthful descriptions in that some aspect of the legal and literary texts portrays some aspect of the context in which they were produced and the context they claim to represent. Both constitutional reforms and novel also move beyond the descriptive. The constitution attempts to envision a better criminal justice system, and Volpi's novel sheds light on how the news falsely portrays events.

I also examine the form of both legal and literary texts, and my reading shows that both texts are organized in such a way that they uphold the status quo. I also find *forces of order* in my analysis, which I understand as any social force that upholds the status quo, or what Žižek calls objective violence. The forces of order in the literary and legal texts relate in some way to the forces that claim to ensure Mexican people's security by advancing their own financial interests, distributing arms among multiple sectors of the population, tacitly accepting high numbers of murders, and arresting and incarcerating people who may or may not have committed crimes.

Formal or aesthetic organizing forces in the Mexican constitution and Volpi's *Una novela criminal* uphold the carceral status quo. The constitution, for instance, is divided into opening statements and headings that group articles together. Although it begins by recognizing the human rights of Mexican citizens, it devotes far more space to outlining acceptable punishments and the procedures of punishment. The Mexican Constitution's organizing strategies and content relate to the forces that impose a violent social order in the world outside the constitutional text. Volpi's novel, for its part, is structured into sections and chapters that relate events in a nonchronological fashion. The narrator relates the ways the Mexican state has imposed order on the lives of the characters by adopting an authorial and authoritative voice, which makes for an organized account.[9] The violent acts of the narrator in *Una novela criminal* mirror the structural violence that underlies the events in the novel.

The Mexican Constitution and *Una novela criminal* also include formal strategies that challenge the *existing order*, a phrase I use interchangeably with terms such as *violent status quo*, *objective violence*, and *structural violence*. The most notable strategy of disorder in the Constitution is that the articles are not organized in a linear way. The constitution is, like most constitutions, divided into sections and articles, but readers must still make connections between segments that present very disparate ideas. The Mexican Constitution is disjointed, in an aesthetic sense, just like Volpi's novel. *Una novela criminal* moves rapidly between topics, and in the span of a single paragraph it can move from microscopic examples to commentary on political themes. Volpi's text becomes even more disjointed as it employs intertextuality, inserting press coverage and other documents into the text and quoting and reinventing parts of key interviews. He frames his own meandering attempts around the issue of "truthfulness," or his attempt to accurately describe the two crimes in the novel: the kidnapping and the staged arrest. The literary text uses resources available to try to convince others of its version of events, including certain elements of the detective genre, literary nonfiction, and the Crack literary movement. Volpi's novel also returns us to metafictional strategies, such as the narrator's constantly referring to himself and speaking to the reader, as well as intertextuality. I engage with both form and content to examine the tension between organizational strategies (or maintaining the existing order) and disorganization. That tension between forces of order and forces of disorder, then, relates to the context in which the novel and the constitutional reforms were produced and offers insight into potential avenues for further and more productive change.

I would now like to spend a moment discussing the events that immediately preceded the arrests of Vallarta and Cassez. Their arrests took place in

2005, toward the end of President Vicente Fox's term (2000–2006), about six months before Felipe Calderón was elected in July 2006—amid credible allegations of electoral fraud—and a year before Calderón was sworn in to office.[10] Calderón was Mexico's second president from the Partido de Acción Nacional, or PAN, which had first come to federal power only six years earlier, after a nearly seventy-year hold on federal power by the Partido Revolucionario Institucional. He took office surrounded by armed guards and faced significant opposition from the leftist Partido de la Revolución Democrática, and its candidate Andrés Manuel López Obrador (AMLO, coincidentally the president of Mexico today).[11] Calderon's party held just under half the seats in the Chamber of Deputies, 206 of 500, and 51 of the 128 Senate seats. That Calderón's party did not have a majority in either legislative chamber meant that, as president, Calderón was in a position to respond to new coalitions that might form in either chamber.

The Calderón administration was obsessed with security. It deployed the term amid its rhetoric of "safety and security" to justify the ways that it controlled the lives of the Mexican people. According to the journalist Dawn Paley, his administration set off "an unprecedented array of bone-chilling episodes."[12] Mexican people were terrified, and their fear "create[d] fertile ground for new forms of social control."[13] That social control, repression, and terror have since become a situation of total extermination. Even as crime was going down, Calderón doubled down on security rhetoric, and Mexico became even more dangerous.[14] Indeed, "el Estado comparte sus tecnologías y técnicas de dominación y administración de la muerte con los sujetos de la violencia privatizada—en particular los criminales" (the state and privatized forms of violence employ the same technologies and techniques to dominate others and administer death, particularly with regards to criminals).[15] The obsession with security preserved a very dangerous status quo and exacerbated the country's problems.

Volpi's novel represents the social, political, and historical events surrounding Calderón's 2006 election. As *Una novela criminal* represents these events, it highlights how Calderón created a powerful enemy, drugs, to distract from the circumstances of his election. *Una novela criminal* re-creates Calderón's inaugural speech, in which he reportedly stated: "Las soluciones a los problemas deben construirse por la vía de la paz y la legalidad . . . dentro del marco de las leyes e instituciones que nos hemos dado los mexicanos y no fuera de él" (The solutions to these problems should be constructed via peace and legality . . . within, rather than outside of, Mexico's laws and institutions).[16] Reforms to legal matters and institutional expansion would be hallmarks of his tenure. Calderón—as recounted by Volpi—

goes on to state: "Sé que reestablecer la seguridad no será fácil ni rápido, que tomará tiempo, que costar mucho dinero, e incluso y por desgracia, vidas humanas. Pero ténganlo por seguro, ésta es una batalla que tenemos que librar y que unidos vamos a ganar a la delincuencia" (I know that reestablishing security with be neither easy nor fast, that it will take time, cost a lot of money, and, unfortunately, human life. But rest assured, this is a battle that we have to win, and that together we will win, over delinquency).[17] Calderón would gain significant support by echoing US rhetoric of the so-called war on drugs, which imagines the issue of drugs as a battle for freedom and human lives, rather than a battle to enrich the already wealthy. On the next page, the narrator comments on historical events, connecting Calderón's rousing speech to the president's subsequent actions that began using the army in the so-called war on drugs: "Diez días después, el 11 de diciembre de 2006, sin que nada en su campaña lo anticipase, el nuevo presidente ordena que el ejército—una institución que gozaba de un respeto casi unánime por su auxilio a la población en caso de desastres naturales—abandone sus cuarteles y, al lado de la Policía Federal, se involucre en el combate frontal al narcotráfico" (Ten days later, on December 11, 2006, before anyone in his campaign anticipated it, the new president ordered that the army—an instituted that had near unanimous support from the population, because of its assistance during natural disasters—abandon its bases and, join the Federal Police in its fight against drug trafficking).[18] In the historical context, the president turned to the army, an institution with far more public credibility than the police force, to assist him in his crusade. As the novel reminds us, Calderón's decision to use the army in the purported war on drugs helped the Mexican people shift their focus from the dubious circumstances of his election. The narrator explains, "En la guerra contra el narco, Calderón descubre una amenaza más inquietante que los desafíos de su rival: un enemigo que encarna el mal absoluto y que le permitirá reunificar al país en torno a una causa común" (Calderón found that the war on drugs was a more troubling threat than his rival: it was an enemy that incarnated absolute evil and a common cause that would allow him to unite the country").[19] The drug war was a specter Calderón invoked to unify the Mexican people. As the novel claims, it seemed at the time that even the people who believed he and his party had committed electoral fraud were swayed by his commitment to human life and the fact that he was willing to deploy the army as part of the so-called war on drugs, as the public supported the military far more than the police. Only with time would the connections among security rhetoric, armed violence at the hands of the military and police, and deaths become as clear as it is in the novel.

One way that Calderón's administration claimed it would increase respect for human life and deal fairly with those who participated in the drug trade was through a series of sweeping constitutional reforms that dealt with the criminal justice system. A brief word about the constitution before turning to analyze its text and Calderón's reforms to it: the Mexican Constitution gives a framework for the rights of Mexican people and the government's responsibilities toward them, and in Mexico, elected officials modify the constitutional text more regularly than is done in, say, the United States. In this sense, reforms under Calderón were part of a long tradition—even as the parts of the constitution that his government revised related to his particular context. In June 2008, two years after he was elected, Calderón's administration modified Articles 16–22, 73, 115, and 123 of the constitution.[20] The amendments to the ten articles pertain to the criminal justice system. They encompass arrests, pretrial detention, court cases, and sentencing. One of the articles, Article 20, is especially significant because it transformed Mexico's civil law system, and traditions of case research and paperwork, into an adversarial system based on oral arguments, as in US law. As *Una novela criminal* observes, it transforms the "modelo inquisitorio en uno acusatorio, introduciendo los juicios orales, los jurados populares y la presunción de inocencia" (inquisitorial model into an accusatorial model, introducing oral arguments, juries of the defendant's peers, and presumption of innocence).[21] In this way, the Mexican legal system begins to mirror the legal system in countries in the common law system, including the United States.

This fact is not an accident. Rather, it is part of a broader strategy in US foreign aid. Indeed, the US government has invested significant sums of money to ensure that other countries adopt a US-style system, as it works to improve security and the rule of law in those same countries. Dawn Paley interviewed Oscar Castrejón Rivas, president of the College of Lawyers in Chihuahua in 2011, and his comments show the potential and pitfalls of these reforms. Castrejón said, "Just as within globalized commerce [the US] wants a world where everywhere there is a McDonalds, an Applebee's, a Home Depot, a Walmart, a Sam's [Club]; they also want a world where tribunals are the same everywhere as they are in the United States, so that whatever legal issues they have can be dealt with perfectly well by a legal firm from the United States, which can operate in the US, in Puerto Rico, in Argentina, in Chile, and so on."[22] These reforms, though, come out of a colonial mindset. The US government only obliquely acknowledges its work to remake other countries' legal systems in its image. Experts from the US claim that these US-style reforms will allow it to better respond to complaints from US citizens in other countries. These experts find it convenient to ignore the very close relationship between the reforms to legal systems in other countries (always under the rule of law) or the use of security rhetoric and colonialism.

The constitution would be the overarching guide for other laws, and, as perspectives on these other laws change, so too does the constitution. The constitution begins with a statement from Revolutionary president Venustiano Carranza, who oversaw Mexico's first constitution under a new type of government in the twentieth century. Carranza's words introduce the material that follows in the 1917 constitution and in every subsequent revision. The current constitution, like previous revisions, is a series of paragraphs. They are grouped first into titles, then into chapters, and finally into articles, which are loosely grouped by theme. Some constitutional articles are several short paragraphs, and others are mere sentences. In a given article, the first paragraph establishes whether the article deals with government responsibilities, individual rights, or collective rights, and then goes on to specify the nature of those responsibilities or rights. The subsequent, equally short paragraphs are often numbered and offer further details. When considered together, legal scholars conclude that it is a document that contains the values that undergird the rule of law in Mexico: sovereignty, liberty, legality, divisions of powers, equality, and others.[23]

There is significant potential for interpretation in the Mexican Constitution. From the perspective of a literary scholar, the constitution describes both Mexico as it is and Mexico as its authors wish it were. It is an aspirational and a descriptive document, at once fantasy and narrative nonfiction. I extend Levine's observations about competing forms in a single text to the question of genre here. As she stated, no form has a monopoly on a time period or work of literature; rather, each form is capable of disturbing the other's organizing power.[24] The literary critic Anne Gulick observed that postemancipation constitutions in the Atlantic world represented a gesture toward "new political identities that were well beyond the realm of possibility in a colonial/imperial imagination."[25] I extend her observations to the Mexican Constitution, which was rooted in massive social changes in the mid-nineteenth and early twentieth centuries. For this reason, the aspirations within the Mexican Constitution are better understood as examples of fantastic literature rather than as policy statements. The document that endures in the early twenty-first century is also one that is wildly optimistic about the possibilities for a better future in Mexico. The Mexican Constitution begins "En los Estados Unidos Mexicanos todas las personas gozarán de los derechos humanos reconocidos en esta Constitución" (In the United States of Mexico, all individuals will enjoy [have] the human rights recognized in this Constitution).[26] The way that the Mexican Constitution begins thus recognizes the human rights of all people in Mexico. At the same time, there is tension between the optimistic recognition of these rights and the way the state intends to regulate them. The very same paragraph of the very first article goes on to state that these rights cannot be restricted "salvo en los casos y bajo las condiciones que esta Constitución establece" (except in the cases and under the conditions established by this Constitution).[27] The tension between the world as it is and the world as it ought to be is present from the very beginning of the constitutional text. I am reminded of Toni Morrison, who stated in an interview with Elizabeth Farnsworth that "utopias are designed by who is not there, by people who are not allowed in."[28] A utopian or aspirational text is more descriptive than it would initially appear. Thus, in the constitutional text, these two genres exist in tension with each other, and it is difficult to categorize the constitution as either entirely descriptive or entirely aspirational.

The remainder of the Mexican Constitution is divided into *títulos*, or sections, and then articles, and some articles are further subdivided. Each section continues to exhibit the tension between the aspirational and the descriptive. The aspirational, following Morrison's line of thinking, is an indirect description of the present by those who are marginalized by those in power. The first section continues with the right to nondiscrimination, then is followed by indigenous autonomy, a discussion of the nature of the Mexican federation of states, and the nature of the Mexican family. It continues with descriptions of liberty of employment, thought, and opinion; restrictions on public employees; freedom of assembly; freedom to use arms; and a comprehensive discussion of the criminal justice system. The discussion of individual human rights even includes a discussion of eligibility for the presidency.[29] Then, in a second grouping of constitutional articles, the text outlines national sovereignty and the forms of government, in other words, how the government will respond to guarantee those rights.[30] The third grouping deals with the division of power and further details the functioning of government.[31] The fourth section deals with the civil service, and the fifth section further details the relationship of federal government, states, and the capital of Mexico City.[32] The sixth section outlines the nature of work in Mexico, and the seventh section gives general guidelines about the limits on individual rights for those who have committed crimes.[33] The text then discusses the circumstances under which the constitution can be reformed, and it concludes by describing the precise nature of constitutional inviolability.³⁴ This brief outline shows sharp contrasts in the constitutional text, for instance, between the articles that describe freedom of expression and freedom of assembly, which are followed by a discussion of the criminal justice system. Similarly, after outlining the nature of the civil service and the division of power at state and federal levels, the constitution explains how to deal with criminals. At every turn, the constitutional text imposes an order or reminds readers of the violent status quo.

The headings and subheadings in the text facilitate the somewhat-abrupt shifts in theme between how Mexico could be and how Mexico is. I imagine the headings and subheadings and general disjunctures as textual elements that facilitate and interrupt the flow of reading. The term *flow* comes from the work of Raymond Williams, who in 1975 described watching television as "total flow," that is, seamless connections between different shows.³⁵ In 1991, Frederic Jameson brought the observations to bear, calling constant television streaming, and the lack of critical distance it encourages, total flow.³⁶ I think of the constitutional text and the "total flow" created as one reads it as analogous to the flow of late twentieth-century television that these theorists describe. The headings and subheadings are like the opening credits of new shows every hour or half hour on television, and commercial breaks are similar to subheadings. The headings, credits, and breaks remind readers and viewers that there is a new idea before them, but they do not break the format or encourage critical distance from the television show—or the constitutional text. Sayak Valencia goes even further than these thinkers, showing that in the twenty-first century, media "fabrica no solo contenidos sino formas de pensar, gustos y comportamientos que legitiman ciertas perspectivas por encima de otras por medio de la psicopatía y la cultura de la celebridad" (creates not only content but also ways of thinking, taste, and behavior that legitimize certain perspectives rather than others, through psychopathy and celebrity culture).³⁷ Reading the constitution with these remarks in mind, I conclude that the headings and subheadings lull readers into believing that the articles follow a recognizable logic. At the same time, they prevent reading the constitution from beginning to end without stopping. The headings and subheadings may also encourage less critical distance between the reader and the text.

The gaps between sections are not so extensive as to allow for all the creative wanderings of the reader's imagination, yet they do encourage some level of critical thinking. Let us take, for example, the third article. The text follows the lengthy second article, which deals primarily with Indigenous rights, and ends with subsection C on the rights of Afro-Mexican people, which text tells us was added on August 9, 2019.³⁸ Article 3, in bold, follows this explanatory text, telling us that everyone has the right to education at the preschool, primary, and secondary levels. The next paragraph tells us that education is to be inclusive, public, free, and secular. A third paragraph was removed. A fourth paragraph describes the emphasis of education on human rights and equality.[39] A fifth paragraph was added in 2019 to emphasize that education takes into account the interests of children. The sixth paragraph describes teachers, and the following two paragraphs deal with their training.[40] The text then moves from teacher training to describe school buildings and specific policy platforms, and to reiterate equal access to education for all children. The third article of the Mexican Constitution concludes by describing councils that function like school boards.[41] Article 4, which recognizes men and women as equal before the law, follows Article 3. This lengthy article is representative of other articles within the constitution's text. It cannot be read closely without noticing these constant shifts in topic, nor can a series of articles be read while being lulled into Jameson's flow. Paying close attention to the content of each article shows that the headings and subheadings are a necessary organizing force. Without them, the text would not make sense. The emphases on rules and regulations within the text mirror the structural organizational strategy of the Mexican Constitution. The aesthetic and political forms come together in the opening articles of the constitution.

The constitutional text was insufficient in terms of preserving the status quo in the early twenty-first century, and thus, Mexican politicians passed multiple constitutional reforms, particularly pertaining to Articles 16–20, which deal with the criminal justice system. Legal scholars such as William Hine-Ramsberger have noted that the legal reforms aimed to respond to a situation of extreme violence and absent rule of law.[42] What legal scholars call "bringing about the rule of law" meant aligning it with the common law system. According to its narrator, "[en] el sistema anglosajón—o la mayor parte de los sistemas jurídicos del mundo . . . la presunción de inocencia es un principio básico y el fiscal ha de probar la responsabilidad del inculpado" (in the common law system—or, the majority of judicial systems in the world . . . the presumption of innocence is a basic principle and the prosecutor has to prove the defendant is guilty).[43] The new system, according to Volpi's novel, contrasts sharply with the system Mexico had before 2008. At that time, the narrator goes on to state of the civil law system: "Se presume la culpabilidad y es el acusado quien se ve obligado a demostrar su inocencia" (it presumed guilt, and it is the accused who is obliged to demonstrate their innocence").[44] Lawyers presented their cases in writing before a judge: "la mayor parte de las diligencias se llevan a cabo por escrito en una jerga tan opaca como las salas de audiencias adjuntas a las cárceles" (the majority of cases are carried out with a written legal jargon that is as opaque as the rooms in the jails where hearings take place).[45] The judges have exceptional power, as there are no juries: "absuelven o condenan al tiempo que imponen las penas" (absolve or condemn when they impose penalties).[46] As all cases were adjudicated on the basis of written submissions, rather than oral arguments,

> Podría decirse que existe una especie de jerga judicial, alejada por completo de la lengua literaria, cuyos principales rasgos son la devoción por los gerundios, las interminables oraciones coordinadas y subordinadas y el uso arbitrario de los tiempos verbales. Un estilo similar, acaso sólo un poco menos desgarbado, prevalece en las transcripciones de discursos. (*One could say that there is a type of legal jargon, completely unrelated to literary language, whose key characteristics are a devotion to gerunds, endless sentences with coordinate and subordinate clauses, and arbitrary use of verb tense. A similar style, only a little less ungainly, prevails in the transcriptions*)[47]

The accused remain incarcerated throughout the process. Mexico's punitive criminal justice system produces lengthy legal briefs and prisons full of inmates with long paper trails explaining why they ought to remain there.

Legal scholars understand that the rule of law would align the Mexican system with the system that prevails in the United States.[48] The novel alludes to the parallels between Mexican and US systems by referring to famous cinematic trials in US film, with somber courts: "al fondo de un salón, por lo general de madera de encino, advertimos un amplio estrado; un secretario anuncia el arribo del juez, el cual avanza con su toga negra y provoca que todos los presentes se levantan" (there is a dais located in the depths of a oak-paneled room; a secretary announces the judge's arrival, who advanced with his black robe, and whose presence causes everyone in the room to rise).[49] After the opening ritual, the court case begins: "En los días posteriores presenciamos un encarnizado duelo verbal . . . Días después viene la deliberación de los jurados y a la postre la sentencia" (In the days that follow there is a verbal duel . . . Days later, the jurors deliberate and the sentencing comes at the end).[50] The narrator of *Una novela criminal* concludes that court cases are speedy and courtrooms are interesting—at least as represented in *To Kill a Mockingbird* and *Twelve Angry Men*.[51] In *To Kill a Mockingbird*, a white lawyer aptly defends an innocent Black man, and the man is still sentenced to death. This film likely made many white Americans aware of the lack of civil rights for Black Americans.[52] For its part, *12 Angry Men* showed the problems and the potential within jury trials, that is, for such trials to lead to unjust rulings, unless there is a figure who, like the protagonist of that film, urges their fellow jurors to carefully review the evidence. The fact that Volpi's novel compares Mexico's new system to *To Kill a Mockingbird* and *12 Angry Men* suggests that legal reforms could change Mexico's court rituals and bring them in line with those representations of US courts.

The 2008 revisions to the ten constitutional articles do bring the Mexican criminal justice system in line with that of the United States, on paper. Articles 16–22 are part of the first subsection, which deals with individual rights. The revision to Article 16, for instance, explains when, where, and under which circumstances police may arrest private citizens.[53] The article concludes by stating that in times of peace people cannot be forced to house armed forces. Article 17 then begins by outlining that the legal system is to be speedy and impartial, and article 18 outlines how, and under which circumstances, people may be imprisoned before a trial.[54] These reasonably sequential articles offer some latitude of interpretation. The subsequent Article 19 reminds readers of the order of prison, clarifying that prison is a place for rehabilitation, and that even there, Mexicans have rights.[55] Article 20 is divided into three lettered subsections, which give an overview of the criminal justice process and then details the rights first of the accused and then of the victims.[56] The constitution continues in this vein and then turns abruptly to organized crime in Article 22. The minimal reforms to Article 73 and 115 establish that the federal government is the entity in charge of federal crimes and give police greater power to arrest and detain people.[57] The amendments that reformed the criminal justice system were meant to bring about substantial change. The aspirations in these articles are much more modest and respond to an understanding of Mexico as full of violent organized crime. The reforms, however, do not question the misguided belief that Mexico is a violent country. Instead, the amendments allow the police and court system to violently impose the status quo in new ways.

The legal reforms have not accomplished the stated goals of improving access to justice; rather, they have ensured the imposition of state-sanctioned violence. As Hine-Ramsberger states, "Without an efficient and successful implementation of the provisions that seek to establish an accusatory criminal justice system, the 2008 amendments threaten to further decrease the rule of law in Mexico."[58] Indeed, Volpi's novel also portrays the challenges associated with legal reforms: "Las resistencias para aplicarlo han sido, desde entonces, incontables. Los mexicanos somos juzgados hoy con este modelo patizambo" (There is nearly endless resistance to applying them. So, we Mexicans today are judged by this bow-legged model).[59] In other words, it is worse now than it was before because the legal system combines both styles in an unhelpful way. After 2008, lawyers still file "una avalancha de diligencias por escrito, incomprensibles cuando no invisibles" (an avalanche of motions, which are incomprehensible, if not invisible).[60] For this reason, "los juicios se prolongan por años, violando el precepto constitucional que aboga por una justicia rápida y expedita" (cases take years to resolve, which violates the constitutional guarantee of a speedy trial).[61] Legal scholars—although they do not cite this novel—agree with Volpi's conclusions. They state that the reforms were implemented under the subsequent presidential administration.[62] Thus far, the reforms have not improved the legal system, for either alleged defendants or alleged victims. They mean that the constitutional text is applied only insofar as it can be used to impose a violent structure.

The constitutional text presents significant descriptions of Mexico as it is and aspirations for the Mexican nation. The tension between nonfiction and fantasy is present in the constitution as a genre, as well as in its structure. The headings and subheadings jolt readers out of complacency and smooth over the extreme shifts in content within and between articles and sections. The content of the constitutional text mirrors these aesthetic concerns as well, recognizing the rights of all Mexicans and establishing the ways the federal government may impose order on the people within Mexico's borders. Both legal scholars and Volpi's novel show that these changes have been successful in imposing a new kind of order; they have been much less successful in allowing Mexican people to achieve their own aspirations.

*Una novela criminal* is similar in some ways to the Mexican Constitution. In the following I describe these similarities in terms of the tension between organization and disorganization. The novel reflects the forces of order in the ways it reflects conventions of the novelistic genre, as well as subgenres of detective fiction, narrative nonfiction, and creative nonfiction. Some of its formal elements, as well as the way the narrator moves between topics, challenge these forces of order and call to mind Mexico's Crack literary movement of the 1990s and the Latin American historical novel of the mid-twentieth century. The narrator organizes these meanderings, yet even the narrator is overpowered by systems of incarceration and policing.

Volpi's work reflects the forces of order, as it is recognizable as a novel. After the copyright page and dedication, the novel includes an epigraph, a warning, and is then divided in a conventional way. There are five parts, and each part is divided into several chapters, for a total of twenty chapters. Notes, acknowledgments, a list of characters, an index, and a table of contents follow at the end of the novel. The epigraph, a quote by Paul Valéry, "Le mélange du vrai et du faux est énormément plus toxique que le faux pur" (The mixture of true and false is enormously more toxic than pure falsehood), sets the tone for a novel that blends truth and fiction.[63] The "Advertencia," or warning, addresses readers and acknowledges that the novel is a blend of truth and fiction. These paratextual elements at the beginning of the literary text mirror those at the end, which further question the issues of truth and fiction. The playfulness of these elements are recognizable to readers of Latin American fiction, as they reflect some of the traditions of the novels from the Latin American Boom. These include authors such as Julio Cortázar, whose 1963 work *Rayuela* (*Hopscotch*) famously skipped between story lines, or Macedonio Fernández, whose *Museo de la novela de la Eterna* (*The Museum of Eterna's Novel*; 1967), with its multiple prologues, nonlinear story line, and narrator's self-reflection, construct a metaphorical museum over the course of the text.[64] In addition to these elements, the novel includes recognizable elements: a narrator introduces characters, develops a plot, and moves through time and space via numbered and ordered chapters. As with other novels with multiple story lines and complex narrators, each chapter deals with a specific subplot, group of characters, or location.

*Una novela criminal* is further recognizable as a novel as it shares several tendencies with novels from the Crack literary movement, in which Jorge Volpi had participated. This literary movement was named after a manifesto that Volpi wrote together with Ignacio Padilla, Pedro Ángel Palou, Eloy Urroz, and Ricardo Chávez Castañeda in 1996.[65] They meant to shake up the Mexican literary scene, to break with the past and redefine the literary field.[66] The novels of the movement are best described by Pedro Ángel Palou: "There is no adjectival novel. . . . The only true novel is a phagocytic organism. It gobbles down everything and spits it up, disrupted and transformed."[67] To do so, they wanted to combine the pleasure of reading with a type of aesthetic that would exploit the breaks or fissures in the novelistic genre, engaging with aesthetic or formal innovation.[68] These novels self-consciously recognized that they would never accurately portray reality—self-conscious because, as he continues, the novels were rooted "in the heroic failure of the short story, which aspires to the impossibility of imperfection. The short story is to utopia what the novel is to dystopia. The novel will continue to triumph by assuming and embodying the dystopian imperfection of reality."[69] *Una novela criminal* evokes many of these remarks about Crack novels; nevertheless, it is less formally experimental than some other novels of the movement from the 1990s, because it is relatively readable from start to finish and does not require nearly as much work to interpret as, say, the experimental novels of the Boom by Cortázar or Fernández. In this way, *Una novela criminal*, as well as other novels from Crack writers, shares similarities with other types of Latin American novels. It is not necessarily logical or easy to read.

*Una novela criminal*'s formal innovation combined with readability also draws on the Latin American historical novel. The novel's publicity materials proclaim: "Todo lo que se narra en esta novela ocurrió así, todos sus personajes son personas de carne y hueso, y la historia, desentrañada con maestría e iluminada hasta sus últimos recovecos por una ingente tarea de documentación, es real" (Everything narrated in this novel occurred as described, all its characters are flesh-and-blood people, and the real story, which masterfully unravels and illuminates all of its nooks and crannies, through impressive documentation, is real).[70] Volpi's fictional re-creation of events is based on extensive research. Waters Hood surveys the rigorous process Volpi undertook to represent these events that may be neither representable nor understandable: "Over a three-year period [Volpi] read everything written about this episode, reviewed all related media, and interviewed many of the principal participants. With this preparation, he thoroughly dissects this highly controversial and complex case, introducing numerous institutions and powerful individuals within and outside the Mexican government who played, or may have played, a role in this ongoing injustice."[71] Waters Hood calls to mind the tradition of the Latin American new historical novel, which acknowledges the impossibility of knowing historical truths or reality even as it represents them.[72] The critic H. Rosi Song summarizes postmodern literary techniques succinctly: "cuestionar la representación de la realidad a través del discurso literario o histórico, presentando un texto reflexivo, consciente de su propio proceso de construcción y la naturaleza ficticia de su discurso" (to question the representation of reality via literary or historical discourse, presenting a reflexive text, conscious of its own construction, and the fictional nature of its discourse).[73] *Una novela criminal* employs several techniques that call to mind the tendencies of these novels, as well as the formal strategies or aesthetic described earlier with regard to the constitutional text. Its own narrator professes that his conclusions are unreliable and tells readers that events have been told in a nonchronological fashion. The novel also includes portions of other sources in its version of events, such as a police report in its discussion of a journalist's investigation into the circumstances surrounding Israel Vallarta's arrest in the years immediately following the events.[74] The way the narrator seamlessly inserts the journalist's observations within a subplot creates connections between what would initially seem disparate moments in time: the 2005 arrest, the 2006–2007 journalist's investigation, and the 2018 novel. This insertion also brings together the question of truthfulness in reporting with the carceral order of policing and incarceration. The narrator thus creates connections between discrete time periods and disparate ideas and continues to do so throughout the novel.

The narrator communicates the impossibility of knowing historical truths. The way the novel questions truth—a metafictional technique—relates to Latin American literature and to other parts of the author's oeuvre, and is a widely recognized tendency in Latin American literature, usually present in novels categorized as magic realism, or "the marvelous real."[75] It is also part of Volpi's other novels, including *En busca de Klingsor* (*In Search of Klingsor*), in which the protagonist engages in a metaphysical search for truth.[76]

In *Una novela criminal*, the narrator is the protagonist and the key figure who searches for truth about Israel Vallarta. Early on, the narrator states, "Al comenzar esta novela documental o esta novela sin ficción no sé, no puedo saber, si Israel Vallarta y Florence Cassez son inocentes o culpables del secuestro de Valeria" (By beginning this documentary novel, or nonfiction novel, I don't know, I can't know, if Israel Vallarta and Florence Cassez are innocent or guilty of Valeria's kidnapping).[77] Uncertainty is part of the novel from the beginning, which brings about an ambivalent tone to the literary text. Then, the narrator returns to the question of storytelling by stating, "De que sólo antes del siglo XX era posible concebir narradores omniscientes, dotados con toda la información posible sobre las historias que se disponían a contar" (only before the twentieth century was it possible to believe in omniscient narrators, who had all the information necessary to tell their stories).[78] Even after exposing the entire case, he is still uncertain: "Yo, que llevo años examinando su historia, que he podido visitarlo y hablar con él en los tenebrosos locutorios de El Altiplano, no tengo una respuesta certera. Si hubiese escrito una novela normal, una novela de ficción, a estas alturas tendría que haber dibujado de cuerpo entero a mi protagonista y, en vez del enigmático sujeto de las primeras páginas estaría obligado a exhibir ante mis lectores un personaje sólido y redondo" (I, who have spent years examining his story, who has visited him, and spoken with him in the gloomy rooms in El Altiplano, do not have an answer. If I had written a normal novel, a fictional novel, by this point I would have had to reveal my protagonist, and, instead of the enigmatic character I present in these first few pages, I would be obliged to share a solid and well-developed character with my readers).[79]

Israel's body, however, remains elusive. It does not exist as a concrete historical truth: "Israel apenas me parece menos borroso que al principio ... su carácter aún me resulta inaprensible" (Israel seems hardly any clearer than he was at the beginning ... his character still remains elusive).[80] The narrative does not—indeed, cannot—capture Israel's body and spirit. This tendency for the narrator to question his own assertions, then, bookends the text and relieves the narrator of the responsibility of omniscience. These imaginings also include Israel's life before he was incarcerated and during his incarceration. The narrator questions historical truths to such an extent that he creates a type of literary freedom for a character who is denied every opportunity for movement.

In addition to the way the narrator questions the truthfulness of the events surrounding Israel's arrest and detention, he does not recount the events in a logical or chronological fashion. The nonlinear or disorganized narrative prohibits easy acceptance of the status quo. As the narrator juxtaposes disparate events, he acts as what the Alfaguara Prize committee called "el ojo que se pasea sobre los hechos y los ordena. Su mirada es la pregunta, aquí no hay respuestas, solo la perplejidad de lo real" (the eye that passes over the facts and organizes them. His gaze is the question, here there are no answers, only the perplexity of the real).[81] This juxtaposition interrupts what was "flow" for Raymond Williams, "endless streaming" for Jameson, and the *régimen live* in more recent years for Sayak Valencia. It upends the neoliberal rhetoric that, according to Irmgard Emmelhainz, "normaliza la violencia, crea modos de ver al mundo a partir de un sentido común que justifica la destrucción y el despojo, con nociones de progreso y desarrollo" (normalizes violence, creates ways of seeing the world from a common sense that justifies destruction and dispossession with notions of development and progress).[82] Disorder thus interrupts a violent status quo, and the disorder in the text is a type of aestheticized violence in its own right that challenges the forces of order that violently impose their own violent logic.

One way the novel goes out of order is by moving from the minutiae of a character's life to a larger social commentary. For instance, the first chapter recounts the experiences of Valeria, the alleged first victim of Cassez and Vallarta. It describes her experiences of pressing charges at a police station, after which the narrator states that she participated in "un sistema tan complejo y meticulosamente regulado como ineficaz. Y una metáfora perfecta del país" (a system so complex and meticulously regulated so as to be inefficient. And a perfect metaphor for the country).[83] The way it moves seamlessly from a character's lived experience to a damning commentary about Mexico is repeated throughout the text. In this way, the novel conforms to the critic Brian Chandler's claim about Volpi's 1996 novel *En busca de Klingsor*, that it "connects history writ large to a personal, humanized perspective of one man condemned to die in obscurity, demonstrating how the narration eases from the macro to the microscopic."[84] It also reminds us of Roberto Ángel G.'s observations regarding Volpi's 2006 novel *No será la tierra* (*This Will Not Be Earth*), which connects human experience to broader historical trends.[85] The way the novel shuttles from micro to macro, and vice versa, is a formal move that reminds us that the intimate personal violence the characters in the text experience, as well as the ways they challenge the larger forces of order, are part of a larger aesthetic tendency that I am proposing regarding twenty-first century Mexican fiction and legal texts.

*Una novela criminal* also moves between distinct elements in a way that is dizzying and hard to follow. As a reader I can no longer trust my own instincts and am encouraged to trust the narrator. For instance, in chapter 9, "En guerra," the narrator goes back and forth between evidence such as medical reports, sworn statements in front of a judge, and personal anecdotes. The narrator describes the medical exam conducted on the victim Ezequiel. The forensic report reproduced in the novel states that his skin markings came from "una petequia y no una cicatriz por punción previa" (a petechia [red spot] and not from a scar from an earlier injury).[86] The narrator then interprets the medical report: "En otras palabras: una mancha en la piel" (In other words: a mark on his skin).[87] The narrator continues, reproducing the report of voice-analysis experts, which, according to the novel, contradicted the police. The novel stated there was nothing in common with earlier phone recordings and the negotiations surrounding the victims' release.[88] Later on, this same chapter of *Una novela criminal* reproduces a character called Eduardo Margolis's sworn statement before a judge in Mexico City. The narrator imagines that Margolis, a wealthy businessman, gave off the impression that the whole thing was a waste of time. The novel reproduces his sworn statement and claims that, at that time, the police considered his responses adequate.[89] The sworn statement implies that Margolis caused the characters' televised—and actual—arrests. The fact that it was placed immediately after a medical report confirms the violent nature of the duo's arrest and the consequences for both characters. The way that *Una novela criminal* employs intertextuality, then, is part of its strategies of disorder. These strategies that confront the social order are an integral part of how the novel exposes the violence inherent in the status quo.

The fact that the novel inserts multiple such statements merits closer examination. It inserts these sources to lend a sense of truthfulness to

Volpi's account, which, like the Latin American historical novel, upends an official narrator. The narrator of *Una novela criminal* effectively curates a variety of materials to establish his version of the truth. One way that he does so is by inserting legal documents, portions of interviews, and citations regarding the case in the media. The novel's footnotes begin with an unnumbered paragraph that summarizes the intertextuality evident throughout Volpi's work. According to the narrator, the novel is based on "los expedientes judiciales de Florence Cassez y la familia Vallarta . . . así como en las transcripciones de discursos, declaraciones y entrevistas de los protagonistas de esta historia" (Florence Cassez and the Vallarta family's case files . . . as well as transcribed speeches, sworn statements and interviews with this story's protagonists).[90] The narrator's assertion that he relied on legal documents to construct his account jolts readers out of complacency, as I noted earlier, and makes the novel seem more truthful. As with the new historical novel's use of other texts to question official narratives, Volpi's novel also questions the official version of events.

The novel inserts a written version of the televised arrest, which is portrayed in such a way that it supports the novel's perspective rather than Televisa's version of events. Toward the end of the second chapter, *Una novela criminal* offers an interpretation of December 8 and 9 for a character called Israel Vallarta. Then, it begins its third chapter, "El canal de las estrellas" (The Star Channel) by describing what these channels broadcast: "la madrugada del 9 de diciembre de 2005, cuando millones de personas atestiguaron, en los dos noticiarios matutinos de mayor audiencia en la televisión mexicana, *Primero Noticias* y *Hechos AM* la 'captura en vivo de dos peligrosos secuestradores' y la 'liberación de sus tres víctimas' gracias a la heroica intervención de los agentes de la AFI en el rancho Las Chinitas" (early in the morning on December 9, 2005, when millions of people were watching, the two morning news shows with the most viewers in Mexican television, *First News* and *Facts AM* the "live arrest of two dangerous kidnappers" and the heroic AFI's "liberation of their three victims" in a rancho called Las Chinitas).[91] On *Primero Noticias*, Carlos Loret de Mola claimed the arrest was "'un duro golpe contra la industria del secuestro': la liberación en vivo de tres víctimas y la captura de dos secuestradores en una casa de seguridad en el sur de la Ciudad de México" (a heavy blow for the kidnapping industry: live release of three victims and capture of two kidnappers in a secure location in southern Mexico City.).[92] Immediately following this sanitized, chronological version, the narrator says it was all fake: "la madrugada del 9 de diciembre la AFI no capturó a nadie y no liberó a nadie" (the AFI did not arrest or liberate anyone in the early morning of

December 9).⁹³ In effect, it was "una ficción en la cual todos los participantes desempeñaron un papel previamente escrito para ellos por las autoridades" (a fiction in which each participant played the part designed already written by the authorities).⁹⁴ As the reviewer Pablo Ordaz highlights, the novel establishes "la liberación de sus supuestas víctimas no fue más que un teatro a mayor gloria de la Policía Federal y en provecho de la audiencia televisiva" (the liberation of their supposed victims was nothing more than theatre to glorify the Federal Police and to increase their television audience).⁹⁵ This particular example of intertextuality—the news clip—is inserted into the text in such a way that the literary representation reminds readers of Vallarta and Cassez's violent arrest the day before it was filmed by Televisa. In this way, intertextuality conforms to the novel's overarching perspective.

The novel offers other examples of intertextuality and stories-within-the-story that confirm that Televisa televised a staged arrest the day after the "real" one had taken place. These metafictional techniques function as both strategies of disorder and techniques for uncovering what the novel considers a truthful version of events. The narrator confirms: "según la confesión posterior del propio director de la corporación (Televisa), Genaro García Luna (Secretaría de Seguridad Pública), la policía recreó —es decir: escenificó, manipuló, *inventó*— una captura y una liberación que nadie sabe cómo y cuándo se llevaron a cabo" (according to the eventual confession from the director of the corporation [Televisa], Genaro García Luna [Secretary of Public Security], the police re-created—that is, staged, manipulated, *invented*—a capture and liberation such that no one knows how and when it really took place).⁹⁶ This seems to be a purposeful joke, as Televisa is widely ridiculed as an arm of the state, and the sentences makes it difficult to discern whether García Luna is aligned with Televisa or the police. The conflation of the television channel and the police implies that both are arms of the state, as well as implying that the police are a corporation, supported by Televisa. Toward the end of the novel, the narrator adds: "como me confirmó [Luis] Cárdenas Palomino, aquel día no ocurrió ninguna detención ni ninguna liberación que pudiesen ser repetidas a petición de los medios" (as [Luis] Cárdenas Palomino confirmed, there was no discovery or liberation that took place that day that could be repeated at the media's request).⁹⁷ Quoting important people involved in the case lends the novel legitimacy and validates its perspective on what Žižek calls objective violence—in other words, the violence inherent in the status quo.

Chapter 20, "Israel," relates what has happened in the ten years between the alleged kidnapping and Volpi's undertaking his research. The narrator inserts a 2015 letter purportedly from the publicist Carlos Alazraki to Florence Cassez in an unspecified avenue of the Mexican press, in which he criticizes her cowardly behavior.[98] After reproducing Alazraki's short letter with ellipses, the novel reproduces other interpretations of the case. For example, it reproduces portions of the dialogue in Daniel Ruiz's 2014 film *Duda razonable* (*Reasonable Doubt*).[99] Using these sources gives credibility to *Una novela criminal*.

The most striking intertextual element is a character called Yuli García, a Colombian journalist based in Mexico City.[100] The novel reveals its version of the truth, which it establishes by inserting the journalist's reactions to Televisa's version of events, her interviews, documents she employed in her research, and her commentary on both types of sources. Her nationality and profession are key to understanding how and why Cassez legitimizes Volpi's perspective. As Paley reminds us, much of Mexico's violence in the early 2000s was similar to the violence Colombia had experienced in the 1990s.[101] The novel relays the facts that in 2005, the character Yuli worked for the famous Mexican journalist Denise Maerker, a historical figure and a character in the novel. That year, in the historical context, the journalist Maerker moved from Televisa to the show *Punto de Partida* on TV Azteca. According to the novel, the character Yuli García followed the character Maerker as she switched television channels. These years of experience and mentorship under a prominent Mexican journalist meant that García's trained eye immediately noticed that the televised arrest was false. The novel quoted the fictional García as reacting in the following way: "No puede salir todo tan perfecto" (Nothing could come out that perfectly).[102] The journalist's astute observation is crucial to the way that the novel establishes that, when it later quotes her interviews or sources, it will be telling the truth.

The narrator imagines situations in which Yuli García interviews other characters connected to the case. These interviews are further examples of intertextuality that legitimize its point of view. Disorder is part of the truth that the forces of order, including strategies in the literary and legal texts, would prefer to cover up. At one point, Yuli interviews Florence's lawyer, Jorge Ochoa, and this provides the first truthful version of events in the novel, that is, the version of events that is closest to what unfolded in real life. According to *Una novela criminal*, they meet at the Café La Habana, a significant location in Mexico City. When I last visited the café in 2018, I saw photographs on its walls attesting to meetings there between Che Guevara, Fidel Castro, and Mexican communists. Back in the novel, the narrator portrays Ochoa as very nervous, as if he had a shameful secret to share: "No sé si Jorge Ochoa suda profusamente, pero así lo imagino cuando Yuli se sienta frente a él" (I don't know if Jorge Ochoa was likely to sweat profusely, but that is how I imagine his interview with Yuli seated in front of him).[103] The novel's portrayal of his demeanor gives Yuli García's interview with Ochoa an air of mystery. As Ochoa relays the events to her, "A cada momento [Ochoa] se levanta a revisar el local, fingiendo ir al baño, y luego vuelve a sentarse, agitado y paranoico" (Ochoa constantly got up to survey the location, pretending to need to use the bathroom, and then he returned to his seat, agitated and paranoid).[104] The narrator implies that Ochoa intuits that something about Vallarta's case and about García's questions is extraordinarily bad. As he sits in the café, Ochoa tells Yuli, "Tu vida corre peligro . . . la mía también" (Your life is in danger . . . mine is too).[105] According to the narrator, this nervous man explains to Yuli that Cassez had first been detained a day earlier than the television release and that he had the documents that proved García's understanding of the true order of events. Later on, García interviews *another* key player, Daniel Cabeza de Vaca, head of the Mexican Procuraduría General de la República (PGR, or attorney general's office).[106] This bureaucrat's surname evokes that of Álvar Núñez Cabeza de Vaca, who wrote *Naufragios* (1555), a famous account of colonization about a shipwrecked crew of Spaniards. The bureaucrat's surname and the colonizer it evokes align with the novel's portrayal of the journalist, clinging to bits of truth in a sea of misinformation. Yuli García and a group of camerapeople and producers from *Punto de Partida* go to Cabeza de Vaca's office, where García has a meeting. Once they sit down, Yuli asks Cabeza de Vaca whether he stages all of his arrests. In other words, if he employed Televisa's production to justify his false arrest. He never responds, so she repeats her question. The narrator adds, "Daniel Cabeza de Vaca mira a la menuda reportera de arriba abajo" (Daniel Cabeza de Vaca looks the petite reporter up and down).[107] This comment suggests that Cabeza de Vaca attempts to disarm García. She returns the favor, showing him the documentary evidence. In response, "el procurador tartamudea un par de excusas y pide acabar la entrevista" (the prosecutor stutters a few excuses and asks to end the interview).[108] These characters' behaviors, and Yuli García's interviews with them, further confirm that the novel's strategies of disorder are part of its truth claim. That is, the way that the novel challenges the existing order is part of the way the narrator establishes what we should believe as the truthful version of events.

The narrator also inserts sources into his discussion of Yuli García that further confirm his version of events. At one point, she reads a police blotter, and the narrator's commentary suggests that the blotter is more truthful than Televisa. After Yuli reads the blotter, she discovers "que Israel y Florence no fueron detenidos a las 06:47 en el rancho Las Chinitas, como dejaban entrever las imágenes noticiosas" (that Israel and Florence were not detained at 06:47 at Rancho Las Chinitas, as the news footage implied).[109] The police blotter—which is not reproduced in the novel—reportedly stated "los agentes aseguran haber detenido a Israel en la carretera federal y afirman que fue el propio Israel quien les abrió la puerta ... mientras que en las imágenes televisivas ésta era forzada por los miembros de la AFI en un espectacular operativo tipo SWAT" (the agents swore to have detained Israel on the highway and affirmed that it was Israel who opened the door for them ... while in the television footage the AFI pushed down the door in a spectacle that evoked a SWAT operation).[110] The blotter directly contradicts Televisa's version of events. Its "live action" began at 6:47 a.m., "28 minutos antes de que, según el informe, los agentes de la AFI hubieran siquiera arribado a Las Chinitas" (twenty-eight minutes before the report states that the AFI agents had even arrived at Las Chinitas).[111]

The novel continues to portray Yuli's search by inserting another document to prop up its perspective. After significant effort, a young man who works at Televisa's archive gives Yuli a videotape while she is working in her office at her own computer.[112] Televisa is reluctant to share the evidence that it had filmed a false arrest. The fact that the television station refuses to share such an incriminating videotape with one of its own staff members is as much proof as the recording itself: "El video no sólo contiene las imágenes transmitidas por *Primero Noticias* la madrugada del 9 de diciembre, sino otras, grabadas minutos antes, que no llegaron a salir al aire" (The video not only has footage aired on *Primero Noticias* on the morning of December 9, but it also contains footage from a few moments earlier that was not ever aired).[113] The novel identifies the voice of Carlos Loret de Mola, host of *Primero Noticias*, ordering around police officers and other reporters. The video unequivocally proves—for the narrator of Volpi's novel—that the media and police coordinated with one another the day after the initial arrest. It also aligns with the narrator's perspective: "Aquí, a nadie le parece importarle que la AFI, la Policía Federal y la PGR hayan mentido una y otra vez o que hayan tramado esa argamasa de verdades y ficciones que hemos llamado el montaje o la puesta en escena" (Here, it does not seem important to anyone that the AFI, the Federal Police, and the Attorney General's Office have lied again and again, or that they have woven an amalgam of truth and fiction that we have called the montage, or the mise-en-scène).[114] It is almost incredible that there would be a single videotape documenting the arrest in Volpi's multilayered fictional account. The interviews with Ochoa and Cabeza de Vaca, the police blotter, and the videotape, then, give the narrator's point of view the weight of truth.

The narrator attempts to organize these metafictional strategies, or disorderly conduct with divisions in the text, by portraying himself as a detective on some occasions and as author on others. *Una novela criminal* employs chapter headings and longer paragraph breaks within chapters to organize its version of events, just as Mexico's constitution tries to structure an understanding of society through headings and subheadings. More than that, it explains how and why it is telling these events in this way. The metafictional self-reflection in *Una novela criminal* makes the narrative meanderings into evidence that supports the narrator's point of view. The narrator-detective legitimizes his account of events by inserting his reflections and commenting on relevant material. The notion of narrator as detective is a twenty-first-century iteration of the typically omniscient character in detective fiction. In the late 1980s, D. A. Miller observed that fiction's detectives typically take on the role of omniscient narrator.[115] Volpi's narrator exists in tension between identifying himself as a detective and making claims based on his own supposed omniscience. The narrator reveals the events in the following way: "Primero, referiré a los hechos que condujeron al descubrimiento del montaje o la puesta en escena y sólo después intentaré reconstruir la transmisión del 9 de diciembre" (First, I will refer to the facts that led to the discovery of the montage or the mise-en-scène, and afterward I will attempt to reconstruct the news that was aired on December 9).[116] He justifies the disorderly novel by stating: "Si escribiera una novela tradicional, quizá contaría los hechos de este modo, detallando la captura de Israel Vallarta y Florence Cassez, así como la liberación de Cristina Ríos, su hijo Christian y Ezequiel Elizalde tal como se vieron en pantalla" (If I were to write a traditional novel, perhaps I would narrate the events in this way, detailing Israel Vallarta and Florence Cassez's arrest, as well as the liberation of Cristina Ríos, her son Christian, and Ezequiel Elizalde, exactly as shown on television).[117] In other words, the narrator of *Una novela criminal* recognizes that he has not told events in a linear fashion. Yet he maintains that he has been truthful. The narrator adopts an authorial voice to an even greater extent when he explains the sources he used in his research. There is a list of sources at the end of the novel. The narrator introduces them toward the end of the novel, adopting an authorial voice and explaining: "Al ser ésta una novela y no un ensayo, decidí no indicar entre corchetes las partes omitidas" (As this is a novel and not an essay, I decided not to use square brackets to show what I had eliminated).[118] The authorial character also admits to revising his sources for content and grammar: "en numerosas ocasiones me he tomado la libertad de eliminar palabras, oraciones o incluso párrafos completos que me han parecido superfluos o redundantes con el fin de acentuar los argumentos centrales de cada declarante" (on a number of occasions I have removed words, phrases or even complete paragraphs that seemed superfluous or redundant, with the goal of highlighting the central arguments of each individual or text).[119] Ever mindful of writing legal fiction, the authorial voice continues, defending himself: "En mi descargo sólo puedo añadir que he hecho hasta lo imposible para que estos cortes jamás alteren la intención o el sentido que los declarantes querían darle a sus dichos. Por esta misma razón, salvo algunas conjugaciones ilativas, en ningún caso he añadido palabras que no estuviesen presentes en las transcripciones originales" (I can only add that, in my defense, I have done the nearly impossible so that the sections I have eliminated do not alter the individuals' intention or meaning. For that same reason, barring some illative conjunctions, in no case have I added words that weren't present in the original transcriptions).[120] By admitting that he has done so much editing, he hopes to make his account even more trustworthy. As the narrator with an authorial voice states, "Como escritor de ficción—y de ficciones ambiguas, sin finales unívocos—debería ser consciente de que la verdad absoluta es imposible, de que la verdad se edifica a partir de un cúmulo de verdades fragmentarias" (As a fiction writer—of ambiguous fictions, without clear endings—I must be conscious that absolute truth is impossible, that the truth is only the cumulation of partial truths).[121] These organizing strategies toward the end of *Una novela criminal* legitimize the narrator-author's perspective. The way he reflects on his own research smooths over anything that may have seemed confusing during his meanderings or through the disorderly insertions of other types of evidence, such as the police blotter.

The narrator's explicit discussion of genre—and the issue of genre in general—is another organizing strategy in the novel. There are several ways to classify the novel, and each possible genre (or subgenre), whether detective fiction, narrative nonfiction, or creative nonfiction, organizes the text for readers in some new way, as the conventions of each different genre encourage different modes of reading. Detective fiction, for example, typically involves a believable detective, who is somewhat an outsider to a local police force and uses unconventional methods to arrive at the truth. Taking *Una novela criminal* as a detective novel, readers are inclined to believe the narrator's version of events. This is especially true if readers are familiar with other examples of Mexican detective fiction, such as works by

Jorge Ibargüengoitia or Paco Ignacio Taibo II. The critics Roberto Gómez Beltrán and Rubén Varona point out that characters in Ibargüengoitia's and Taibo's novels uncover crimes committed by the political party in power, and by authority figures more generally.[122] Volpi's *Una novela criminal* also follows a tendency that the critic Alberto Vital noted in Taibo's: highlighting the fact that police are unjust actors.[123] The narrator in Volpi's *Una novela criminal* similarly challenges the political party in power (in Volpi's case, the PAN), authority figures (in his case, at Televisa), and unjust politicking practices. Readers of *Una novela criminal*, were they familiar with detective fiction, would likely believe the narrator's version of events. This claim follows Worden's understanding of literary nonfiction and detective fiction, which sustains that the form and content of literature and art produced under neoliberalism replicate the fractures of a society living with the effects of neoliberal economic policy. The fragmented narrative can be understood as results of the massive social changes brought about by these economic policies. The *crónica* genre, as the critic Polit Dueñas reminds us, is one way that many twenty-first-century journalists record social suffering. Categorizing the novel as a *crónica* encourages taking the novel's version of reality at its word. The similarities between Volpi's novel and the detective genre, as well as other nonfiction genres including the *crónica*, impose the narrator-protagonist's vision, and also understanding of who is at fault, onto the text. Genre, then, is another strategy that I think organizes the chaotic events the novel portrays.

The detective genre is particularly useful for analyzing the text. My genre based analysis of *Una novela criminal* builds on the works of other critics who have analyzed other examples of Volpi's work as detective fiction. Their work on genre in Volpi's oeuvre gives us some parameters for thinking about how readers, engaging with an unfamiliar text, might be able to understand its meaning more easily because they are already familiar with the conventions of detective fiction. I extend the critic Clemens Franken Kurzen's observation about Volpi's other novel *En busca de Klingsor* as a detective's search to *Una novela criminal*, which represents a detective's search for truth.[124] Furthermore, establishing the narrator as a detective follows several predetermined patterns of detective fiction, which makes the meanderings understandable. The narrator of *Una novela criminal* searches for truth about two crimes, the false reporting that framed Vallarta and Cassez, and their alleged kidnapping of Ríos, her son Christian, and Elizalde. The narrator-protagonist, like most protagonists in detective novels, is not a member of a police force. Because of his outsider status, he is able to solve the crime. Indeed, the narrator's work follows the observations of Ramírez-Pimienta and Villalobos on the importance of a single individual in examples of detective fiction. For these critics, "Ante la nula procuración de justicia convencional, las obras estudiadas proponen la indignación individual como el detonante de cambio" (In light of the complete absence of conventional justice, the works studied here propose individual indignation as the trigger for change).[125] The narrator of *Una novela criminal* suggests that Eduardo Margolis, a wealthy businessman, kidnapped the three individuals, and in addition to incriminating Margolis, the novel incriminates Mexico's leaders and their emphasis on security. The way the narrator points out that Margolis, not Vallarta, is likely the guilty party aligns with the critic Daniel Worden's description of detective fiction: "The crime is solved, the event is made visible."[126] Worden adds that the guilty parties and characters that detective fiction typically implicates in these violent structures do not, however, admit guilt. This is exactly what occurs in *Una novela criminal*—the guilty character (Margolis) remains free. Volpi's account also lacks closure—a closure that, according to Worden, normally disguises the "structural conditions of exploitation that target the poor and [the] traumatic events that cannot be resolved or achieve closure."[127] This pattern of search and resolution common to detective fiction is also present in *Una novela criminal*. The fact that the novel has a familiar pattern allows readers to follow its events more easily, and the pattern is sufficiently familiar to readers so as to ensure a clear understanding of its portrayal of events and to allow them to follow the development of the story line.

*Una novela criminal* also engages in extensive social and political critique, which further conforms to aspects of the genre of detective fiction in Latin America, and also in Spain, as well as the related terminology of police fiction. As the critics Clemens Franken Kurzen and Magda Sepúlveda would have us believe, "estudiar el género policial es hacer una crítica a la violencia, a la justicia y al derecho" (studying police fiction means criticizing violence, justice and the law).[128] In this vein, the narrator of *Una novela criminal* begins the novel with a forceful critique: "Con algo de suerte, espero concluir estas páginas con una idea más clara de los hechos. Por mi parte, inicio este relato, mi propia investigación literaria del caso, como debieron hacerlo la policía y las autoridades judiciales en su momento: con la presunción de que Israel Vallarta y Florence Cassez son inocentes mientras no se demuestre lo contrario" (With a little luck, I hope to conclude these pages with a clearer idea of the facts. I began this account, my own literary investigation of the case, in the way that the police and legal authorities should have: with the assumption that Israel Vallarta and Florence Cassez are innocent until proven otherwise).[129] Indeed,

Volpi's novel implies that in addition to the wealthy businessman Margolis, the government and a government-supported television channel are also guilty. In this way, *Una novela criminal* criticizes multiple institutions. This criticism means that it complies with remarks by the critics Gianna Martella and Jacky Collins on detective fiction, as condemning "governments, the military, the police, and government agencies in general."[130] Narrators in detective novels relentlessly search for the truth, exemplifying what Martella and Collins call "an obsession with unmasking those guilty of past injustices—for example, wars and torture."[131] *Una novela criminal* conforms with these aspects of detective fiction as well. After all, Volpi's novel criticizes corruption, ongoing dictatorship, abuse of power, and inequality.[132] Thus, the novel conforms to multiple aspects of the genre of detective fiction, particularly in the ways that genre has critiqued powerful institutions in Latin America. By aligning in certain ways to the genre, the novel and its criticisms of systems of incarceration and policing are part of an identifiable literary tradition, and as *Una novela criminal* conforms to certain aspects of this genre, it makes other parts of it more understandable for readers. Moreover, approaching the novel as an example of detective fiction offers is an important counterbalance to more challenging aspects of its aesthetics, particularly the ways that *Una novela criminal* shifts in time and space.

The novel also presents its version of events as nonfiction, which aligns it with several tendencies in Latin American literature and culture, such as the *crónica*, and other genres such as creative nonfiction, narrative nonfiction, and documentary fiction. The narrator employs the terminology of nonfiction novel told in reverse order.[133] Literary and artistic nonfiction has become more common in works of art and literature published since the 1960s, as, according to Worden, it is a way to try to make sense of the realities imposed by the massive social, political, and economic changes associated with neoliberalism.[134] I use the terminology of documentary fiction in relation to *Una novela criminal* because it complies with several strategies that Worden outlined in his *Neoliberal Nonfictions*. According to Worden, those strategies reveal both the personal experience and the broader social structures of "extraction, dispossession and exploitation that make ... postmodern spectacles possible."[135] The "warning" at the beginning of *Una novela criminal* and the narrator's later assertions together declare that the novel is a work of nonfiction, which aligns it with the genre Worden analyzes. The narrator's blending of Israel Vallarta's life with a version of the author's investigation into Vallarta's case—which aligns with Worden's description of the personal experience—illuminates the structures of exploitation inherent to neoliberalism. By bringing Volpi's work into dialogue with Worden's theories, it becomes clear that the novel relates that what it conceives of as a truthful account is part of the way it shows the structures, or the violent status quo, that underlie the high levels of violence in Mexico.

At the content level, the constant threat of prison prevents anything from getting too out of hand. Chapter 9 fictionalizes the author's experience of writing the novel and his initial attempt at interviewing Israel Vallarta in prison. Initially, the author's reflections draw readers into the story: "Tras más de un año de leer una y otra vez su nombre en miles de fojas de expediente, de identificarlo en diarios, revistas y tabloides—donde sin falta se la asume culpable" (After more than a year of reading his name time and again in thousands of files, of seeing it in newspapers, magazines, and tabloids—he is always assumed to be guilty").[136] The narrator had become convinced that Vallarta's case was important, which drove him to obsessively "imaginarlo, estudiarlo, analizarlo, entreverlo—y preguntarme en silencio quién es en verdad" (imagine, study, analyze and glimpse him—and ask myself in silence who is he, really).[137] The author-as-narrator thus engaged in sustained research on the subject, and *Una novela criminal* was the result. The novel humanizes Israel Vallarta: "A diferencia de las fotos que he repasado una y otra vez en el expediente, luce más maduro, con las mejillas ensanchadas y el cabello cortado al ras, un poco como yo" (Unlike the photos that I've reviewed again and again in his files, he looks older, with wider cheeks and close-cropped hair, a little bit like me).[138] The narrator connects disparate events: "Israel conserva una energía casi avasalladora aun cuando se quiebra" (Israel has an almost overwhelming energy even at his breaking point).[139] The narrator compares aspects of the prison to food and to the weather, which rhetorically disarms the power of the prison. These reflections are a force of order attempting to impose itself on the disorder in the crime and in the televised version of it.

Prisons are a devastating/harsh/deadly example of social organization. Prisons, as Jei Alanis Bello Ramírez and Germán Parra Gallego explain in their sociological study of incarceration in Colombia, are integral to the system: "[la prisión] produce la muerte a través de un ejercicio sistemático de la violencia y el terror, configurando campos donde los derechos se suspenden y los cuerpos de las personas son reducidos a cosas" ([prison] produces death through the systematic exercise of violence and terror, configuring camps where rights are suspended and the bodies of people reduced to things).[140] Prisons allow those who are not incarcerated to live with the fiction that they are free. Arresting Vallarta and Cassez—and keeping them in prison until such a time as they could be released in a way that let the government save face—kept people believing in security.

The first prison Volpi's novel describes is a pretrial detention center in Mexico City's Colonia Doctores, near Café La Habana, where Yuli had interviewed Ochoa. The pretrial detention center was originally established elsewhere in 1983 for dangerous criminals who may have been associated with organized crime. They were to be detained there for up to three days. Later, the laws changed to allow for detentions up to ninety days.[141] The pretrial detention center then moved to its current location, in Colonia Doctores, in 2003. There, detainees meet their duty counsel, similar to a public defender in the United States. According to the narrator, these lawyers typically represent the interests of judges and police rather than their clients.[142] The novel's criticism of the pretrial detention center in Colonial Doctores can be extended to a broader commentary on the Mexican criminal justice system as one that violently ensures the social order.

The next prison the novel describes is called El Altiplano, located in the State of Mexico. In prison, the narrator interacts with Vallarta and reflects on how prisons ensure a troubling social order. This particular prison is famous because El Chapo was incarcerated there, escaped, and returned before being extradited to the United States.[143] The narrator continues to share his thoughts and feelings. He remarks on the weather, stating that the prison exists "bajo el agreste sol del invierno mexicano, que te calcina a la intemperie pero es incapaz de confortarte en la gélida penumbra" (under the harsh sun of Mexican winter, which burns you out in the open but is incapable of comforting you in the icy gloom).[144] The prison that looms in front of them is akin to winter. He even goes so far as to compare the prison to "un cúmulo de moles cuadrangulares, de hormigón, esparcidas en el páramo bajo la custodia de torres de vigilancia desparramados como hongos; a la distancia, unos montes yermos ponen límites a la planicie amarillenta" (watchtowers, scattered like mushrooms, survey a cluster of four-cornered concrete buildings, scattered around the flat yard, where one can see some barren hills, which limit the yellowish plain).[145] Describing the prison's watchtowers as a fungus overseeing something—the concrete buildings made of *hormigón*, which means "concrete" but also evokes an anthill, or *hormiguero*—only multiplies its malevolent power.

The prison system, then, asserts its full level of control in layers of bureaucracy that are not unfamiliar to any Mexican person, an experience that is a reminder of remarks by the anthropologist David Graeber about bureaucracies in so-called liberal democracies. As Graeber states, "government policies intending to reduce government interference in the economy actually end up producing more regulations, more bureaucrats, and more police—can be observed so regularly that it is a general sociological law. I propose to call it 'the iron law of liberalism.'"[146] In other words, twenty-first-century political leaders suggest that smaller government involves shifting bureaucracy. In Volpi's novel, the bureaucratic shift has occurred with regard to the prison system. As the narrator-protagonist explains, "Mostramos nuestras identificaciones al primer oficial, cruzamos la verja que da paso al estacionamiento y caminamos en fila india por un pasillo al aire libre" (We show our identification to the first official, pass the gate that leads to the parking lot, and walk single file in an open-air hallway").[147] This is only the first step; in the reception room other steps follow: "Entregamos nuestras identificaciones, firmamos los documentos que nos presentan los guardias de seguridad, atravesamos los escáneres y nos dejamos fotografiar por cámaras anónimas instaladas en el techo antes de conseguir el ingreso" (We hand over our identification, sign the documents the security guards give us, go through the scanners, and allow ourselves to be photographed by anonymous cameras installed in the roof before obtaining entry).[148] They have performed four further steps to confirm their identification: showing their ID cards, signing documents, going through a scanner, and being photographed, so that the prison can record and review their visit—although it is highly unlikely that such recordings make anyone safer. Once they have completed these steps, they can enter the prison, and ideally, the narrator-protagonist will be able to interview Israel Vallarta: "Tras un nuevo control, subimos por una escalera para llegar a la sala 3, un aula desnuda y mal iluminada" (We pass through another checkpoint, go up a set of stairs to arrive in room 3, a bare and badly lit room).[149] Once they are in the room, they still cannot see the accused kidnapper face-to-face. Israel is barely visible on a video conference screen: "Al fondo, tras un cristal polarizado, verdoso, dividido en una suerte de tríptico —en los extremos la rejilla es densa, apretada, y sólo al centro se abre una especia de ventana donde los barrotes se espacian unos milímetros—, atisbo una silueta oscura que, fijando la vista, me devuelve los rasgos de Israel" (In the background, behind a polarized greenish screen, divided into a type of triptych—at the ends the grating is dense, tight, and only in the middle is there a kind of window with a few millimeters of space between the bars—and I glimpse a dark silhouette staring at me that reveals Israel's features).[150] Israel is only a shadow of a man.

The bureaucracy ensures that after all these dehumanizing steps, the narrator-protagonist and the characters who accompany him will not actually be able to meet with Israel: "El secretario toma la palabra y explica, en la deslavazada jerga de los leguleyos mexicanos, que el juez no podrá llegar por exceso en su carga de trabajo —cuando fue él quien fijó el día y la hora de la audiencia— y, para colmo, que el sistema de videoconferencia se halla culpado y no podrá utilizarse" (The secretary begins to speak and explains, in the washed-out jargon of bad Mexican lawyers, that the judge will not be able to arrive because he is too busy—even though the judge was the one who set the date and the time—and, to top it off, that the video-conferencing system is broken and cannot be used).[151] Israel arranges with his court-appointed lawyer to change the date of the interview: "El secretario se enreda para justificarse, argumenta que éste saldrá de vacaciones en unos días y él mismo a continuación, y pospone la nueva audiencia para fines de enero de 2017" (The secretary goes into tangles to justify himself, arguing that the judge will leave for vacation in a few days, and so will he, and so the new hearing is postponed until the end of January 2017).[152] The prison, as part of the legal system, then, quashes any attempts at disorder that would defy the status quo.

The novel goes on to compare Israel Vallarta's situation to that of other Mexicans, to show that the novel is not portraying a single incident: "en el fondo, él no es sino uno más de los miles de mexicanos que han sufrido abusos por parte de las autoridades y han sido víctimas —sí, víctimas— de la corrupción y la desvergüenza de quienes le han impedido tener un proceso justo" (in the end, he is but one of the thousands of Mexicans who has suffered abuse at the hands of the authorities and have been victims—yes, victims—of the corruption and shamelessness of those who have denied due process).[153] As Israel explains: "'Mi historia no es única', me dice. 'Por varias razones se conoció más que otras, pero hay muchas personas en situaciones similares'" ("My story is not unique," he tells me. "For many reasons my story is better known than others, but there are many people in similar situations").[154] Israel declares that he is only interested in being released on his innocence.[155] The narrator lauds Israel's ideological purity even as he pities him. This pity is present in the final prison scene in the novel: "Israel avanza por el patio de cemento hacia la última reja de El Altiplano. Frente a él se extiende la vasta polvareda de la tarde" (Israel advances along the cement patio toward the final gate of El Altiplano. The endless afternoon dust is all that is beyond him).[156] Prison imposes its logic and maintains the status quo for all people, not just those who are incarcerated.

The novel cements the relationship between the representation of prison and the status quo when it shows the rewards characters received for collaborating with high-level officials. Genaro García Luna, a character in the novel crucial to the portrayal of the release on television, became secretary of public security a year after the "rescue" once Calderón was sworn into office.¹⁵⁷ He was Calderón's right-hand man in the war in drugs. Calderón also awarded the high-ranking security official Cárdenas Palomino—involved in the Televisa staging—a medal for police merit.¹⁵⁸ Another key actor in the case, Isabel Miranda de Wallace, is introduced in such a way that she reveals connections between those in power and the purported guilty Eduardo Margolis.¹⁵⁹ A reporter from Mexico's Jewish press asks her if she has any connection to him, as he is a Jewish businessman, and she says she does—this is one paragraph after the narrator has stated that Margolis "recibió de manos de Calderón el Premio Nacional de Derechos Humanos y unas semanas después, la candidatura del PAN a la jefatura de Gobierno del Distrito Federal" (received from Calderón's own hand the National Prize for Human Rights, and then, a few weeks later, the PAN candidacy for the Federal District's head of government).¹⁶⁰ She reappears during the case only to accuse the Supreme Court of letting guilty parties go free on technicalities, technicalities that, the narrator explains, amount to torture.¹⁶¹ According to the novel, twelve years later, as the text was being finalized, these characters had uniformly done very well. Their participation in the state worked for them. García Luna lived in Florida and Cárdenas Palomino became the head of security for TV Azteca.¹⁶² The most likely candidate for kidnapper, Eduardo Margolis, "continúa siendo dueño de su conglomerado de empresas y de su agencia de autos blindados" (still is owner of his business conglomerate and his armored car agency).¹⁶³ Collaboration with the security state—including its lip service to human rights—paid off.

In portraying the experiences of Israel Vallarta following his arrest, and televised arrest, *Una novela criminal* investigates his personal experience and explores the underlying violent social order. One of the ways that it reflects on the broader social context is by explicitly referring to the 2008 constitutional reforms. As I mentioned toward the beginning of this chapter, these reforms were designed to "improve" procedures for arresting and detaining alleged criminals. The amendments did not accomplish their stated goal. Rather, they led to higher numbers of people being incarcerated. Analyzing *Una novela criminal* in conjunction with the constitutional text reveals other similarities as well. Both texts have a difficult aesthetic, which challenges the violent status quo. The novel is illogical, disjointed, and disconnected in some ways. This disorganization is similar to the constitutional text, whose sections, subsections, and articles require several signposts to encourage legibility. The headings that interrupt a continuous reading of the constitution remind readers of the topic for a series of articles, just as the chapter divisions in the novel bracket off its representation of distinct portions of Israel Vallarta's experiences in twenty-first-century Mexico. The narrator-detective also offers a certain level of guidance to readers to conduct us through the text, as well as employing conventions of literary genres, such as narrative nonfiction and detective fiction, to provide an idea of how to read and understand the text. These strategies exist in tension with the metafictional literary devices of intertextuality and the story-within-a-story of the journalist character Yuli García. In the novel, the forces of order push back against any deviations from the order. The status quo, represented by the prison, effectively ensures that readers follow the narrator-protagonist's guidance, just as his own character passed through multiple layers of security and saw Vallarta himself before being told that he would not be able to interview him. The narrator's imposition of order criticizes the prison so that readers will agree with the narrator's point of view and conceive of the narrator as a heroic detective offering a truthful version of events. If readers venture to disagree, then incarceration is the viable alternative. Similarly, in the constitutional text, the reforms devote such significant attention to how a person can and should be arrested, detained, and prosecuted that any and all mention of the rights to due process and legal representation are clouded.

The aesthetics in the literary and legal texts that create a sense of disorganization, and those that create a sense of organization, depend on each other. One does not exist without the other. Indeed, the tension in the aesthetics and in the content of the texts reflects the preoccupation with security that was rising at the time the constitutional reforms were passed in 2008, which had reached impressive heights a decade later, when the novel was produced. *Una novela criminal* draws on resources from narrative nonfiction, detective fiction, and the established precedent of the Crack literary movement, as its narrator comments on the version of events as it is representing them. The tension in the disjointed events and endless narrative commentary in the novel relates to the organizational structure of constitutional text in contrast to its content. The constitutional reforms and Volpi's novel mirror the obsession with security in Mexico in the twenty-first century. It is possible to emphasize policing and extensive security measures only if the population believes—and is destabilized by—a constant, unknowable threat.

CHAPTER 2

# Women Dream in *¡Basta!* and in Antiviolence Laws

This chapter continues the exploration of the first two decades of the twenty-first century and specifically focuses on the experience of women. The chapter compares literary and legal texts, highlighting the tension between formal strategies and the political context. It proposes that the aesthetics mirror the surrounding context in imposing and reinforcing subjective violence and in presenting challenges to the violent social order from 2000 to 2021 in Mexico.

The violent social order, as it pertains to women, is the tacit acceptance of all forms of violence—at home, in the workplace, and in public spaces. It encompasses everything from the division of labor to unfunny jokes, from intimate partner violence to rape and murder. In 2020 in Mexico, men killed approximately eleven women each day; men also raped eighty-seven women each day.[1] Moreover, 99.7 percent of rapes are unreported, because women believe that reporting is a waste of time: they distrust the authorities, believe the authorities will be hostile, or understand reporting involves too much paperwork.[2] No law or reform appears to have changed the staggering numbers of violent deaths of women. In 2006, when the law guaranteeing women a life free of violence was being discussed in Mexico's Congress, it was estimated that year that 1,293 women had died and were presumed murdered. In 2009 the annual number had risen to 1,858.[3] In 2007, and in 2020, the annual number of women's violent deaths had barely changed.

Women's experiences of violence have led to protests as well as significant political, artistic, and cultural production that testifies to their experiences. These include events for International Women's Day under the banner of #JuntasyOrganizadas (Together and Organized) and online campaigns in which women describe their experiences.[4] These include #NiUnaMenos (Not one woman less), which was adapted from the words of the murdered poet and activist Susana Chavez, #MiPrimerAcoso (My First Assault), and #SiMeMatan (If They Kill Me), in which women posted what they thought authorities or media outlets "would say to discount their lives if they were murdered."[5] Women have also organized movements to search for their missing and murdered daughters in movements like "Nuestras hijas de regreso a casa" (We Want Our Daughters to Return Home).[6] They have written to the president asking for help and written short stories as well. The term *femicide*, or the murder of women or girls by virtue of their gender, has entered legal discourse.[7] These efforts show us that violence is a systemic issue. Each person who protests, tweets, or writes a letter or a short story brings to light a facet of violence in women's lives.

Politicians, for their part, have passed laws to address violence in women's lives and to recognize the terminology of femicide. The 2007 Ley General de Acceso de las Mujeres a una Vida Libre de Violencia (General Law Guaranteeing Women Access to a Life Free of Violence) places femicide at the core of its definition of violence, stating that it is "la forma extrema de violencia de género contra las mujeres, producto de la violación de sus derechos humanos, en los ámbitos público y privado, conformada por el conjunto de conductas misóginas que pueden conllevar impunidad social y del Estado y puede culminar en homicidio y otras formas de muerte violenta de mujeres" (the extreme form of gender-based violence against women, the product of the violation of their human rights, in the public and private spheres, made up of the set of misogynist actions that can lead to social and state impunity and can culminate in homicide and other forms of violent death for women).[8] Politicians also recognized femicide as a specific crime, separate from homicide, in the criminal code.[9]

This chapter, "Women Dream in ¡Basta! and Antiviolence Laws," compares that 2007 law with women's letters to the president that describe experiences of violence and literary fiction that dreams of another world. In each type of text, there is significant tension between maintaining the status quo of violence and disorder. Voyeurism characterizes the way texts uphold the existing order, as well as their allusions to police and business protection. Women testifying to their own experiences, protesting injustice, and escaping their situations upends the violent social order. The following examines these competing structures and approaches to show what is at stake and how it might be changed.

## WOMEN'S EXPERIENCES OF VIOLENCE IN MEXICO

Women's experiences of violence preserve the social order, the smooth functioning of government, and capitalist expansion. Violence in women's lives is, as Kathleen Staudt explains, "an exposé of the state, masculine privilege embedded therein, and unequal gender power relations in state and society."[10] My analysis of women's experiences of violence in Mexico relies on the work of Staudt and other social scientists and cultural theorists. In this way, violence in women's lives in Mexico is framed within a broader understanding of violence against women. Such a broad understanding contextualizes analysis of how the legal, epistolary, and literary texts disrupt and maintain the brutally misogynist social order.

The patriarchal social order manifests in multiple forms of violence. Indeed, in Mexico, women are kidnapped, killed, tortured, and raped in large numbers by men who may be family members, intimate partners, or involved in criminal networks.[11] A man can be violent toward a woman by harassing her, assaulting her, raping her, or murdering her. Women in stigmatized occupations, such as sex work, are particularly vulnerable. This violence takes place within a system of power dynamics that includes relationships of gender, sex, race, and class.[12] The theorist Julia Monárrez Fragoso explains that the deaths of women and girls are the result of "la relación inequitativa entre los sexos: la superioridad genérica del hombre frente a la subordinación genérica de la mujer, la misoginia, el control y el sexismo" (the unequal relationship between the sexes: man's gender-based superiority and woman's gender-based subordination, misogyny, control, and sexism).[13] Violence in women's lives is so pervasive that it often goes unnoticed, yet it is crucial to the way that society functions—violence ensures smooth social functioning, and this point is not counterintuitive. When women accept that they are responsible for preventing their own rape or murder, they are more likely to accept less drastic forms of violence, such as lower pay for equal work, laughing at jokes that are not funny, taking on a disproportionate percentage of domestic and affective labor, and controlling behavior of male family members or partners.

Indeed, violence in women's lives is one of the types of systemic violence that ensures a specific social order: correct functioning of the capitalist system. The way that women accept lower pay, extra work, or multiple mistreatments directly enriches the people—usually men—who hold power in the workplace, in the home, in the political realm, and in licit and illicit businesses. The critic Sergio González Rodríguez analyzes the situation of extreme violence that women experienced in Ciudad Juárez. His vivid description remains pertinent for analyses of violence that women experience in other contexts. Using Gilles Deleuze's and Félix Guattari's concept of a war machine, González Rodríguez describes the violence women experience as a femicide machine, one in which violence is a cog that is integral to the larger structure.[14] González Rodríguez's work acknowledges that misogyny is a parasite, which is a social feature rather than an aberration. He demonstrates that misogynist violence finds ample nourishment in our society. As he goes on to explain: "Ciudad Juárez's femicide machine is composed of hatred and misogynistic violence, machismo, power, and patriarchal reaffirmations that take place at the margins of the law or within a law of complicity between criminals, police, military, government officials, and citizens who constitute an a-legal old-boy network."[15] Women's experiences of violence, including their deaths, are integral to the social fabric—in Mexico and elsewhere.

The epidemic is crucial to capitalist expansion.[16] According to Alice Driver, people in important positions in various powerful structures, from government to business, act violently and collude with one another to ensure impunity. She states that "there is a level of complicity between wealthy business owners and politicians that demonstrates the way in which sovereign power has become something shared by the parallel structures of government and big business."[17] The corporate takeover of the Mexican government becomes more apparent with the high numbers of missing and murdered women in Ciudad Juárez in the years after the North American Free Trade Agreement went into effect. Multiple US-based companies built factories along the Mexico-US border. Along with economic growth, women began to die. Alicia Gaspar de Alba puts it succinctly: companies are making a killing while young, poor brown women are dying.[18] The young women assume incredibly high levels of risk for relatively minor economic gain, and in light of widespread poverty, if one of them dies, there is always another woman willing to work in the factories. That women factory workers bear the risk means that those who run the companies can extract additional profit and preserve their power, and the Mexican government refuses to deal with the ways that companies benefit while women die. Mexico's minimum wage does not correspond to the cost of living, and no level of government ensures safe transportation or safe housing. The government benefits too strongly from the companies' presence in Mexico—

through taxes, bribes, or other forms of corruption—for it to do anything about the issues. The collusion between state actors and those in the private sector preserves the power of the people at the top and comes at great cost to vulnerable women factory workers.

## MEXICAN GOVERNMENT RESPONSE TO VIOLENCE

The Mexican government has not been completely silent on the matter of violence against women. I examine some of the ways that the Mexican government has attempted to rectify the high level of violence in women's lives.[19] New laws are the main way that legislators in the Chamber of Deputies and the Senate have responded to the Mexican people's appeals for justice and the eradication of violence. The Ley General de Acceso de las Mujeres a una Vida Libre de Violencia was signed on February 1, 2007, by President Calderón, and is a top-down response to Mexico's particular incarnation of misogynist social norms. It comes out of over a century of Mexican women advocating for their rights. Mexican women began agitating for suffrage in Yucatán in the nineteenth century. They held an international feminist congress there in 1916 and gained the right to vote in that state in 1923.[20] They gained the right to vote in municipal elections in 1947 and on a national level in 1953.[21] Women gained equality before the law in 1974.[22] A law was also passed guaranteeing equality between men and women in August 2006.[23] Each of these laws is a move toward a different type of society. Yet since the Ley General de Acceso de las Mujeres a una Vida Libre de Violencia comes from the top, it is unlikely to change the lives of ordinary women who live with violence, particularly if those men who exert power over them do not change their behavior and those women who uphold patriarchal social norms continue to do so.

Mexican deputies and senators discussed the law in the months prior to its enactment, including examples of Mexico as it is and Mexico as they think it should be. These discussions were particularly timely, as newly elected representatives began their terms in September 2006, a few months before President Felipe Calderón was sworn into office that December. In the span of two months, Congress established the nature of the violent status quo and expressed its members' hopes for the future. Much of the discussion was spearheaded by representative Marcela Lagarde, from the left-leaning Partido de la Revolución Democrática, or PRD.[24] Others involved were also from the PRD, and its coalition parties, the Workers' Party (Partido de Trabajo) and Convergencia. Lagarde and the PRD's advocacy was important in the context of women's rights and in asserting their general opposition to the new president Calderón. As discussed in Chapter 1, Calderón won the election under highly questionable circumstances. Members of the Partido Revolucionario Institucional (PRI), and its allied Green Party (Partido Verde), aligned with the PRD for the purposes of the Ley General de Acceso de las Mujeres a una Vida Libre de Violencia. Alberto López Rojas, a PRD representative from the State of Mexico, was one of the first representatives whose remarks established the systemic nature of women's experiences of violence. On October 16, he stated that that social norms and legal texts reproduce masculine supremacy and violence.[25] The law's implied goal, then, would be the eventual eradication of misogynist male supremacy. Two weeks later, the Partido Nueva Alianza representative Mónica Arriola echoed his remarks. She mentioned proverbs or sayings, and jokes, as a way to illustrate the widespread nature of violence against women in everyone's lives.[26] A week later, in the senate, Green Party senator Ludivina Menchaca Castellanos was even more explicit about the systemic nature of violence: "La violencia contra la mujer deriva de aspectos sociales y culturales, de normas que colocan a las mujeres en una situación de injusticia, desigualdad e inequidad ante los varones; es producto de una socialización diferenciada que considera inferior y más débil a un sexo frente al otro" (Violence against women has social and cultural roots, with norms that place women in situations of injustice, inequality, and inequity vis-à-vis men; it is the product of a differentiated socialization that considers one sex to be inferior to and weaker than the other).[27] These comments, taken together, exemplify Mexican politicians' understanding of women's experiences of violence as part of the status quo. Their speeches mirror the ideas of social scientists and cultural theorists, and in Mexico, it is much more common for politicians of every political party and coalition, from leftist to conservative, to pay lip service to feminist ideals even if their actions contradict their professions that women's experiences of violence are a systemic social issue.

These legislators also remind us that laws reflect aspirations for a better society. Indeed, in the same speech, Menchaca Castellanos made clear that legislators have a duty to change these systemic issues: "Estas manifestaciones constituyen actos de desvalorización y discriminación de la mujer, así como un menoscabo a sus derechos humanos y a su autodeterminación, por lo que es labor de los legisladores contribuir a finalizar estas prácticas" (These manifestations are acts of devaluing and discriminating against women, as well as an impairment of their human rights and self-determination, and for this reason it is the task of legislators to contribute to putting an end to these practices).[28] Legislators will end these violent practices by passing a new law. The words of Convergencia representative Jorge Godoy Cárdenas encapsulate the law's aspirations: "Es menester destacar que esta ley es emanada de una situación grave, producto del franco desinterés evidenciado por generaciones respecto a la violencia contra las mujeres" (It is important to highlight that this law emanates from a serious situation, which is the product of the flat disinterest of generations with respect to violence against women).[29] In his view, only a new law will be able to "superar los lastres que han perjudicado a la sociedad, por ello contempla ... reformas jurídicas que permitan a las mujeres ejercer plenamente sus derechos humanos y sancionar a quienes los transgreden acorde a los delitos especiales que atiende el proyecto que obra" (overcome the burdens that have harmed society, and for that reason contemplate legal reforms that allow women to freely exercise their human rights and punish those who transgress them as a special type of crime identified in the project at hand).[30] Godoy Cárdenas's comments crystallize many efforts to recognize women's experiences of violence. The tension between describing violence and creating a better society is evident in the legal text as well.

## LEY GENERAL DE ACCESO DE LAS MUJERES A UNA VIDA LIBRE DE VIOLENCIA

Lawmakers eventually passed a law that goes into more detail about the problem of violence in women's lives and imagines ways to transform women's experiences of violence. The Ley General de Acceso de las Mujeres a una Vida Libre de Violencia exhibits significant tension between description and aspiration in terms of its form and its content, and ultimately, in the legal framework, the descriptive forces of order overrule the aspirations. This law is both descriptive and proscriptive, as are many laws. The law strives to create a framework in which Mexico might be able to eradicate violence against women, in every part of Mexico. Its formal structure divides these ideas into a series of articles, even as the divisions creatively imagine a better future. The repeated emphasis on policing throughout the text overrules the creativity necessary for imagining a better future for Mexico.

The law also begins in an aspirational way, elaborating on how the law will ensure that Mexico is as it should be. The text explicitly states its objective, as "establecer la coordinación entre la Federación, las entidades federativas, el Distrito Federal y los municipios para prevenir, sancionar y erradicar la violencia contra las mujeres, así como [establecer] los principios y modalidades para garantizar su acceso a una vida libre de violencia" (establishing that every level of government will work together to prevent, sanction, and eradicate violence against women, as well as [establishing] the principles and modalities that could guarantee her access to a life free of violence).[31] In other words, the Mexican federal government will ensure women a life free of violence. Once women are able to live without violence, they will be able to access the promises of the Mexican Constitution. The law affirms that eradicating violence in women's lives will improve conditions throughout Mexico when it adds that these principles and modalities will favor women's development and well-being, and as such, will be implemented: "conforme a los principios de igualdad y de no discriminación, así como para garantizar la democracia, el Desarrollo integral y sustentable que fortalezca la soberanía y el régimen democrático establecidos en la Constitución Política de los Estados Unidos Mexicanos" (according to the principles of equality and nondiscrimination, as well as guaranteeing democracy, and a holistic and sustainable development that will strengthen the Constitutional establishment of Mexico's sovereignty and democratic regime).[32] In this way, women will be able to fully participate in every aspect of life. Here the legal text puts its stated goal—guaranteeing women access to a life free of violence—in an optimistic framework. This represents a hopeful position that, in the future, women might be able to live their lives without violence. That is, if the law creates the desired social framework, women may be able to flourish.[33]

The law's subsequent articles also describe Mexico as it is. The switch from the aspirational mode to a descriptive one is jarring and creates a sense of discontinuity that, moreover, ensures readers are paying close attention to what follows. The law's sixth article describes Mexico as it is by detailing multiple forms of violence, all of which echo the politicians' remarks in the debates. The law mentions psychological, physical, property, economic, and sexual violence. It concludes by adding: "Cualesquiera otras formas análogas que lesionen o sean susceptibles de dañar la dignidad, integridad o libertad de las mujeres" (any other types [of violence] that denigrate or could damage women's dignity, integrity, or liberty).[34] The law also mentions the various places where violence occurs: at home, at work, at school, in communities, in institutions, and in the political realm.[35] The law's comprehensive description of violence in women's lives reminds us that Mexico is deeply imperfect. The ways that these articles of the law align with the descriptive genre exist in tension with the lofty goals the law sets out for itself in its first article.

The Ley General de Acceso has a formal structure that organizes its ideas, one similar to the structure of the Mexican Constitution. The headings in the legal text create a sense of order for the reader and cover up certain leaps of logic between the different articles. That is, the parts of the text that are in bold and use roman and Arabic numbers are noticeable and help the very dense text make some sense for the reader. The law begins with a title, which is located at the top of its first page. The way the title appears on the page, along with the combination of fonts, use of bold, and roman and Arabic numerals is normal for Mexican legislative texts. Then, after the title, the text states that it was signed by Felipe de Jesús Calderón Hinojosa, president of Mexico. The president's signature places the law within the context of his administration. The law is then divided into *títulos* (titles) and *capítulos* (chapters). They are written in different fonts and also use bold. As such, the title and chapter markers function as headings that guide the reader. The sections are further subdivided into *artículos* (articles). The Arabic numerals that accompany each article group paragraphs together, which would otherwise be disjointed (i.e., the headings are key to making the law make sense). As the entire law is about a single topic, there are only forty-eight articles. So, the framework of headings makes the articles' description of violence understandable for the reader, who may wish to avoid such a painful topic. It categorizes violence by type, ranging from psychological to physical, and by location, ranging from the workplace to the home. Each article that deals with a type of violence or location where violence occurs is usually four to seven lines of text. The organizing structure thus calls to mind some aspects of the Mexican Constitution, as it connects an individual article's allusion to a relatively broad topic, such as the shift from violence at home to violence at school. These divisions in the text, then, serve an important organizing function: they contain the more aspirational elements of the text and try to keep those aspirations more in line with the world as it already is.

The organizational structure of the law also disrupts a sense of flow and makes the reader question certain aspects of the law or pay closer attention to these shifts. Article 6, for instance, is quite different from Article 7. Article 6 uses roman numerals to enumerate six types of violence.[36] The subsequent article is much more specific, as it deals solely with intrafamily violence. It begins by defining family violence as "el acto abusivo de poder u omisión intencional, dirigido a dominar, someter, controlar o agredir" (the abusive act of power or intentional omission, designed to dominate, subject, control or attack).[37] There is a logical connection between a list of types of violence in Article 6 and a specific definition of family violence in Article 7. However, the headings in the legal text interrupt any possible flow from one article to the next. Article 7 appears at the beginning of Title 2. In slightly larger bold font and in all uppercase letters, the legal text states:

## TÍTULO II
## MODALIDADES DE LA VIOLENCIA
## CAPÍTULO I
## DE LA VIOLENCIA EN EL ÁMBITO FAMILIAR.

*(Title II, Types of Violence, Chapter 1, On Intrafamily Violence)*[38]

The headings are in a text that is clearly different from other texts. They bridge the list of all types of violence and the definitions of specific types of violence. They disrupt an easy acceptance of the information and remind the reader to pay attention again. Throughout the legal text, the headings allow the reader to understand how and why the law moves from one topic to the next.

The law also describes the types of punishments the state and victims may seek for aggressors. I posit that the text's constant emphasis on punishment, policing, and incarceration grounds it in the descriptive rather than aspirational genre. First of all, each subsection that deals with a specific type of violence ends with a list of ways that the federal and local governments will ensure compliance with the law. The final item at the end of every single subsection involves sentencing or reporting the violent incident in a woman's life to some kind of authority.[39] The law goes into more detail regarding arrest and detention when it establishes the procedures for restraining orders in the very last chapter of Title II. The title thus follows the same pattern as each individual chapter, which also describes a type of violence and ends with a statement related to sentencing or incarceration. The title begins by defining a restraining order in Article 27, then what types of restraining orders exist (i.e., differentiating emergency and other situations) in Article 28, and in Article 29 it gives further definition.[40] The law recognizes that women have a right to a life free of violence. Its structure and content, however, illustrate the perspective of those in power. For them, the only way to remedy the situation is with a show of strength. Reliance on policing and incarceration is the fatal flaw at the heart of this law.

The third title describes the ways that the Mexican government will deal with violence in women's lives. The articles in this section include aspirations for how women's lives ought to be and descriptions of how abusers might be punished for violating this federal guarantee that women's lives be free of violence. Article 38, for instance, lists a series of strategies that the federal government will undertake to improve women's lives throughout the country. The thirteen-item list there, with roman numerals, begins with examples of education and special programming for victims; shifts to emphasize investigation, recording, and reporting data; and concludes with a summary of the holistic and punitive approaches to dealing with violence in women's lives.[41] Article 38, Item II, states that programming for eradicating violence against women will transform Mexican society and culture. Then, Article 38, Item III, states that the law will ensure that police and the legal sector receive education about violence against women.[42] Further subsections elaborate on how to transform social and cultural beliefs and how the law will educate police and the legal sector. Articles 41 and 48 recognize that Institutos de la Mujer are places that provide legal assistance to women who are victims of violent crimes.[43] In addition to explaining how women might navigate the legal system, Articles 42 and 44 offer proposed reforms to policing in Mexico. Article 44 states that in the future, Mexican police will pay closer attention to women when they report; moreover, it will create special police forces.[44] In this law, then, policing is an integral part of a better future for women. Policing, together with the bureaucracy enshrined in the Institutos de la Mujer, is part of the status quo that upholds structural violence. Policing and bureaucracy have the final word and supersede the earlier enumerated tensions between order and disorder. The aesthetic forces of order ultimately align with the violent forces (e.g., policing) that order society in early twenty-first-century Mexico.

## LITERARY AND ARCHIVAL REPRESENTATIONS OF WOMEN'S EXPERIENCES OF VIOLENCE

Both legal and archival texts include representations of voyeurism, allusions to policing, and disappointments with the criminal justice system. Moving now to explore a short-story collection and archival documents reveals that, in some ways, the aesthetics in the short-story collection, the archival strategies, and the violence to which both letters and short stories allude all maintain the violent status quo. In other ways, the structure of the literary texts and the letters disrupt these tendencies.

Literary texts and letters that deal with violence in women's lives also exhibit a tension between organization and disorganization. This tension exists in terms of both their form or aesthetic qualities and the subject matter they represent. In some cases, the disorganization or disorder may be a deliberately created crisis that allows those in power to accumulate more capital. In others, the disorganization or disorder in a literary text jars the reader out of complacency and encourages critical interrogation of the literary text and the social, political, and historical context it represents. The forces of order are any that support the violent status quo that profits off misogyny—whether a joke or a femicide. The forces of disorder, as I analyze in these texts, are any strategies that challenge the patriarchal order that subordinates women and the misogynist component that hates women.

The literary texts and letters analyzed in this book were written in the first two decades of the twenty-first century in Mexico, a time and a place when women's rights were part of cultural discourse. They were written by women from a variety of social classes and occupations rather than by politicians, who work within a framework that recognizes the state's right to violence. As the short stories and letters come from such diverse backgrounds, they represent distinct ideas about the nature of violence in women's lives and what ought to be done in response. Women have written many letters and literary texts that testify to the violence that they experience and that dream of better futures. The letters I look at in this chapter are part of the *peticiones presidenciales* (presidential petitions) collection in Mexico's Archivo General de la Nación (AGN, or National Archives), and the short stories I analyze are from a collection called *¡Basta! Cien mujeres contra la violencia de género*. The letters form part of a much larger collection that includes any letter that a Mexican person has sent to a president from the tenure of Lázaro Cárdenas (1934–1940) to Felipe Calderón (2006–2012). As such, the letters that I look at that tell the president about violence in women's lives are only a small portion of the many concerns that Mexican people have brought to the president over the course of almost a hundred years.[45] Each letter is approximately one page long and is archived together with a cover letter and the government's response.[46] The stories in *¡Basta!*, for their part, are also brief. They are less than a page long, and as such can be classified as flash fiction.[47]

The *peticiones presidenciales* that deal with violence in women's lives are only a few of the tens of thousands of letters that Mexican people write the president. They may write letters or emails or fill out an online form. They ask questions or beg him for justice. The interactions between Mexican people and their president follow a colonial-era tradition in which people would petition the Spanish king or his vice-regal representative in New Spain in *audiencias*. The king or vice-regent had the power to intervene and occasionally did so.[48]

The archives classify the correspondence between Mexican people and the president in what I would call a dehumanizing way.[49] Similarly, the Mexican AGN reduces moving accounts of devastating violence to a series of numbers and letters. The way that the AGN classifies the letters, moreover, amplifies existing issues with the correspondence between the

Atención a la Ciudadanía program and the letter writer. In the AGN, petitions to the president—and the government's responses—are held in the same file folder. The first page in the folder is a cover letter from Atención a la Ciudadanía, which classifies the letter writer by age, sex, city of residence, and so on. The second and third pages are a copy of the letter from the petitioner. Communications between government agencies about the letter and the government's eventual response to the petitioner round out the file. Each of these documents dehumanizes the letter writer. The cover letter likely exists for the government to prove that it is meeting the needs of the Mexican population of every age and from every state in the republic. It serves the secondary purpose of facilitating discrimination based on the letter writer's profession. Ultimately, Atención a la Ciudadanía may not even respond to a given letter. The bureaucracy maintains the status quo by sending letters to other government agencies and back to the original petitioner, and where the bureaucrats rarely address the issues outlined in the letters.

One particularly poignant account in the archive is from María Antonia Márquez Hernández, a woman seeking justice for her murdered daughter. Márquez Hernández alleges that her daughter's boyfriend and his brother murdered her daughter in front of their young children and had not yet been convicted.[50] Analyzing this letter and file reveals how the bureaucratic forces of order organize the relaying of events. I will also explore the aesthetics of Márquez Hernández's letter and the response from Atención a la Ciudadanía, to show how deploying formal conventions upholds the violence inherent to patriarchal social structures. The fact that the letter describes a woman's experience of violence, and her mother's search for justice, disrupts the socially acceptable level of violence, even if only slightly.

The archive makes Márquez Hernández's situation understandable by employing the same organizing strategy used by the bureaucracy. The file begins with the cover letter from Atención a la Ciudadanía and its version of events identifies Márquez Hernández as a housewife and gives her address.[51] The fact that she is a housewife gives anyone who reads her file a reason to denigrate her, or to pay less attention to her needs. Moreover, the fact that Márquez Hernández's letter is a single page in a file that contains only six pages shows that the bureaucracy overwhelms the individual who would seek to use what little possibility she had to make powerful people pay attention to her. In this way, the archival strategy aligns with that of the bureaucracy to ensure that whatever appearance might be given to allow people the opportunity to converse with their head of state, they would not disrupt the status quo.

The letters, for their part, also follow many formal conventions of letter writing. These organizational strategies are part of any correspondence a Mexican person might wish to have with anyone with power, in particular, with anyone in power in a government ministry. The letters typically begin with the address and date in the top right-hand corner, and then, a few lines below, the presidential address, on the left-hand side of the page. Márquez Hernández omits the formal salutation and moves to her opening paragraph. It gives her name and then states: "en mi carácter de ofendida en la averiguación previa que se cita al rubro" (as the offended party, in the preliminary investigation, cited here).[52] This woman, likely from a marginalized background, explains why she is writing the president. Her letter is typed; yet she makes small errors, such as, "Ruego de ud. Su valiosa intervención" (I beg of you Your valuable intervention).[53] Márquez Hernández's letter may have been typed by another person and signed by the letter writer. It concludes with variations of Spanish phrases common to formal letters: "Por su atención quedo ante usted muy agradecida" (I am grateful for your attention to this matter) and then, several lines of empty space below the letter, "Atentamente" (Sincerely), her signature, and below the signature, her name is typed in uppercase letters. Her letter thus conforms to and is constrained by common letter-writing strategies, particularly as she is likely from a marginalized background. The generic elements of the letter reveal her social class and educational background, and that she is desperate enough so as to write to a person at the top of the hierarchy to resolve her issues.

The content of the letter aligns it further with powerful individuals and social systems—which impose violence and order—through its references to the constitution, legal case numbers, and courtroom experiences. Márquez Hernández's letter does not quote feminist theory or align with the debates about the law that would be passed a year later. It does remind the president of other ways that the constitution guarantees justice for all Mexicans and demonstrates a high level of bureaucratic literacy. Her second paragraph asks the president to intervene because he has promised to ensure that the constitutional guarantees for crime victims are enacted: "En virtud de que nuestra máxima constitución consagra derechos a favor de las víctimas de los delitos como se desprende del artículo 20 constitucional y así mismo los derechos de recibir una procuración pronta y expedita" (By virtue of the fact that our esteemed constitution establishes rights for victims of crimes, as shown in constitutional Article 20, and similarly grants the right to prompt sentencing).[54] As with Israel's situation in Volpi's *Una novela criminal*, however, speedy justice is a pipe dream at best. Márquez

Hernández continues in the same paragraph, and reminds the president that he has promised to uphold these guarantees as part of his role: "ud. sr. presidente como máxima autoridad en el país se ha comprometido a velar por el cumplimiento de nuestra constitución" (you, mr. president, as the highest authority in the country have committed yourself to ensure the fulfillment of our constitutional guarantees).[55] The letter repeats its reference to the constitution likely in hopes that, by mentioning such a significant document, the president will be more likely to respond. Márquez Hernández reiterates what she understands to be: "del compromiso de ud. [p]or defender los derechos de las mujeres y evitar mas [sic] muertes por causa de violencia familiar" (your commitment to defend women's rights and avoid further deaths from intrafamiliar violence).[56] The way that she refers to the constitution foreshadows the debates that would take place in Congress a year later. She also chastises the president as she reminds him that he had promised to reduce the numbers of murdered women. Márquez Hernández also encourages him to uphold Mexico's laws. Indeed, were he to uphold these laws, he would align himself with what the letter writer states is his "franca y abierta manifestación de no permitir la corrupción y mucho menos que se dejen los delitos impunes" (frank and open statement that he would no longer permit corruption, much less that he would leave offense unpunished).[57] The letter writer is aware that the president has made public declarations against corruption and impunity, and so she reminds him of promises he has made, and of his role, which is to uphold Mexico's law. The way Márquez Hernández refers to the law and the constitution aligns the letter's contents with the forces of order. Moreover, it affirms her understanding that were the president to "correctly apply" force, good would prevail.

The letter then details Márquez Hernández's version of events. This woman voices her own experiences of violence so those in power will pay attention. In this way, her letter disrupts the violent status quo, upheld by the bureaucracy, by the archive, and by other social structures. Márquez Hernández's letter, and others, thus "contrarrestar el paternalismo y la misoginia inherente a México; combatir la desmemoria y la historia oficial de los acontecimientos; y producir material original al respecto" (push back against Mexico's inherent paternalism and misogyny; combat forgetfulness and the official history of events; and produce original material in this regard).[58] It states that her daughter was assassinated by her *concubino* (partner) and his brother on February 12, 2004.[59] She has put her version of events on the public record, and no one can take away the power of that courageous declaration.

At the same time, the forces of order are omnipresent within the letter. The subsequent, equally short paragraphs consistently refer to case numbers, police procedure, and events in courtrooms. Márquez Hernández's multiple mentions of policing and the criminal justice system further brings the letter in line with prevailing ideas of order and the notion that the state has the sole legitimate monopoly on violence. After giving the case number, she adds that the men were charged because her grandchildren testified. Then the letter relates how things started to go downhill. The case went forward, and the judge ordered the accused men to be arrested and held in pretrial detention. The men were to be held in a location similar to where Israel Vallarta was detained in *Una novela criminal*. Once they were charged, however, the local police commander was totally uninterested in apprehending them. The alleged murderers sued for *amparo*, and their detention order was removed. The judge reissued the order, but the men were not apprehended. The accused in fact filed a second *amparo* that challenged the children's testimonies. Márquez Hernández's letter concludes by asking the president to intervene and ensure that the men who were charged are arrested and incarcerated. Her experiences remind us that when women do report on their lived experiences of violence, the authorities are usually uninterested in proceeding with the case. Even as the letter illustrates the futility of reporting, it does express a desire for the president to correctly apply the forces of order to arrest and convict those responsible for her daughter's death.

The process through which the government responds to Márquez Hernández's letter is yet another act of violence. It compounds the police's unwillingness to apprehend her daughter's partner and his brother or to put them on trial. The Atención a la Ciudadanía program, at that time called Atención de la Red Federal de Servicio a la Ciudadanía, dealt with each piece of correspondence the president receives and ultimately creates a paper trail that justifies its own inaction. In light of Márquez Hernández's request, someone in that office sent information about the case about her daughter's murderers to the Procurador de Justicia (attorney general) in the State of Mexico. Several bureaucrats entered information into a database. One, Arturo Cruz Noyola, summarizes her account. On January 9, 2006, he states that the case has been concluded because the Procuraduría de Justicia has asked that the State of Mexico police force to arrest the alleged criminals.[60] On June 19, the database was modified to reflect that the government is satisfied that she was given the attention required. While it is useful for a government to keep track of citizen interactions with the president, the supposed resolution of Márquez Hernández's legitimate complaint is problematic. It shows that the database is set up so that writing a letter back is considered sufficient—even if the letter does not address the petition in a substantive or meaningful way. The machine of bureaucracy has thus effectively organized a problem out of existence.

The content of the letters further illuminates the nature of bureaucratic violence. Adriana Cabrera Santana, personal secretary for the *procurador general de justicia* (attorney general) in the State of Mexico, sends the Atención a la Ciudadanía program a letter responding to Márquez Hernández. Cabrera Santana uses bureaucratic language to her advantage to avoid responsibility and completely ignores Márquez Hernández and her daughter. Instead, Cabrera Santana states that there were 135 cases of misapplication of justice in the State of Mexico between January 1 and February 15, 2006.[61] Her office considers these cases closed because they have followed up with the people who wrote letters. They have, as she goes on to explain, given special attention "a aquellos en los que se solicita la agilización en la integración y resolución de la averiguación previa correspondiente" (to those who asked for expedited resolution to the preliminary inquiry, as requested).[62] The letter implies that arrests have not been possible in every case. Cabrera Santana then exculpates the Procuraduría de Justicia by claiming: "En otros muchos casos o faltan elementos probatorios o algún dato que debe presentar u ofrecer el propio denunciante, o falta que ratifique su denuncia o querella o la naturaleza del asunto . . . implica que estas averiguaciones previas dilaten en su resolución" (In many other cases there may be missing evidence of lack of some other type of information that the complainant must present, or, it must be ratified, or there is something to do with the nature of the matter . . . any of these issued can lead to delays in a case).[63] The bureaucracy exculpates itself. Should this nonsensical statement be insufficient to cover Márquez Hernández's case, Cabera Santana's brief letter adds that other cases in which women were victims are still pending: "estos asuntos no pueden quedar indefinidamente pendientes, por lo que solicitamos su amable comprensión para que se puedan dar de baja" (these matters cannot be outstanding indefinitely, and for this reason we ask for your kind understanding so that the matter can be resolved).[64] The letter completely fails to recognize the petitioners. The closest thing Márquez Hernández receives to a response is Cabrera Santana's statement: "El Secretario Particular del C. Procurador solicita se concluya el presente asunto, en virtud de que en su momento se le dió [sic] la atención correspondiente" (The Prosecutor's Personal Secretary asks that the present matter be resolved, as it has already been given the necessary attention).[65] They are reduced to a collective of people who have filed complaints. The painful experiences she shared do not even make it into the government's response, and the government's attention certainly did not resolve Márquez Hernández's legitimate complaint. The bureaucrats' failure to address her needs in a meaningful way could mean that, for them, writing a letter was a sufficient response. Rhetorical violence and bureaucratic inaction mirror the inaction and corruption that Márquez Hernández had outlined in her letter to the president.

In Márquez Hernández's case, the archival strategies mirror the bureaucratic method for dealing with matters pertaining to citizen complaints. The valiant efforts of women such as Márquez Hernández testify to the extreme incidents of violence that women experience in Mexico and bring to light all-too-common aspects of society that some may wish would remain hidden. The conventions of letter writing, as well as the constant references to policing and court procedures, align her brief letter with forces that ensure an unjust social order. In Márquez Hernández's letter, then, the constraints, as well as the bureaucracy and the archive, reinforce or uphold the constraints imposed by the police's understanding of the desirable social order.

The short-story collection ¡Basta! exhibits some of the same tension between accepting and disrupting the status quo as in Márquez Hernández's letter to the president and in the bureaucracy's failure to respond to her in a meaningful way. The stories in ¡Basta! exhibit formal strategies that contain the fictional accounts even as they are organized in such a way that there are ample opportunities for reader reflection. There is a similar tension in the stories' content, where they expose everyday violence in women's lives and occasionally do so using literary voyeurism, which dehumanizes the female characters in the short stories. The tension in ¡Basta! between maintaining and disrupting the status quo mirrors the tensions in both the legal texts and the archived letters analyzed so far. The way that ¡Basta! refers to policing and other structures of power as an integral part of women's experiences of violence overshadows its form and content that point to a better future.

The structure of the short-story collection necessarily restricts the depth and breadth of each entry. Together, the hundred very short stories in ¡Basta! are the eighth installment in a series of collections of short stories with the same title, ¡Basta!.[66] Each collection includes one hundred accounts that "resist dominant narratives of many types of gender violence, from symbolic and discursive, to physical and fatal violence in each of their micro-short stories."[67] The stories in the collection are about the same topic.[68] In Lauro Zavala's understanding, this type of organization is less expansive than a collection of unrelated short stories but more expansive than short stories with so many commonalities in plot, character, or setting that they could be read as part of a novel. The overarching structure of the short-story collection, then, contributes to a sense of order.

The stories in ¡Basta! are ordered in a way that increases the sense of containment. The first story in the collection, Adaliz Patricia Estrada Torres's "Ojos ciegos a oídos sordos" (From Blind Eyes to Deaf Ears) deals with quotidian discrimination, and the last story, Yuyu/Carmen Castro's "Única" (Unique) offers a sense of closure. "Ojos ciegos a oídos sordos" deals with the division of labor at home and at work. In it, Estrada Torres describes a man and a woman who are married to each other and who work at the same employer and have the same job. They even began their positions on the same day. Yet they are treated differently. Moreover, as Torres points out, the woman character has already been working for several hours—performing domestic labor and childcare—before she even goes to work.[69] Such a story validates female readers by assuring them that their experiences are normal. "Única" implies that women share many of the same life experiences. The story is told in a series of verbs in the second-person singular form, *tú* (informal *you*), a narrative voice that suggests that some outside power is ordering women's lives. "Naces, comes, duermes; lloras, comes, duermes . . . menstruas . . . te casas . . . tienes hijos . . . olvidas comer, te olvidas de ti" (You are born, you eat, you sleep; you cry, you eat, you sleep . . . you menstruate . . . you get married . . . you have children . . . you forget to eat, you forget who you are).[70] These verbs reflect key moments and experiences in many women's lives: birth, menstruation, marriage, having children, and forgetting oneself to take care of others. The author's first name, Yuyu/Carmen, is split. The first of these names, Yuyu, suggests something personal, and the more common name Carmen, which would be shared with other women, could point toward the collective nature of the experiences in the story. The double name implies a tension between a woman who wants to make herself known outside of these key life moments and shared experiences. The examples from Estrada Torres's "Ojos ciegos a oídos sordos" and Castro's "Única" are similar to many women's lived experiences. The stories bookend a very slim volume of work, one with ninety-eight more examples of violence in women's lives.

The collection also alludes to larger social structures outside of the collection through the one-line author biographies at the bottom of each story. In some cases, the author's biographies are as long as the stories themselves. They show that the authors "nacieron y radican en diferentes estados del país, además de [mencionar] las profesiones y actividades tan diversas a las que se dedican" (were born and live in different states in the country, in addition to mentioning the many professions and activities to which the authors dedicate themselves).[71] Some of them are well-known writers, such as Martha Bátiz Zuk, whose work has been published in English and Spanish in several countries.[72] Others are journalists like Emma Irene L. Martínez, academics such as Rebeca Monroy Nasr, and activists like Laura Edith Saavedra Hernández.[73] These professions highlight the authors' relatively prestigious social locations and thus insert the collection into a certain level of acceptance of the status quo.

The collection—like most short-story collections—does not have a single narrator to make meaning for its readers in the way most novels would. I consider the editor in a similar way to the archivist mentioned earlier. The editor controls narratives and presents stories by authors who have a similar social class and level of educational and professional attainment. Thus, the reader must engage in interpretive work in order to understand how and why the stories fit into a broader whole. Each story has the same structure, of a title, a short account, and a biography of the writer. The stories are frustratingly short. In some stories, there is more blank space on the page than writing. The blank space may give the reader time to pause and think. It also, like the leaps of logic I noted in the legal text and in the constitution, is a way to make any potential disconnections between individual stories less noticeable.

Several of the stories, like all the letters to the president, are written with the understanding that someone with authority could fix the situation if he wanted to. Now, the stories and letters that most obviously express the desire for presidential intervention are those that deal with the extremely high numbers of murdered women in Ciudad Juárez. Three stories portray widespread violence, Carmen Nozal's "Ciudad Juárez," Hortensia Rosas Pineda's "Desde aquel día" (Since That Day), and Gabriela Morales Ríos's "Duelo eterno . . ." (Eternal Mourning). These three stories bring to life the tension between the extremely high level of murder, typically unknown victims, and collective or social issue of violence in women's lives. Like other stories in the collection, the stories that portray Ciudad Juárez typically have anonymous protagonists. In them, the narrator, even when a narrator-protagonist, often focuses on the character's body at the expense of her thoughts.

The narrators in these three stories, and letters to the president about murdered women in Ciudad Juárez, exhibit a type of exploitation of violence that is common in examples of cultural production that shed light on violence against women. Alice Driver has applied the term *porno-miseria* (porno-misery), a term first used by Colombian film critics to describe the exploitation of poverty in film, to portrayals of violence against women in

Ciudad Juárez.[74] Her observations apply to ¡Basta! as well. The portrayals of women's deaths in the three stories I've highlighted are less personalized that those of individual murders represented by other short stories or by other letters as they allude to an impersonal victim. These three short stories and letters to the president about Ciudad Juárez focus on the sensationalist aspects of violence (even though violence at home or in the workplace affects many more women). The stories and letters to the president align with Driver's contention that "graphic, violent descriptions and images of feminicide, although they may be represented as an effort to preserve the memory of the dead or to promote justice, contribute to the exploitation and objectification of the female body and reify the idea of the spectral, ghostly condition in which women in Juárez are depicted, hovering somewhere between life and death, a state that Judith Butler describes as 'precarious life.'"[75]

The stories and letters also follow Segato's observations about crimes in which women are victims: "se presentan como crímenes sin sujeto personalizado realizados sobre una víctima tampoco personalizada, un poder secreto abduce a un tipo de mujer, victimizándola, para reafirmar y revitalizar su capacidad de control" (they are presented as crimes in which an impersonal attacker acts violently toward an impersonal victim; a secret power abducts a certain type of woman, and victimizes her, in order to reaffirm and reanimate his sense of control).[76] Various stories focus on specific physical markers of violence and overtake characterizations of the victims as whole people. They also mention the numbers of dead women as a collective, without recognizing that they are also real people who have died. Bureaucratic strategies of violence, such as the lack of response as well as the sense that a problem can be organized out of existence by creating a new government ministry to deal with it, are also present in the letters that portray violence women experience in Ciudad Juárez. Here the voyeurs are women in a higher socioeconomic position who perceive the most precarious women and children as an impersonal, nonindividualized mass that is simply a problem. The fact that the concerned women occupy a relatively more privileged position than the women who are murdered mirrors the difference in power between the concerned women and the president.

Nozal's "Ciudad Juárez" focuses specifically on the reality of that city and reminds us of some of the remarks of theorists like Sergio González Rodríguez who vividly describe the femicide machine. Her story, using González Rodríguez's terminology, deals with the intricacies of the femicide machine, and it is dedicated to the city's dead women.[77] In "Ciudad Juárez," death is inevitable. Its first-person narrator states that is waits for women, "como quien espera una cerveza helada" (like someone waiting for a cold beer).[78] The narrator looks at her own body as if she were outside of herself and notes her state of affairs: "la ropa hecha jirones y el cuerpo descarnado, lleno de sangre y tierra" (clothing in tatters, and a gaunt body, full of blood and dirty).[79] Bells keep time as three hooded men rape her. They half-bury her body and leave her on the side of the highway. Nozal's story exhibits techniques of *porno-miseria*, then, as it describes an unnamed female protagonist's body and the final impression is of the woman's body at the side of the road. The protagonist also lacks specific identifying features. She may have been a poor brown woman, as Gaspar de Alba states, and no one will ever really know what happened to her. They will only remember the graphic description of her body.

"Desde aquel día" focuses on graphic violence in an unspecified location. The story exemplifies an exploitation of violence, as the narrator explicitly connects the vivid portrayal of the protagonist's body to the experiences of other women. "Desde aquel día" begins by describing the protagonist Sara, who is disoriented in a small, dark, and silent place. The narrator asks, "¿Cómo llegó allí? Iba de regreso a casa cuando . . ." (How did she get there? She was headed home when . . .).[80] Then, the story snaps back to reality by describing her body and a horrible smell: "Horrorizada, logra verse mutilada, su sexo desangrando. No se reconoce, piensa que no es ella" (Horrified, she is able to see herself mutilated, her genitals bloody. She doesn't recognize herself, she thinks it is not her).[81] Once her body has been mutilated, it is as if it were no longer hers. Then, "De pronto ya no existe el dolor, aquel olor ha desaparecido y ya no le atormenta la muerte" (Then suddenly there is no more pain, the smell has disappeared and she is no longer tormented by death).[82] The story concludes: "Sara no regresa a casa . . . Ellas tampoco . . . Luisa, Marisol, Martha, Rosario, Jacinta, Claudia, Lucía, Elena" (Sara doesn't return home . . . Neither do the others . . . Luisa, Marisol, Martha, Rosario, Jacinta, Claudia, Lucía, Elena).[83] Their bodies will also no longer be their own. They will become public bodies, and, applying Wright's assertions to "Desde aquel día," they would likely be perceived as public women, who had done something that made them deserve to die. The way the end of the story connects Sara's experience to that of other women is a pointed reminder that violence occurs so frequently in women's lives that it could be the experience of almost any other woman. On the one hand, Rosas Pineda's short story dehumanizes its protagonist. On the other, by depicting the dehumanization of women in relation to violence, the law, and the state, it pushes back against patriarchal structures that would prefer to completely ignore violence in women's lives.

The protagonist of Morales Ríos's "Duelo eterno . . ." gestures toward the systemic nature of violence in women's lives, which is crucial to the smooth functioning of society. The narrator states: "Había desaparecido, como muchas otras, como miles de mujeres que también desaparecieron y no merecieron más que una nota pequeñita en el periódico local de Chihuahua" (She had disappeared, like so many others, like thousands of women who also disappear and whose deaths are only worth a short note in Chihuahua's local newspaper).[84] It encourages readers to pay attention to these stories in newspapers as it reinforces that the women who appear by the thousands in newspapers were real people. Their deaths are much more newsworthy than those of the women whose intimate partners likely killed them.[85] Newspapers or other forms of news media are also loath to admit that any individual person would be complicit in the ugly social problem of widespread violence in women's lives. The fixation on these women's disappearances is one element of voyeurism, in which concerned women focus on the violence women of other social classes or economic backgrounds experience as a way to ignore the everyday violence that they are subjected to and that may also preserve their social position.

Women in Mexico in the early twenty-first century experience various types of violence that may lead to their death. One of these women's lives makes it into the letters written to the president. In March 2006, Gloria León Hernández wrote about violence against women to the president. León Hernández's mother was murdered by someone at her work rather than an intimate partner. Her short account is simply entered into the online platform. The brief missive is filled out in capital letters and includes confusion of *s* and *c* spellings, a common indicator in Mexico of not having a high level of formal education. The brief letter describes the events and the ways that the president ought to rectify the injustice brought about by other state actors: "mi madre, la señora María del Carmen Hernández Bravo, la cual fue asecinada [sic] en una forma violenta de la manera más cobarde por un individuo que la sorprendió a traición por la espalda quitándole la vida de un machetazo en el cuello (my mother, Mrs. María del Carmen Hernández Bravo, was violently assassinated by a cowardly individual who came up behind her and killed her with a machete across her neck).[86]

The letter writer contextualizes these events by explaining a problem with her mother's work as an *elote* seller in a market. León Hernández was supposed to be the only woman allowed to sell *elote*, but after an unspecified period of time, another woman was selling the same product in the same small market. The letter implies that León Hernández's mother understood that the presence of a second seller of the same good violated some sort of agreement and felt that it was unfair for another woman to cut into her business. León Hernández states that her mother had been on her way to speak with the market director about her unfair competition, to resolve the problem of too many people selling *elotes* in the same market. Then, she was killed. León Hernández alleges that the murderer was a family member of the other *elote* seller, which suggests that there is a relationship between her mother's work and her untimely death. The woman's death highlights more obvious examples of police corruption than Márquez Hernández's situation: the police in charge of the case asked for money to move it along. León Hernández states that her family does not have enough money to solve the problem. Police are unwilling to do their job without an additional incentive. They may also be colluding with the market director, in a small-scale version of the collusion between government and business that Driver explored in Ciudad Juárez and found had deadly effects on women's lives.

The government offers appears to respond to León Hernández. The Atención a la Ciudadanía's bureaucratic inaction evokes Graeber's notion of a bullshit job, as no one from the program addresses León Hernández's valid plea. Moreover, the cover letter and its eventual response reinforce existing violence in the letter writer's lived experience. León Hernández's grief over her mother's death comes through in her letter's plaintive cry for justice to the president: "Me ayude a que se le haga justicia" (Help me get justice for her).[87] The database entries are similar to those I mentioned with regard to Romo Fregoso's letter. Here, the cover letter from Atención a la Ciudadanía directly refers to the events that took place in the market and the murder of León Hernández's mother. Adriana Cabrera Santana, in 2006 still the secretary for the *procurador general* in the State of Mexico, explains that the matter has concluded because the aggressor's home was abandoned.[88] The government appears invested in resolving problems on a rhetorical level, but its inaction is evident. The letter, moreover, implies that finding the accused in a place that is not his home was simply too difficult to contemplate. Misogyny is embedded in society, which includes the criminal justice system, the police officers, and the office that purports to respond to citizens. If they do respond to people's needs, it is clear that the next level of justice system could easily reverse these decisions, deliberately fail to act, or cover up inaction with a robust bureaucracy. León Hernández's account, then, echoes the short stories and shows that when a woman lives outside of the boundaries that have been set up for her by social structures, her life is at risk; if someone harms her in any way, that person will face no consequences. That the government fails to respond to León Hernández's plea, just as it had failed to respond to every other plea anyone brought to the president via Atención a la Ciudadanía, implies that this fear is well founded.

Widespread violence in Ciudad Juárez is also a concern outside of the literary sphere and the ¡Basta! collection. It appears in the *peticiones presidenciales*, with several letters to the president asking him to do something about the problem of women's deaths in Ciudad Juárez.[89] In the subsequent paragraphs, I analyze two women's exchanges with the Mexican government via the Atención a la Ciudadanía program in Ciudad Juárez. These two women, Guadalupe Campos Villa and Adriana Laura Romo Fregoso, express grave concern about these women's deaths. I show that the way that they express their concern mirrors the voyeuristic approach in the short stories, in that the letters reduce women to their deaths. Campos Villa's and Romo Fregoso's letters also refer to other structures that maintain the social order, such as the law, policing, and the possibility of presidential intervention. The responses to their letters from federal bureaucrats pass on these requests to new government ministries and special prosecutors. The bureaucrats who write intragovernmental memos and responses to Campos Villa and Romo Fregoso on behalf of the Federal Government want to pretend the crimes never happened. They hope to organize the crime out of existence rather than organize the world so crimes like murdering women in Ciudad Juárez would no longer happen.

The letters to the president are based on the idea that state intervention is possible and necessary. Romo Fregoso and Campos Villa implicitly recognize what the journalist Diana Washington Valdez has observed: "Corrupt officials have covered up the crimes and protected the killers. Because of such official complicity, the deaths truly are crimes of state."[90] The letter writers want the state to start enforcing the laws that already exist. Desperate Mexican people want the state to apply its laws to their particular situations. It is as if on an intuitive level they realize that when the state does not enforce its laws, it is "deciding which lives have value and which do not."[91] Campos Villa and Romo Fregoso remind the Mexican federal government that these lives did have value.

Campos Villa's letter exemplifies common tropes in raising awareness about violence against women, and she portrays violence in women's lives from the same voyeuristic standpoint as the short stories analyzed previously. Campos Villa recurs to her participation in an ideal family structure and expresses a voyeuristic type of shock at the situation that deviates so far from her lived experience. The letter shows that she is part of the ideal Mexican family. It states that she is the mother of two girls, and she signs her letter with her married name, Guadalupe C. de Contreras, which would be her socially preferred, rather than legally changed, surname. She then goes on to state that she identifies with the mothers of the missing and murdered girls: "no me pongo en el lugar de esas madres que han perdido a sus hijas de una manera tan brutal." (I cannot put myself in the place of these mothers who have lost their daughters in such a brutal way).[92] At the same time, she could not write even a short paragraph without using a word like *brutal*, which falls back on porno-misery tropes to describe these women's experiences of violence. In addition to the way her letter reduces these women to their deaths, the letter also emphasizes the usefulness of state force. In her own words, she is frustrated to see that "por incapacidad, corrupción o complicidad (no lo sabemos) ningún caso ha sido resuelto hasta el día de hoy" (no cases have been solved, because of incompetence, corruption, or complicity (we do not know which)).[93] The letter exhibits respectability, in that the writer situates herself within an ideal family, as well as references to state use of force. The way the letter focuses on violence in other women's lives, rather than in her own, reinforces the letter's references to these other structures—of the family and policing—that uphold a violent status quo.

Romo Fregoso's letter reiterates these issues in September 2004. Romo Fregoso's letter reduces the women to their deaths and expresses a reliance on presidential power to right what had gone wrong in the country. That is, the technique of voyeurism complements emphases on presidential power. Romo Fregoso asks the president to end the kidnapping and assassination of women in Ciudad Juárez and in the city of Chihuahua. These women are reduced to their kidnapping and deaths. The letter goes on to refer to presidential power as the way to solve the problem, in part because the president himself had professed an interest in human rights. Romo Fregoso states: "Su gobierno ha manifestado su compromiso de promover la protección de los derechos humanos en todos los ámbitos. Sin embargo, estos casos pueden restar credibilidad a dicho compromiso" (Your government has proved your commitment to promoting the protection of human rights in every area. These cases, however, can undermine the credibility of that commitment).[94] His administration is hypocritical, and for this reason, Romo Fregoso implies he is not a very good president. Her letter reflects an interest in the women's deaths in Ciudad Juárez that aligns with parts of Driver's use of the term porno-miseria and it underlines the letter writer's belief that the man with the most power in Mexico can prevent further deaths.

The government's response to Romo Fregoso echoes the responses of Atención a la Ciudadanía to Márquez Hernández. Communications from the Atención a Ciudadanía program to bureaucrats in other parts of the

Mexican federal government, as well as the bureaucrats' response to Romo Fregoso, do not address her concerns. The bureaucrats attempt to streamline the problem of women's deaths in Ciudad Juárez into a database rather than address any of Romo Fregoso's valid concerns. The bureaucrats from one area of government pass the responsibility on to another area of the federal government and avoid taking responsibility for the problem. The anthropologist David Graeber chronicled a similar type of government expansion in the area of human rights in an era of austerity in *Bullshit Jobs*. He shows that an expanding bureaucracy allows people to believe that they are doing good and shows that the proliferation of such jobs prevents people from realizing that they are not doing good.[95] He adds that politicians, such as those invested in law and order, do not find that solving the underlying problem of crime is in their best interest.[96] Indeed, if police or prosecutors were set up to solve crimes in a way that created a more just society, there would not be nearly so many parts of the government. The AGN would not have recorded nearly so much intragovernmental communication.

After Atención a la Ciudadanía receives Romo Fregoso's letter, it sends it to the Procuraduría General de la República, or PGR. The communications within the PGR about Romo Fregoso's letter prove Graeber's point: it is not politically expedient for politicians, bureaucrats, or law enforcement officials to solve crime. Four bureaucrats write letters to one another about Romo Fregoso's concerns: Jorge Leonel Sánchez Ruiz, Benigno Aladro Fernández, Fernando Blumenkron Escobar, and María López Urbina. Sánchez Ruiz receives the letter because he works in a part of the PGR that deals with citizen complaints. He forwards Romo Fregoso's concerns to Aladro Fernández, who is from the federal Subprocuraduría de Derechos Humanos (Deputy Attorney General's Office for Human Rights), a subentity of the PGR.[97] Aladro Fernández eventually contacts Blumenkron Escobar, a *coordinador de asesores* (coordinator of advisers) in the PGR's division of victim and community services. Blumenkron Escobar then passes on the complaint to López Urbina, in the Fiscal Especial para la Atención de Delitos Relacionados con los Homicidios de Mujeres en el Municipio de Juárez, Chihuahua (Special Prosecutor's Office for Homicides of Women in the Municipality of Juárez, Chihuahua), another subdivision of the PGR.[98] Each bureaucrat turns over the letter to a more specialized subdivision. The first subdivision suggests that there are significant complaints against the PGR to warrant a special section of the PGR; the second, that there are high levels of human rights violations; and the third, that homicides against women are such a problem that they are considered separate from the issue of human rights as a whole. Taken together, they represent a bureaucratic approach to problem solving. These three subsections of the PGR align with the bureaucratic tendencies that Graeber outlines. The three subsections also mean that the PGR can appear to take the issue of women's deaths in Ciudad Juárez seriously without evaluating why the existing legal system did not previously address women's violent deaths.

López Urbina ultimately responds to Romo Fregoso. The letter—sent a year after Romo Fregoso's initial plea—is written in a patronizing way that falsely assures Romo Fregoso that the Mexican government is looking into the situation in Ciudad Juárez. López Urbina's letter is an example of bureaucratic incompetence and further confirms Graeber's observations about the expansion of government bureaucracies. López Urbina, from the office of the special prosecutor investigating women's deaths in Ciudad Juárez, begins by addressing Romo Fregoso as *señora*, which ignores Romo Fregoso's stated professional title of *ingeniero* (engineer) and reduces her to a social title. This is disrespectful in Mexican culture, which is deeply attached to titles, and represents the misogynist assumption that women cannot or should not be engineers. López Urbina, whose signature does not include a professional title, may address Romo Fregoso without her title to subtly undermine her. López Urbina's patronizing letter assures Romo Fregoso: "Puede tener la certeza de que estamos hacienda y haremos, nuestro mayor esfuerzo institucional y personal en la atención, seguimiento y en los casos en que legamente seamos competentes, la determinación jurídica de cada uno de estos casos que han ofendido gravemente a la sociedad y especialmente a las mujeres mexicanas" (Rest assured that we have been giving this case, and other cases where we have legal authority, our highest institutional and personal effort, and will continue to do so. These cases have seriously damaged society, and, in particular, Mexican women).[99] The fact that López Urbina's letter mentions possibility of action rather than action itself suggests that the PGR does not want to act, and so it blames the legal system. Moreover, in light of the high numbers of unsolved crimes in Mexico, it is clear that bureaucrats, politicians, and law enforcement never want to act. Romo Fregoso undoubtedly realizes that López Urbina's letter is nothing but an empty promise. Her letter is an example of a bureaucrat exerting violence on a citizen. López Urbina's letter to Romo Fregoso is part of a series of letters that, taken together, illustrate the problem of an expanding bureaucracy that fails to address the high numbers of murdered women in Ciudad Juárez. The way that each bureaucrat's letter reduces women to their deaths relies on the expanding bureaucracy to uphold the status quo.

The AGN also includes letters two groups of women wrote to the president about missing and murdered women in Ciudad Juárez. These petitions exhibit problematic literary tendencies, such as reducing women to their violent deaths, to persuade the president that widespread violence in women's lives is a problem he should pay attention to. The responses reinforce the government's lack of a meaningful solution by ignoring the content of the letters or the female letter writer's preferred names, or by suggesting that the government's hands are tied, so it cannot end the high number of women's deaths in Ciudad Juárez. The letters are part of a charade of a government that responds to its people, when in reality it does so only so that people will not notice that nothing has really changed.

A group of women's organizations called Coordinadora de Organismos No Gubernamentales en Pro de la Mujer (Coordinator of Nongovernmental Organizations in Favor of Women (and Women's Rights) drafted a letter to the president in February 2003. In it, they outline the many issues in Ciudad Juárez and how the government could do better. The strategies the group used to communicate with the president and draw attention to its cause dehumanizes the women who have been murdered. The letter reached the president in an unusual fashion. Six months after it was written, in July 2003, the actress Cristina Michaus hand-delivered the Coordinadora de Organismos' petition to the president.[100] It implicitly criticizes the mushrooming government programs and subprosecutorial agencies that ostensibly respond to women's experiences of violence. Indeed, the group directly challenges the government by boldly proclaiming, "Las autoridades responsables de impartir la justicia, se justifican mas que detener esta ola de terror que sacude nuestra Ciudad" (The authorities responsible for imparting justice justify themselves more than detaining this wave of terror that is hitting our City).[101] They remind the president that the justice system has not addressed any problems in a meaningful way. Instead, the legal authorities: "culpabilizan a los grupos que exigimos seguridad, de lucrar con el dolor de las victimas y exagerar el asesinato de mujeres al que consideran 'normal'" (blame the groups that demand security, implying that they profit from victims' pain, and exaggerate the murder of women, which they consider "normal").[102] They recognize the status quo is unacceptable. The letter, then, calls to mind Sergio González Rodríguez's notion of the femicide machine where women's deaths are a cog in the machine. As the letter argues, "El terror se ha apoderado de la población y la violencia sexual y física hacia niñas pequeñas o adolescentes es alarmante" (Terror has overcome the population and sexual and physical violence toward young girls and adolescents is alarming).[103] They explain the situation as one in which terror has taken over the lives of some of the most vulnerable people—young women and girls—and with this word, the letter takes away some power or agency that the victims may have had. They explain: "Hay una psicosis colectiva que no encuentra eco en sus demandas de justicia y seguridad" (There is a collective psychosis that is not echoed in their demands for justice and security).[104] That is, violence against women is so extensive that it has led to collective psychosis. Not only are the women who have died reduced to their embodied experience, so are the people who fight to have their deaths recognized. That is, the letter is constructed in such a way that it reduces the writers to an abnormal mental state. The rhetoric of this letter differs from theoretical contributions I examined earlier, yet it implicitly supports Gaspar de Alba's work, that businesses and politicians profit from the deaths of young women who work at factories along the Mexico-US border, and González Rodríguez's understanding that femicide is integral to the social fabric. Throughout the letter, they reduce the complex lives of tens of thousands of women to violence and death, and their own lived experiences to a type of psychosis. The Coordinadora de Organismos' fixation, then, on women's violent murders reproduces voyeurism or porno-misery.

In the files for this letter, the government passes on the communications until it reaches the appropriate person. The AGN record shows that five bureaucrats communicate about the matter: Laura Carrera Lugo, Santiago Creel Miranda, Miguel Rodarte de Lara, Daniel Cabeza de Vaca, and Ricardo J. Sepúlveda Iguíniz. Their communications illustrate bureaucratic expansion in the neoliberal period. The first instance of bureaucratic inefficiency appears in Atención a la Ciudadanía's initial response to the Coordinadora de Organismos. After Michaus delivered the letter to the president, the bureaucracy began to act. Laura Carrera Lugo, head of Atención a la Ciudadanía, wrote a letter the very next day. On July 17, Carrera Lugo wrote to Secretary of the Interior Santiago Creel Miranda.[105] Creel Miranda did not respond to Carrera Lugo's letter. Rather, it was sent to the part of the Secretaría de Gobernación (SEGOB, or Secretary of Home Affairs) that deals with other government agencies. Miguel Rodarte de Lara worked in that office, and on July 23, he forwarded Carrera Lugo's letter to another part of SEGOB. Carrera Lugo's letter and the petition from the Coordinadora reached Daniel Cabeza de Vaca, *subscretario de asuntos jurídicos y derechos humanos* (undersecretary for judicial matters and human rights), shortly thereafter.[106] Cabeza de Vaca is also introduced earlier in this book. Two years after receiving Carrera Lugo's letter, he would become Mexico's attorney general (2005–2006). Cabeza de Vaca also appeared in Volpi's *Una novela criminal*.

In the case of the letter, Cabeza de Vaca's office does not deal with it. Instead, he passes off Carrera Lugo's letter and the petition from the Coordinadora to Ricardo J. Sepúlveda Iguíniz, head of yet another area of SEGOB: Unidad para la Promoción y Defensa de los Derechos Humanos (Unit for the Promotion and Defense of Human Rights). Sepúlveda Iguíniz, the fourth bureaucrat to receive the petition from the Coordinadora, responds to the group. The subdivision that responds is so specialized that its very existence could be used to proclaim that the Mexican government has effectively dealt with women's murders. It also reminds us of the subdivisions of the PGR the government invoked to respond to Romo Fregoso's letter. The parts of the bureaucracy that relate to law and order proliferate in times of austerity.

The Mexican government's eventual response to the Coordinadora further upholds the status quo—in this case, the violent structure of bureaucratic inaction. Sepúlveda Iguíniz writes two letters. On July 30, he sends one to the members of the group. In it, Sepúlveda Iguíniz expresses his desire to "hacer de su conocimiento que el Ejecutivo Federal condena enérgicamente los actos violatorios de derechos humanos." (make it known that the Federal Executive energetically condemns actions that violate human rights).[107] He completely ignores the fact that the violations of human rights have led to such high levels of women being murdered that the letter writers from the Coordinadora have rightly likened women's murders in Ciudad Juárez to a state of constant terror. As Sepúlveda Iguíniz goes on to state, his office "facilita a las autoridades competentes todo el apoyo humano y material requerido para el pronto esclarecimiento de los hechos y el castigo de los culpables" (gives the pertinent authorities all the human and material support required to clarify events and punish the guilty in a timely manner).[108] Sepúlveda Iguíniz does nothing to address the Coordinadora's specific, valid concern. His pretense of action is also typical of the government's claims to respond to people's complaints. In another common move, Sepúlveda Iguíniz mentions that other government programs might be suitable for solving the problems, including a new subentity in the National Commission for Preventing and Eliminating Violence against Women: the Subcomisión de Coordinación y Enlace para Prevenir y Sancionar la Violencia Contra las Mujeres en Ciudad Juárez, within the PGR.[109] The new subcommission is yet another way that the government pretends to deal with women's deaths in Ciudad Juárez rather than actually facing the staggering loss of life. Sepúlveda Iguíniz's letter completely ignores the Coordinadora's request that the government do something. The archival record includes a second letter Sepúlveda Iguíniz wrote on August 12 to the Coordinadora in which he reiterates that the government is committed to dealing with the problem and details the ways different government agencies will coordinate to address women being murdered in Ciudad Juárez.[110] In both letters, Sepúlveda Iguíniz claims that the Mexican government is committed to human rights, which would be laughable if the effects of this inaction were not so deliberate or so devastating. Sepúlveda Iguíniz's letters to the Coordinadora—as well as the intragovernmental communications with Carrera Lugo, Rodarte de Lara, and Cabeza de Vaca—are part of the government's elaborate performance that completely absolves itself of any responsibility for causing the high number of women's deaths in Ciudad Juárez.

The Coordinadora was not the only group that sent a petition to the Mexican president begging him to stop women from being murdered in Ciudad Juárez. Indeed, a private citizen, Teresa Gómez Ibarra, delivered a petition to the president that contained 12,240 signatures. Gómez Ibarra's letter adopted different rhetorical strategies than those of the Coordinadora. She employs activist rhetoric as she suggests that, were the government to better use Mexico's existing legal framework, it could improve the situation of extreme violence in Ciudad Juárez. Gómez Ibarra begins by reminding the president that a number of international actors and the international women's community have condemned the high level of violence in Mexico. These organizations include "la agrupación Amnistía Internacional, a las Naciones Unidas que han mostrado su interés para que se solucione el caso de las mujeres asesinadas y el gobierno mexicano asuma su responsabilidad" ([from] Amnesty International [to] the United Nations, who have shown their support for solving the case of murdered women and having the Mexican government take responsibility).[111] Here Gómez Ibarra reminds the president that the numbers of women murdered in Ciudad Juárez are so high that the international community has condemned the Mexican government's response—or lack thereof. Gómez Ibarra then offers a solution: the president's professed belief in the rule of law. Her letter explains, "Cuando el espíritu de la ley se esquiva, la ley pierde su razón inspiradora, la norma pierde su dimensión transformadora, se vuelve lastre, instrumento de opresión, es letra muerta" (When the spirit of the law is ignored, the law loses its inspiration, norms lose their transformative potential, become dull, instruments of oppression, the words are dead).[112] In this way, Gómez Ibarra places the law in its context and implies that if support for law is solely rhetorical, the law is meaningless. The letter ends with a hopeful stance and activist cry: "Señor presidente: ¡Exigimos el esclarecimiento y castigo a los culpables del feminicidio en Ciudad Juárez! ¡Basta de impunidad! ¡Nunca una más!" (Mr. President: We demand clarification and punishment for those guilty of feminicide in Ciudad Juárez! End the impunity! Not one more!).[113] Gómez Ibarra's activist rhetoric contrasts sharply with the opening statements of her letter, which had referred to powerful international nonprofit organizations and exhibited a sophisticated understanding of the rule of law. Yet the references to powerful structures are so extensive that they outweigh more grassroots approaches to problem solving.[114] Gómez Ibarra's rhetorical strategies remind us of the tension between using institutional channels, which typically lead to government inaction, and activists' urgent call for change.

The official response reinforces that the power in the presidential office, as well as law enforcement, will solve violence against women. The letter upholds the fiction that policing or other types of law enforcement would lead to less violence, and it reminds us of the organizing structures that maintain an unjust social order. Laura Carrera Lugo highlights the government's concern for this social problem.[115] Her concern does not lead her to change the status quo in any meaningful way, yet her language reflects a desire to rhetorically challenge it. The letter adds that the president "busca atacar las causas estructurales que producen esta violencia de género" (seeks to root out the causes of gender-based violence).[116] The letter continues, reducing these women to their experiences of violence and reiterating that the president, as chief authority, is the person who will end violence in women's lives. Carrera Lugo concludes that the president "ha hecho suya la lucha contra esta incalificable violencia" (has made the fight against this uncountable violence his own).[117] It is much easier for Atención a la Ciudadanía to give vague assurances than to dismantle problematic social structures. All its responses invoke recognized powers within the country, such as the presidential office, special prosecutors, and new human rights programs, as part of these assurances.

Several letters to the president and short stories in ¡Basta! deal with violence against women and women's violent murders in Ciudad Juárez. The way they represent violence that ends in women's deaths upholds the existing status quo. The letter writers rightly refer to the president, and legal structures, as they anticipate that the correct application of the law would lead to a better future for all people in Mexico. Other cases also refer to powerful nonprofit organizations, their own professions, or their position in an ideal family structure to get their point across. These strategies align the stories and letter writers with the forces of order, because they use a strategy within Mexico's feminist movements for creating change through the political sphere.

The responses to the letters—as well as the absent responses to widespread violence in the short stories—show us that the government is committed to an elaborate charade in which it appears to bring about justice for all people in Mexico but is deeply uninterested in changing the status quo in any way. In each case, these bureaucrats failed to address women's experiences of violence and the system in which men kill many women each year. Instead, they pass on petitions to a variety of special commissions and government ministries to deal with the problem, in a particularly neoliberal conundrum of expanding bureaucracy in an era of austerity. In these examples, then, the letters and short stories about Ciudad Juárez inspire a particular type of voyeurism that focuses on Juárez at the expense of violence in other locations and in less dramatic ways. In this way, it aligns with other forces of social order that maintain the status quo.

Rather than offering a solution to the problems of violence against women, the letters and stories calling for better policing reinforce structures of violence, degradation, and silencing. While this is a laudable goal, many scholars and activists have observed that reforming the police is a misguided venture because it does not address the issue of force. Thus, reforming the police, those people who have a state-sanctioned ability to mete out force, can never solve the root of the problem. Indeed, failed policing "derives from and symbolizes flawed governance and criminal justice institutions."[118] I would expand Staudt's observation that good policing cannot come from such flawed institutions. When short stories refer directly to policing, they allude to trauma, police brutality, and impossible standards of evidence. The narrators typically express a desire to change these problematic areas; their continued reliance on these structures aligns the stories with the forces of order.

I briefly return to the *¡Basta!* collection to discuss the possibility of good policing. The stories in the collection that refer to the police represent police as abusers and police as completely ignoring people who report women's deaths.[119] In other words, police are inept at dealing with violence in women's lives. They also imply that policing could be reformed and, in this way, better deal with women's experiences of violent crime. I disagree: Policing is a violent profession, and male police officers often engage in intimate partner violence. Estimates suggest that 40 percent of police officers in the United States are violent toward their intimate partners, who are usually women.[120] Moreover, in Mexico, police are not well compensated, have no educational requirements, and are prone to corruption. Police are not well positioned to deal with women's lived experiences of violence on an individual or systemic basis. Indeed, as Melissa Wright has stated, if victims' families do report victims' deaths, they often "encountered the attitude that the brutal murders and kidnappings represent problems internal to the families and are not public crimes requiring state intervention."[121]

Several fictional accounts of violence in women's lives in ¡Basta! confirm what researchers have established. Rosario Gutiérrez's story "La delegación" (The Municipal Office) describes a woman who goes to the police to report a rape. Its third-person narrator recounts the events: "Su boca en la cara de ella, sus golpes, su miembro penetrándola" (His mouth on her face, the way he hit her, his penis penetrating her).[122] The narrator reflects that reliving the events in front of an indifferent police officer in a cold room was like being a martyr. "La delegación" implies that, until the protagonist was being questioned by police, she had felt that reporting the crime was a good use of her time and energy. The police officer's final question, however, shows that reporting the crime was very much *not* worthwhile for the protagonist. The police officer asks her: "¿Qué hacía usted vestida de forma tan provocativa?" (What were you doing dressed so provocatively?).[123] When the protagonist attempted to break the cycle of impunity, she faced a police officer who was completely willing to uphold his version of order rather than respond to the laws as they were written, and he was completely allowed to do so. The police officer, a state actor, ignored the law. In other cases, whether in fiction or in women's real lived experiences, state actors apply laws in uneven ways. The behavior of the police officer in "La delegación," moreover, aligns with the observations of several scholars. Melissa Wright, for instance, has claimed that "upon reporting a murder or disappearance, families have had to field the following question: 'Did she (the woman/girl in question) lead a 'double life'? A woman who leads a 'double life' is a woman who has a public persona in addition to the private one defined by her familial relationships."[124] In other words, police struggle to criminalize behavior that occurs at home. The only plausible explanation is that a woman acted in a way that they consider inappropriate outside of it. These individual actions form part of a misogynist system, which upholds capitalist expansion.

Two other stories in the collection, Laura Edith Saavedra Hernández's "¿Por qué las leyes son así?" (Why Are Laws Like This?) and Cecilia González's story "Amor, miedo y costumbre" (Love, Fear, and Custom), illustrate an unfair burden of proof in cases where women report their experiences of violence or when their bodies are examined after death.

Saavedra Hernández's and González's stories imply that the system could be changed ever so slightly, which shows a continued reliance on forces of order and a desire to uphold the status quo. "¿Por qué las leyes son así?" shows how women suffer when they report. The anonymous first-person narrator implies that she went to a police station with a friend. Her entire experience was unpleasant. It started because the day was cold and raining. The narrator reflects, "Por un lado, quería hablar de lo que me había pasado, por el otro, tenía miedo y pena de exponer mi caso ante extraños" (On the one hand, I wanted to talk about what had happened to me, and on the other, I was afraid and embarrassed to share my case with strangers).[125] When the fictional protagonist gains the courage to report, she encounters a literary version of what Monárrez Fragoso describes as the "*no lógica* de las autoridades; es decir, en ésta (no lógica) se concentra la censura, el distanciamiento, el desinterés y la indiferencia para tomar en serio lo que se exige y reclama" (authorities' *faulty logic*; that is, in this [faulty logic] we fine censure, distancing, disinterest, and unwillingness to take the cases seriously).[126] The narrator in "¿Por qué las leyes son así?" tells a police officer that her husband had hit her so hard that she became unconscious. She states that when she described her abuse to the police officer, she started crying. The female police officer asked the protagonist "sí había testigos, si traía golpes y sí tenía alguna prueba de la violación" (if there had been witnesses, if she had been hurt, if she had any proof of rape).[127] Since the protagonist in Saavedra Hernández's story had waited an unspecified amount of time before reporting, she had no proof they would recognize. The fictionalized officer, as if a perfect incarnation of Monárrez Fragoso's comments, tells the protagonist, "Si no hay pruebas no se puede levantar una denuncia, ni se puede hacer nada, eso dice la ley" (If there is no proof, you cannot file a complaint, and we cannot do anything, that is what the law states).[128] The police officer's response in Saavedra Hernández's story is the epitome of bureaucratic incompetence and shows that reporting retraumatizes women. The woman in the story—and the women in the entire collection—wonders: "Entonces pensé ¿por qué las leyes son así?" (And so I wondered, why are the laws like this?).[129] The protagonist's final question is rhetorical and implies that a better way of having laws would solve the problem. These measures will always be insufficient because a patriarchal system will always find another way to discredit women. It also shows that impunity flourishes even when there are laws that guarantee women a life free of violence because impunity is the status quo; thus, laws or better policing cannot fix the problem of violence in women's lives.

González's "Amor, miedo y costumbre" portrays a similar story in which the burden of proof is too great. It, too, implies that better legal standards would ensure justice for the victim; in this way, González's account relies on forces of order to create a better world. The narrator portrays the misogyny that leads a man to kill his wife and then the misogyny inherent in impossible standards of evidence in cases where men kill their intimate partners. The protagonist is a woman who achieves more in her profession than her male partner does. He claims that these accomplishments mean that she places herself above him.[130] The narrator does not go into detail about the protagonist's murder but does imply that the protagonist's male partner killed her. "Amor, miedo, y costumbre" goes on to state that the protagonist "fue declarada muerta al día siguiente, las pruebas fueron insuficientes pero presentaba golpes en el rostro y cuerpo" (was declared dead the next day, and although the tests were inconclusive, her face and body bore the marks of punches).[131] The tests were not good enough to convict her partner. The penal system is functioning exactly as it was designed, to uphold the status quo, by having standards of evidence in cases of intimate partner violence that would be nearly impossible. The story expands on how he avoided conviction: "Su victimario quedó libre porque no hubo testigos" (Her aggressor was able to remain free because there were no witnesses).[132] The fact that there were no witnesses but that the protagonist's body bore signs of her murder reminds us that the burden of proof in cases of abuse is often too high. In this way, González's story aligns with what social scientists have observed: the lack of material evidence beyond the body of the victim often means that men are not convicted of violence.[133] The final phrase in the story further condemns policing and the criminal justice system. A police officer states, "Porque si lo conocía, ella se lo buscó" (if she knew him, she was asking for it).[134] The representation of a police officer character aligns with Wright's observations about policing in the story's context: that the criminal justice system does not take crimes inside the home seriously, in part because of the inherently sexist beliefs that would confine women to their homes and thus blame women when they deviated in any way from the expectations that they would remain there. "Amor, miedo y costumbre," then, offers a chilling reminder that until the criminal justice system responds to women's lived experiences, González's story will continue to accurately represent women's experiences of violence. The way that "Amor, miedo y costumbre" incisively critiques policing is important, as it allows readers to shift the narratives around gender-based violence. At the same time, its narrator implies that the criminal justice system is still a valid way to seek justice.

Crimes that do not fit typical patterns exacerbate police tendencies to discriminate against women and their refusal to investigate crimes with female victims. Patricia Karina Vergara Sánchez's story "Violación" demonstrates an unusual problem a woman faced when reporting her rape. Vergara Sánchez's story—like González's—implies that police can be reformed. "Violación" suggests that changing police's homophobic attitudes would lead to better outcomes for women. The female protagonist was raped by a woman, and the narrator-protagonist shows that after the protagonist reports, police officers exhibit homophobia that compounds misogyny. "Las autoridades dictaron: señora, necesitamos pruebas, ¿cómo que fue una mujer? ¿Está loca? Presente pruebas" (The authorities stated: ma'am, we need proof, how could it have been a woman? Are you crazy? Show us proof).[135] The police officers ridicule the protagonist. The way police officers behave in "Violación" is in keeping with what Debra A. Castillo, María Gudelia Rangel Gómez, and Armando Rosas Solís have observed about police behavior. For example, that police give lower priority to prosecuting "homicides of homosexuals."[136] These scholars note that queer and trans people could find solidarity in their communities. Vergara Sánchez's protagonist, however, does not. The narrator elaborates: women question her. Indeed, her friends advised her to forget that it ever happened. Vergara Sánchez's fictional account is in keeping with the findings of sociologist Claire M. Renzetti about violence in lesbian relationships, that women who are abused by other women find it difficult to understand that their relationship was abusive.[137] Indeed, the protagonist's enemies deride her, and other lesbians hope her case does not become well known. She does not even have a friend join her at the police station, as the protagonist—a woman who was raped by a man—did: "¿Por qué las leyes son así?" "Violación" reminds us that even though men are the vast majority of perpetrators in intimate partner violence, women can also be violent. Given the misogynist cultural system, if a woman reports an abusive female partner, she will experience an even more adverse response. In spite of recognizing these problematic cultural patterns, the narrator of "Violación" recognizes also that a better application of the existing system would lead to better outcomes, and that better outcomes in cases of intimate partner violence, would, in turn, lead to a more just Mexico.

Many of these stories follow the same carceral logic as the government's responses to the petitions. That is, they believe that it is hopeful when the guilty are punished through long prison sentences, or they believe that policing can be reformed to encourage justice for women. The stories are likely too short to truly elaborate on why reforming the police and criminal justice system would fail to improve women's lives so I will reiterate it: improving the response of one of the most violent forces that maintains the status quo will not improve people's lives. If it were not impossible, it would simply give the structures that have a state-sanctioned use of force the opportunity to mete out further violence.

The stories also show the way that violence in women's lives is death by a thousand cuts. The portrayal of everyday violence throughout the short stories in ¡Basta! disrupts the status quo by showing that the examples of violence in women's lives are not always present in its most extreme form. Indeed, as the critic Hermosillo Núñez observes: "Es importante resaltar que las autoras y las protagonistas de estas historias son concebidas como receptoras o testigos de prácticas violentas realizadas en su entorno. Esta visión permite que en estas ficciones literarias se retrate lo acontecido en la realidad con respecto a la violencia de género sin estereotipar a las mujeres como víctimas" (It is worth highlighting that these stories' authors and protagonists receive or witness violence in their surroundings. This vision means that the literary fiction portrays what occurs in reality, with regards to gender-based violence, without stereotyping women as victims).[138]

Like the majority of the letters, many of these stories repeat similar experiences, which points toward the systematic nature of women's experiences of violence, calling to mind what Juana Leticia Herrera Ale stated in congress, that the system of gender-based discrimination has structural, institutional, and symbolic roots.[139] The collection, like the legal texts and congressional debates, shows that violence is a spectrum rather than an isolated incident. The widespread nature of violence in women's lives is evident in the range of topics in ¡Basta!. Some stories show that violence can escalate from seemingly friendly comments or compliance with basic social structures like marriage, and end in a woman's death. The stories also portray female characters who remain in violent places of employment, homes, or relationships for their own survival.

The range of topics in ¡Basta! is also one of the ways that it challenges the forces of order. Stories in the collection portray all-too-familiar events, ranging from street harassment to stalking.[140] Adela Margarita Lucero Hernández's "Carne de edecán" (The Assistant's Body) deals with a common sight in Mexico of female product or company promoters on the street. In this case, a female character advertises an auto lubricant while dancing to reggaetón. The first-person narrator reflects, "Me tragué la humillación porque ocupaba el trabajo, ya se acercaba el día de pagar el semestre" (I swallowed the humiliation because it was my job, and my tuition deadline was approaching).[141] She also repeats men's comments to her, such as

"Yo sí me la cojo" (I'd fuck her), which men often call out to women on the street and so will likely resonate with readers. Several stories deal with ways that women have liberated themselves from violent relationships patterns. Other stories represent simple daily pleasures, and others portray women who murder violent male partners.[142] These fictional accounts portray the multifaceted nature of violence, rendering horribly vivid the somewhat dry legal descriptions and definitions from theorists and social scientists. As Petersen states, these narratives in ¡Basta! "are inviting others to renew their social contract and work to shift cultural scripts of gender violence."[143] The range of topics in the short stories reminds us of the lengthy definitions of violence in the"Ley General de Acceso, as well as the legal explanations of the many locations where violence can occur. The stories in ¡Basta! disrupt the social order by showing that violence is part of every facet of women's lives: their homes, their relationships with friends and family, and any time they are in public, from brief exchanges to women's deaths.

The stories also show that violence exists on a spectrum, beginning with a simple comment or joke. In other words, noticeable violence is part of a pattern of escalation. Fabiola Morales Gasca's "Modelo," for instance, exemplifies escalating violence.[144] It portrays a male photographer and one of his female models. He takes pictures of the model and makes her feel beautiful. After they move in together, he begins to act violently toward her. The photographer starts hitting her, and eventually she is hospitalized for her injuries, and upon her return, he takes a photograph of a bullet in her heart. "Modelo" is so short that it does not describe how or why his violence escalates. It simply ends when the narrator states that the photographer has killed her. "Modelo" thus represents what social scientists have shown, that a gun increases the risk of a man killing a woman. Teresa Isabel Ruvalcaba Rodríguez's "Más de tres motivos" (More Than Three Reasons) presents a similar account of escalating violence. Its narrator begins with a backhanded compliment: "Nunca la insultó por sus grandes escotes. Tampoco la golpeó por celos" (He never insulted her for her low necklines. He did not hit her out of jealousy either).[145] Then, he kills her. The narrator makes the story more chilling by beginning by stating that he did not attack her for reasons that male aggressors may use to justify their violence. Angelina Zamudio's "Muñeca" (Doll) for its part, portrays a female character only known as "Muñeca," a term of endearment. She desperately wanted to be married and so married Pedro, even though her family had warned her about him. He eventually became abusive, and her dream of marriage became a living nightmare: "golpes, insultos, otras mujeres, alcoholismo, drogadicción y ninguna ayuda económica" (punches, insults, other women, alcoholism, drug addiction, and no economic support).[146] One night, Pedro comes home drunk and high. He goes to the bed where his wife and children are already sleeping. "Sin darle oportunidad de despertar la golpeó y la violó. Después, frente a los niños que lloraban, la estranguló con un cable de la luz" (He hit her and raped her before she woke up. Then he strangled her with an electrical cord in front of their crying children).[147] These stories make domestic violence seem quotidian and almost banal. The very prosaic nature of what occurs in these stories speaks to the everyday and universalized experience of intimate partner violence.

Women are also murdered in other places, where they are perceived to be threats to men in some way because they advance professionally, earn more money, or have more friends. Women intuit that men might be jealous of their achievements, and so make themselves seem smaller or cater to men's unarticulated needs. Many women act like the protagonist in Elodia Corona Meneses's "Curso de inglés" (English Class) who takes an English class on Saturdays, to access more and better job opportunities. Yet she makes sure to keep things going at home, by leaving food for her husband, so that he does not ask her to stop the class.[148] Other short stories describe male partners who are resentful that women advance in their professions or educations. These include the protagonist of Ruvalcaba Rodríguez's "Más de tres motivos," whose partner killed her when she got into university and he did not.[149] These examples show the spectrum of violence, to which parts of the law guaranteeing women a life free of violence alluded and, in so doing, disorder the status quo that accepts the attitudes of these male characters—even if it would not typically accept the female characters' deaths—which are the end results.

Other stories disrupt socially acceptable violence by explaining how and why women are complicit with it. Women uphold violence as a survival strategy. Indeed, as legal experts remind us, leaving an abuser can be incredibly dangerous. Women often do not stand up to their intimate partners because they know that they might be killed. In Emma Irene L. Martínez's "Sumisión: Enseñanza mortal," an anonymous protagonist learns from a young age that she should submit. Then, she meets José at a dance near her home on Mexico's southern border with Guatemala. They get married when she is only sixteen. Shortly after their marriage, he begins to hit her. Once, he even leaves her unconscious. Her mother refuses to let her come home. The unnamed husband eventually kills the protagonist. "En el funeral, Esther [la mamá (de la víctima)] con voz quebrada le dijo a Luna [la hija]: 'tu madre no supo obedecer'" (At the funeral, Esther [the victim's mother] told Luna [the daughter] in a quavering voice: your mother did not know how to obey).[150] Submission makes remaining alive, near an abuser, somewhat possible. So, when women like Esther, the grandmother, tell their grandchildren to submit to violence, it is because it is a proven survival strategy.

The entire collection—and in particular, "Modelo," "Muñeca," "Curso de inglés," "Más de tres motivos," and "Sumisión: Enseñanza mortal"—portray female characters in violent situations. Morales Gasca, Zamudio, Corona Meneses, Ruvalcaba Rodríguez, and Martínez's stories represent a reality that conforms to many aspects of the discussion in the Mexican Chamber of Deputies and the law eventually passed there. They remind readers that violence is incredibly common and seldom begins with death. It begins with socially acceptable behavior that a person's friends or neighbors might not even notice. Showing the spectrum of violence so clearly—and the fact that women uphold it as well as men—certainly disrupts the misogynist status quo.

In a system where women's lives are at risk and perpetrators of violence against women experience near-total impunity, women have few viable options for resolving problems. The short stories in ¡Basta! and the letters to the president show that the system for reporting and prosecuting crimes is set up so that crimes in which men perpetrate violence against women are solved so rarely so as to give people only hope. An important way that the stories disrupt the unacceptably violent status quo is by portraying female characters who escape their lives in creative ways. The characters in the stories follow known trends: women in desperate situations make desperate choices, and those with family or community support are able to leave more easily. Some stories that describe escape include women simply leaving their partners. Others are chilling: they include suicide or murdering violent men. The short stories that represent escape remind us that, for many women who experience intimate partner violence, death or imprisonment is a better option than continuing to be in a violent relationship.

Some literary protagonists in ¡Basta! follow the examples of feminists who died by suicide, like the Argentine poet Alfonsina Storni or the purported case of Rosario Castellanos. For these women who lived a life of pain, suicide, in their decision, was a better option than being violated, as in in Paula Calderón Ramos's "Frente al destino" (Facing Destiny). Calderón Ramos portrays a young woman who could earn money as either a *fichera* or a prostitute.[151] A *fichera* is a cocktail waitress who receives *fichas* (slips of paper) each time a man purchases a drink in a bar or cantina thanks to her.[152] The protagonist of "Frente al destino" opts to work as a *fichera* in part because she remembers that her father used to watch *películas de meretri-*

*ces*, or films about prostitutes, also often called *ficheras*.[153] She occasionally earns extra income by taking her clients to another location, most likely an hourly motel. Then, one day, some men force her to leave the club without her consent. The story implies that they take her somewhere in their car. According to the narrator, "La desesperación por lo que le esperaba la hizo abrir descuidadamente la portezuela del coche y una combi la embistió" (Desperation about what was about to take place meant that she opened the car door and a bus crashed into her).[154] This resolves her problem. Yet death by bus accident is a good solution only because her situation is so desperate. The narrator redeems the protagonist's choice with a beautiful description of her death: "Como ave libre voló por el aire y su cráneo se rompió en mil pedazos al estrellarse, seco, contra el pavimento" (Like a bird she flew through the air and her skull broke into a million pieces as it fell, dry, against the pavement).[155] The protagonist's actions *are* understandable for readers who may have considered death as a viable escape from violence. In this way, Calderón Ramos's story disrupts the many examples of women's deaths in which women had no agency.

Death is also presented as a good option in situations that would be more familiar to readers in a less graphically violent way. The positive portrayal of suicide is troubling; in fact, the numbers of deaths by suicide have only increased in the first two decades of the twenty-first century. The fact that these stories would present suicide as a valid option only reinforces the characters' desperate situations.[156] Ninfa Adriana Estrada Orozco's "La decisión" (The Decision) for instance, portrays Mariana, who is in a bad marriage. The narrator states that one morning she makes a decision, which implies that on other mornings, she had not made that decision and simply lived to fulfill her husband's wishes. Indeed, the protagonist's husband has ensured that the couple will have no children and has isolated her to such an extent that she has no friends. So one morning, "se sentó en el sillón azul de su habitación mientras miraba a través de la ventana con una suave sonrisa en los labios, hasta que de sus manos cayó un frasco de pastillas vacío" (she sat in the blue chair in her bedroom, looking out of the window with a soft smile on her lips, until an empty pill container fell from her hands).[157] She overdoses on pills and dies. The protagonists in Calderón Ramos and Estrada Orozco's short stories die for similar reasons, to escape marriage to violent men. Yet the protagonist in "Frente al destino" is from a lower social class and her death takes place in public. Women in the historical context who experience something similar to what Calderón Ramos represents might have their bodies photographed by a journalist and be understood within the framework of feminicide or that of the staggering numbers of women who have died in Ciudad Juárez. It is unlikely that the death of wealthier woman, like the protagonist in "La decision," would be understood in the same way. If anyone were to report deaths like these fictional accounts to the police, only the friends and family of the first woman would be asked what she was wearing.

Women also reclaim agency against violent men by killing them. Two stories in ¡Basta! represent characters who face equally impossible choices and murder their intimate partners. María Eugenia Merino's "En la cocina" (In the Kitchen) and Leticia Romero Chumacero's "Despierta" (Wake Up) follow a universal precedent of women murdering violent men. The protagonist of Jorge Luis Borges's "Emma Zunz," for instance, kills the man who had murdered her father.[158] It extends to stories as early as Jael or Yael in the book of Judges in the Hebrew Bible, who put a tent peg through Sisera's head.[159] It also calls to mind more recent events, such as Cyntoia Brown, who in 2004 murdered an abusive man in Tennessee when she was only sixteen years old. She was sentenced to life in prison but released in 2004 after serving fifteen years.[160] The short stories in ¡Basta! represent events akin to that. Merino's "En la cocina," for instance, represents an abusive marriage between Manuela and Juan. It opens, "¡Nunca más!, se dijo Manuela, por enésima vez" (Never again! Manuela said to herself, for the umpteenth time).[161] Yet she stayed, as do so many women in situations of intimate partner violence.[162] Juan's alcohol abuse worsened his physical violence. Juan's behavior in the short story is consistent with Lenore Walker's observations about abusive men in the late twentieth-century United States. Walker observes that when abusive men use alcohol and drugs, they become more abusive.[163] In "En la cocina," Manuela is used to the way Juan's behavior worsens when he drinks. After he hit her, she cleaned up her blood on her nose and hands and then washed the dishes. Unlike scholarly accounts of women who eventually leave their partners, Manuela takes a more drastic approach: "No debía preocuparse porque él ya no iba a despertar jamás" (She wouldn't have to worry because he was not going to wake up ever again).[164] Murdering Juan saves Manuela's life. "Despierta" presents murder as a similarly viable option. It opens with the word *corre*, which is the command "run." "Despierta" continues with furniture that crashes loudly, after the ambiguous command "Tumba."[165] The narrator of Romero Chumacero's story clarifies that these are not instructions when it uses the unambiguous object pronoun, *la*. She realizes that he is behind her. They fight, and it is hard to know who is violent toward whom. Ultimately, "Su cuerpo cede. Duele. Y se detiene súbitamente" (The body cedes. Hurts. And slowly comes to a stop).[166] Under recently ironed sheets, she closes her eyes and breathes deeply. Her entire physical experience changes because her aggressor is no longer present: "Mira en derredor, con la confianza de quien ya no tiene razones para huir; con la tranquilidad de quien decidió poner fin a un mal sueño" (She looks around her, with the confidence of someone who no longer has reasons to flee; with the tranquility of someone who finally has decided to end a bad dream).[167] The way that the narrator initially employs a word—*despierta*—that could be a command, or a conjugated verb, makes it difficult to understand whether the narrator describes the protagonist's actions or the character's dreams. Moreover, the fact that the narrator conjugates the verb in the third-person singular, without a clear subject, could refer to the protagonist or her aggressor. I suggest that the deliberately misleading verb use in "Despierta" mirrors the difficulty that people in abusive situations have between understanding the difference between the reality the abuser imposes and their own lived experience.[168]

For the narrators of both stories, murder was the best option because of the devastating effects of the abusers on these women's lives. In this way, the two stories further challenge the troubling status quo that places women in subservient positions. For example, when women have family or community support, or access to money, they do not have to make such desperate choices. Other stories portray much less dramatic accounts of leaving an intimate partner. They eschew the criminal justice system, but because the female characters have some savings or family support, they have simpler choices. Norma Pinal's "Palabras," for example, presents a female protagonist who leaves her husband on a typical day. The anonymous protagonist gets up and takes a shower.[169] Each water droplet "era un recordatorio de lo fea y estúpida que era, de lo poco que valía como mujer" (was a reminder of how ugly and stupid she was, of how little value she had as a woman).[170] Her husband's punches accompany these insults. One day, she got her daughter ready for school and went into her kitchen. She took a knife and then used it to open a can full of enough money for bus fare. In the spirit of what sociologist Tressie McMillan Cottom calls "get-out money," they leave the house.[171] The protagonist implicitly blames herself for her experience of violence: she states that her daughter is sweet, so a man will not cause her suffering. In other words, the adult woman thinks that had she been sweeter, she could have prevented her partner's abuse. Pinal's story, then, reflects discourses of shame and how many women feel that they deserve the violent treatment they receive from men. "Palabras" also calls to mind the story "Sumisión," in which the grandmother stated that if the protagonist might have lived longer had she accepted her husband's abuse. Elizabeth Vivero's "Más allá del vacío" (Beyond the Void) deals with similar events in a series of short sentences describing a female protagonist who leaves her partner: "Se fue. Ella. Sola. Sin nada" (She left. Her. Alone. Without anything).[172] She knew that "Más allá del vacío estaban las palabras" (Beyond the void were words).[173] The narrator thus connects its own version of events to lived experience outside of the text. She too was able to leave. The reference to words implies a higher level of education, which might lead to better employment prospects. A higher level of educational attainment and overall literacy level facilitates her departure. Cynthia Menchaca's "Fibonacci" is a more uplifting story. It recounts a woman taking off her constricting clothes, makeup, and jewelry and stepping into the bath.[174] The protagonist in "Fibonacci"—like those in "Palabras" and "Más allá del vació"—leave violent situations without relying on structures that impose force, like the police, president, or legal system. These stories present exodus as a viable form of resistance to systems of power, and thus do not inadvertently reinforce those structures, as was evident in some of the other stories and some letters to the president.

The stories in *¡Basta!* represent aspects of women's other experiences of violence, in the workplace, at home, and in public. They also show us something that does not necessarily exist in reality—one ends one's life, murders one's partner, or leaves. Justice does not come about through the police or prison system. In the texts I have analyzed, justice is only reached by stepping outside of the system and perhaps even by pushing back in a violent, murderous fashion. Yet examples are so few and far between that it suggests that the discourse around violence against women is fatalistically accepting its inevitability. These examples offer the opportunity to avoid reinscribing the same violence I have been critiquing throughout the chapter and thinking about the possibility of change that does not rely on the state.

The short stories and letters analyzed here are part of problematic social structures. The short stories are organized in such a way that they contain the women's accounts, and the bureaucratic process for writing a letter and receiving a response evokes the colonial period and enacts violence in the present. The letters show that many of women's attempts to report abuse or violence merely reproduce the violent inherent in the social structures—which had caused their deaths in large numbers. Portrayals of women who died in Ciudad Juárez were particularly problematic, as they had even more of a tendency to dehumanize the women while trying to draw attention to their death. Laws in effect before 2007 had had little effect on women's experiences of violence, and the new law was just pretty papering over of an existing problem that the criminal justice system was designed not to handle. So too were the explosion of special prosecutors, undersecretariats, and similar agencies that purported to deal with women's experiences of violence. Much like the special prosecutors and special police forces, these bureaucratic tools diminish rather than increase justice and have no meaningful effect for women in the country. A government that refuses to address the individuals and society responsible is itself criminal.

Some short stories and letters also disturb the violent system by showing that it is not just violence that ends it women's deaths. The female characters in these stories have experienced significant violence before their deaths, which is similar to examples in the historical context, in which women typically experience other forms of violence, such as the workplace, as in León Hernández's letter, before their deaths. Some fictionalized female characters, for their part, manage to leave or kill their male partners, and the women in the letters and stories are the fictional counterpart to the tens of thousands of women who are abused, forcibly disappeared, or murdered each year in Mexico and across the world.

The tension in ¡Basta! and the archives between upholding the forces of order and strategies to disrupt unjust social structures mirrors the tensions in the legal text as well as in the debates about its passage and in the surrounding context. The Ley General de Acceso, the short stories in ¡Basta!, and letters to the president emphasize the forces of order in such a way that they overshadow any attempts to expose the violence inherent in those structures. At the same time, examining the tension between forces of order and potential for change within each type of text offers a better understanding of how violent structures operate. Each text represents the idea that the status quo will not change itself. The legal, literary, and archival texts offer tantalizing hints for possibilities of transformation within these texts.

I end the chapter by describing Eglé Margarita Hernández Grijalva's "Mariposa" (Butterfly), who is "libre como una mariposa" (free as a butterfly).[175] The protagonist dreams of flying freely without persecution. She had once dreamt of being president.[176] She could be a leader who would do more than pay lip service to the rule of law, human rights, and the prevalence of violence in women's lives. She would move beyond a rhetorical commitment to the neoliberal ideas that have led to important debates in government, new laws, and myriad government ministries. Hernández Grijalva's protagonist finds meaningful ways of addressing and repairing violent patterns that uphold the status quo. She imagines a future of justice that transforms rather than a system that punishes.

CHAPTER 3

# Children's Rights and Dreams in *Historias de niñas extraordinarias*

Previous chapters have explored a variety of socially acceptable levels of violence. This chapter explores how socially acceptable levels of violence impact another group: children. The chapter examines sources that portray the experiences of children and seek to improve their lives. It finds both of these tendencies in laws that protect children, letters adults write to the president about children whose rights have been violated, and short stories girls write about their lives. These three kinds of writing show that children's lives in Mexico are precarious, as children experience multiple forms of violence that are embedded in the status quo. They also offer options for how violence in children's lives might end.

The experience of children in Mexico is troubling. According to the Mexican government's own statistics, more than half of Mexican children of all backgrounds live in poverty. Poverty in Mexico is not evenly distributed in people of all racial and cultural origins, as more than 90 percent of Indigenous children live in poverty.[1] A symptom of widespread child poverty, around one-tenth of children participate in the labor force, and half of those do so without being paid. Children's economically vulnerable position makes them vulnerable in other ways as well. The World Health Organization says that, across the world, including Mexico, one-fifth of women and one-tenth of men have experienced child sexual abuse.[2] Children are not immune to the high levels of violence that people experience in Mexico either, as approximately 3.4 children and teens were killed every day in the 2010s.[3] As children experience various forms of violence, it is clear that violence is part of the everyday lives of children in Mexico. As such, violence mediates every interaction a child may have with the individuals and institutions that have power over them.

Politicians, government agencies, nonprofit organizations, parents, and children all have tried to improve violence in children's lives. They have passed new laws, most notably, the 2014 Ley General de los Derechos de Niñas, Niños y Adolescentes, and developed materials to explain those laws to the Mexican public. Parents have written letters to the president when he does not follow the laws, and children have written short stories that reflect their lives, including *Historias de niñas extraordinarias* and *Historias de niñas extraordinarias 2*. All these examples—laws, letters and short stories—exist in a tension between describing the world as it is and describing the world as it could or should be. This chapter explores the aesthetics of these three kinds of texts and shows that they reflect the violence inherent to their context. The texts show that violence in children's lives is embedded in other social structures, such as education and policing, which seek to confine the experiences of children to recognizable patterns. The letters to the president and short stories also sustain that leaders, such as the president, teachers, and police officers, could put an end to violence in children's lives. The texts portray structures that reproduce violence even as they explore the possibility of a world without violence. At some level, the formatting and structural signposts in each text do not limit the expression of a child's lived experience. Moreover, they further disrupt the violent status quo by testifying to the quotidian nature of children's lived experiences of violence and point out that the structures that are supposed to help children, like school, fail to do so.

The letters to the president, the Ley General de los Derechos, and *Historias* and *Historias 2* respond to Mexico's situation of violence. The stories and letters, in particular, show that violence affects girls more than boys. Girls' lives in Mexico (and around the world) are materially harder and statistically more dangerous than boys' lives. According to the National Human Rights Center, in Mexico, as in many other countries, girls and young women have less access to education, nutrition, and physical and mental health.[4] Girls have less access to basic human rights like food and health and are more likely to experience violence, which typically begins at home: "La violencia familiar es un acto de poder u omisión intencional, dirigido a dominar, someter, controlar o agredir física, verbal, psicoemocional o sexualmente a cualquier integrante de la familia; dentro o fuera del domicilio familiar"

(Intrafamiliar violence is an act of power or an intentional omission, which is design to dominate, subject, control or be aggressive in a physical, verbal, psychoemotional or sexual way, toward any member of the family, inside or outside of the home).[5] When violence occurs at home, the perpetrator is usually a paternal figure, like a father or stepfather. Adult men's violence toward girls can also include more extreme examples likely to draw public attention: "con frecuencia son víctimas de diversas formas de explotación social, sexual, en el hogar, y/o de situaciones de extrema violencia, como la trata de personas, la explotación sexual con fines comerciales y la pornografía" (they are often victims of various forms of social, sexual and domestic exploitation, and/or have experienced extreme violence, such as human trafficking, commercial sex work, and pornography).[6] Girls who live in poverty or extreme poverty are more vulnerable to sexualized violence, as they or their parents may earn significant income from these various forms of exploitation. Girls' participation in sex work or pornography may not always be as obvious as sexual abuse. As a result of their lack of access to basic human rights and the fact that they are more likely to be victims of violence at home, girls do not enjoy the same rights, confront inequality, and do not experience childhood and adolescence.[7] Girls are not allowed to be girls, that is: to live their lives to the fullest extent possible. In the United States, girls of color, particularly Black and Latina girls are sexualized at earlier ages than white girls and routinely punished for displaying the same emotions or behavior as white girls.[8] Although the racial context in Mexico is different from in the United States, there are some parallels with the Mexican context. In the laws, letters, and short stories, Mexican girls from marginalized backgrounds, due to race or economic status, also face higher risks than other girls.

The Mexican federal government passed the Ley General de los Derechos de Niñas, Niños y Adolescentes in 2014. The law explicitly states that the rights guaranteed by the Mexican Constitution also apply to children and adolescents. Passing the law was an important political effort in describing the situation children experience, such as multiple forms of violence, as well as a way that politicians articulated a better future for them, through access to safe housing, education, food security, and recreation. The law presents a vast concept of rights and explicitly extends them to children in Mexico. The law is organized in sections and subsections that outline these rights, describe how the state will guarantee them, and lay out consequences for parents, teachers, and other adults in children's lives who fail to meet these goals. The headings and subheadings, as in other laws, connect the disparate lists of rights and create a sense of order in the text. At the same time, the disconnected ideas also disrupt any sense of order the law might create. Moreover, as the law explains that children have rights, including the right to participate in a society, it disrupts the idea that children should be protected by those in power. The law includes elements that connect to notions of order and of disorder, which replicate and challenge social structures in the world outside of the legal text.

Mexico's laws also align with national and international movements that developed an understanding that children have rights and to respond to the lives of children living in Mexico. These constitutional and legal changes come out of what the philosopher Clark Butler explains as a "socially validated by a well-nigh universal consensus [that] establishes specific children's rights from birth onward in customary international law."[9] The international precedents are a series of UN declarations regarding civil and political rights. In 1989, the UN adopted the Convention for the Rights of the Child, which recognizes that rights granted through its own prior declarations, such as rights to equality based on gender and race, also apply to children.[10] In 1980, a paragraph was added to Article 4 of the Mexican Constitution to recognize the need to protect children. Then, in 2000, Mexico followed the tendency outlined in the 1989 UN convention and added a statement about children's right to participate in a society to the same article.[11] The constitution also states that adults in the child's life, such as parents, teachers, and other guardians, are obliged to allow for children's active participation in all realms of society.[12] Children's rights laws are also rooted in the struggle for state-funded daycare for workers in the formal economy, which established a tradition of protection for some Mexican children, in terms of daycare and other social services.[13] There was thus national and international precedent for recognizing children's rights and protecting them, as it was understood that children were in a vulnerable position.

Laws that deal with children's rights align with the general principles espoused by the Mexican Constitution. The first of these laws, the Ley General de los Derechos de Niñas, Niños y Adolescentes (Law for Protecting Child and Youth Rights), was passed in 2000. In 2014, it was reimagined as guaranteeing—rather than protecting—the rights of children and adolescents. The more recent legal text places the law explicitly within the constitutional framework of protecting children's rights and punishing anyone who would prevent violence from affecting children. The law asserts that the Mexican state will guarantee the "protección, prevención y restitución integrales de los derechos de niñas, niños y adolescentes que hayan sido vulnerados" (protection of the rights of children and youth, and will prevent them from being violated, or offer holistic restitution).[14] It emphasizes protection, which reminds readers that children are in a vulnerable position vis-à-vis the state. The legal scholar Gustavo Guerra does not focus on children's vulnerability; instead, he interprets the law as the implementation of "the constitutional duty to promote respect for the dignity of all children and the full exercise of their rights."[15] The law also goes into significant detail about consequences for those who prevent children from exercising these rights. As it states, it will "prevenir cualquier conducta que atente contra su supervivencia, así como para investigar y sancionar efectivamente los actos de privación de la vida" (prevent any behavior that goes against their survival, and will investigate and sanction acts that deny life).[16] In other words, the state will intervene if children are not safe. The legal text recognizes children's rights even as it emphasizes their need for protection from the state.

The law is structured in much the same way as the law granting women the right to a life free of violence. The law for children is more like a list than either the Ley General de Acceso de las Mujeres or the Constitution, and those listlike organizational strategies confine the law. After the presidential declaration, sign, and seal, the Children and Adolescents' Rights Law, is divided into six sections, five of which have subsections and some of which are further divided into articles. The presence of such a significant number of headings, subheadings, and roman numerals (for the lists within articles) makes the law different from others I examine here. Such an extensive number of paratextual notations leaves less room for interpretation, explicitly protecting, and implicitly confining, children and youth.

The formatting strategies in the law confine the subject matter of each section. However, unlike the Constitution or the Ley General de Acceso, the section headings in the Children and Adolescents' Rights Law do not "paper over" disconnections. Instead, they facilitate reading short sentences that already seem related. The first article, for instance, states that the law is "de orden público, interés social y observancia general en el territorio general" (of public order, social interest, and general observation throughout the nation).[17] After describing its scope, the article gives five objectives, each of which carries a roman number. The first recognizes the rights of children and adolescents; the second guarantees their ability to exercise them; the third creates a system to protect them; the fourth establishes how the state will protect children and guarantee their rights throughout the country; and the fifth establishes the nature of the involvement of civil society and the private sector in the issue of children's rights.[18] The article's fragments, then, cover significant breadth of content. Each fragment, moreover, relates to the opening statement in some way, as after the basic definitions, each subsequent fragment refers back to how a specific sector of society will promote and protect these rights. The form structures the content, as a guide rather than as a hammer that connects very disparate ideas.

The second section, on rights, is the longest part of the law. It follows the UN convention, and global precedent, as it extends constitutional guarantees to children and includes rights to identity, to equality, nondiscrimination, and so on. Moreover, this section emphasizes eliminating obstacles that would prevent boys and girls from accessing these rights in an equal fashion. These rights include equal rights to food, education, and medical attention.[19] The law continues, stating that it is particularly invested in eliminating obstacles for girls and teens from "grupos y regiones con mayor rezago educativo o que enfrenten condiciones económicas y sociales de desventaja para el ejercicio de los derechos contenidos en esta Ley" (groups and regions with less educational attainment or that deal with disadvantageous economic and social positions, which would prevent them from exercising the rights contained in this Law).[20] The legal text, then, shows that the state will focus on areas where inequality is more prevalent, and in this way, it will ensure greater equality and access to human rights throughout the country. The third subsection outlines how parents, guardians, and other responsible parties will ensure that the law's promises—its guarantee of a better society—will occur. Legal scholars claim that, "this legislation notwithstanding, the rights of children are not always fully protected."[21] Indeed, at the time the letters and short stories analyzed here were written, even the Children and Adolescents' Rights Law was not being enforced. The definitions of children's rights in the second section of the law are an important gesture. They are the most aspirational part of the text and so extensive that they occupy most of it. The simple fact of the statements disrupts a status quo that disadvantages girls, particularly from rural areas or from lower socioeconomic backgrounds.

Certain parts of the law also uphold the social order. Much of the text is also dedicated to explaining how authorities will ensure that children can exercise their rights. The connection between children's rights and state intervention can have devastating consequences. Legal experts in the United States, for instance, observe that certain protections for children can lead to overpolicing of already-vulnerable families.[22] Every section of the Mexican law emphasizes the punitive nature of legal protection. In the section on rights, the final fragment of every article is a threat that the appropriate authority will intervene if a child is not protected. Moreover, the fourth through sixth sections outline how the state will protect children through special residences for housing children whose rights have been violated, a special section of the Sistema Nacional para el Desarrollo Integral de la Familia (DIF, or National System for Wholistic Family Development) will intervene. DIF is a social services bureau charged with strengthening and developing family welfare in Mexico. In addition to DIF assistance, the Comisión Nacional de los Derechos Humanos (CNDH, or National Human Rights Commission) is also empowered to act in cases where children's rights have been violated.[23] The law also creates special prosecutors who develop cases against individuals and institutions who violate children's rights. The law continues, outlining a national system where local and federal authorities cooperate to protect children's rights. The child protection system is also an aspirational section of the law, in this case, aspiration for increased state intervention in children's lives. Provisions for child protection expand existing bureaucracy and ensure a forceful application of state power through what is essentially a parallel legal system for the lives of children. Even though a system for protecting children is supposed to make children's lives better, the way the law encourages expanding only the parts of the bureaucracy that pertain to the courts and policing suggests that it will instead uphold the status quo. In this way, much as the legal text claims to be advocating for children, its organizational strategy and its extensive focus on punishment and expanding the government only as it pertains to systems of confinement and punitive justice lead it to uphold the forces of order and vastly outweigh any other emphasis within the text.

I now turn to examine the literary and archival texts that shed further light on the lived experiences of children in Mexico, as well as the tension in the texts' aesthetic between confining accounts of injustice and reforms that uphold the status quo to allow for visions of transformation. The two short-story collections I look at were written by children as part of a contest sponsored by the Instituto Municipal de la Mujer (Municipal Women's Institute) in Xalapa, Veracruz, an office of Xalapa's municipal government. The context in which they were produced defines the ways the form of these stories and the way they are collected replicates and challenges systemic violence, as well as the allusions to problematic social structures and forms of escape, throughout both texts.

*Historias de niñas extraordinarias* (2016) and *Historias de niñas extraordinarias 2* (2017) are both anthologies of short stories by girls in the municipality of Xalapa, Veracruz. Each story responds to a prompt about what makes an extraordinary girl. The girls who entered the contest and whose stories were ultimately part of both collections were between six and twelve years old, and they attended public or private schools in the municipality.[24] Most stories in the first anthology were written by seven-, eight-, and nine-year-olds, and most in the second were written by eight- and nine-year-olds.[25] The first collection is organized into three categories: award winners, fantastic stories, and stories to share. The second is organized by topic: award winners, "extraordinary girls, in their own words," "about nature," and "fantasy as inspiration." The stories in both collections were written by ordinary girls who imagined what it meant to be extraordinary.[26]

These collections exist because of a variety of institutions, local schools, a center for adults with disabilities, the Instituto de la Mujer de Xalapa, and the UN-designation of October 11 as International Day of the Girl Child. In this way, the collections were produced by institutions that only marginally challenge the status quo, and so from their beginning they exist in a space of challenge between preserving the status quo and exposing it for what it is. Girls were selected or recruited for participation in the story-writing contest from local schools, so the collections relied on one of the most important structures governing the lives of children. The collections were also published together with artwork from a center for older adults and a center for people with disabilities (I analyze the artwork separately later). In addition to partnering with schools and centers, the Instituto Municipal de la Mujer de Xalapa sponsored the contest. I received copies of the collections from Yadira Hidalgo González, who in 2018 was director of the institute.[27]

Children's literature is seldom written by children. For this reason, it often too optimistic about children's lives. As adults are the main purchasers of children's literature, a significant part of children's literature presents an adult idea of children.[28] Literature for children thus often emphasizes adult protection and the safety of the home.[29] Emphasizing adult protection contradicts the alarming statistics on violence in children's lives. In Mexico, according to Socorro Venegas, in an interview with Emily Hind, books directed at children reportedly deal with a range of topics and attempt to address challenging and violent situations.[30] Yet they likely do so in a way that upholds the status quo. For instance, Daniel Goldin stated—in an interview with literary critic Emily Hind—that his work deals with the contemporary social issues of bullying.[31] Bullying is an uncontroversial subject, and so would likely appeal to the most important book buyers in the country, schools, and state who subsidizes the publication of children's books.[32] Book buyers from the educational sector are especially significant in light of the fact that the literature market for children and young adult has exploded in the twenty-first century, the same time when there is an extremely high level of violence in Mexico.[33] In addition to the fact that Goldin mentioned a relatively "safe" social issue in his interview with Hind, I extend his comment to assume that other works designed for children tailor their material in such a way that they satisfy the needs of those who subsidize and then purchase the books, so as to show that the state is responding to the violent situation rather than enacting policies that would prolong it or make it worse.

Children, when given their opportunity, give their own perspective on their lives and an ideal version of daily life. A project like *Historias* and *Historias 2* is a powerful way to validate and celebrate the girls' lived experiences. The collections are a way for girls to express themselves and counter the way that adults mediate and represent children's experience. The girls' stories challenge the fact that adults control certain types of language and power, in law, and the literary realm, without having much recourse to listen to the children themselves. *Historias* and *Historias 2* thus also question tendencies in much of popular children's literature, which is written by adults, and is a genre that typically represents a romanticized version of childhood. The adult representation of childhood in literature for children can invalidate—or at least discount—children's lived experiences. The stories in *Historias* and *Historias 2* represent what the girls would imagine as an ideal life. Some of them portray the most mundane aspects of everyday life. The short stories that portray everyday life suggest that the narrators and characters want girls to have freedom to enjoy them without a threat of violence. These straightforward accounts respond to what some in the field of children's literature have advocated, which is that children find examples of literature by, for, and about them. A striking example comes from the work of Mary Branley, a poet, playwright, and former teacher. She sought out literature for a classroom of Traveller children, marginalized in her Irish context. Branley facilitated workshops for children to publish a collaborative novel with a press that exclusively publishes work by and for children.[34] The Traveller children have written several works together that reflect their context. Most notable is a class of eleven- and twelve-year-olds who wrote a novel called *Rebellion in the Village* in just nine weeks.[35] The novel's protagonist was a teenager Leon, who lived in poverty and fought against an unjust government in eighteenth-century France.[36] Leon's experiences parallel some of the challenges in their families. Branley notes that her students' portrayal of Leon's daily life was a validating experience for them, and she paraphrases the children saying things like "children understand children better than adults do; they know more about what children like to read."[37] *Historias* and *Historias 2* follow some of the patterns Branley outlines, as the Mexican collections offer similar opportunities for the girls to describe their own lived experiences and to imagine alternative lives.

The collections of stories were based on an idea that the director of the Instituto Municipal de la Mujer had about human nature, an idea that aligns with scholarly observations about children. The institute's director, Yadira Hidalgo González, explains that the institute developed the collection because she knew that girls liked stories, and so the story-writing contest was an opportunity to create stories for girls that did not end with Prince Charming.[38] Educational researchers confirm her intuition, stating that children create stories before they are even able to write.[39] The competition was designed to legitimizes girls' perspectives about their own lived experiences.

Both collections confirm that writing short stories validates girls' understandings of their own lives. Hannia Laiz García's "Triunfos logrados: La historia de la extraordinaria Hannia" (Triumphant Achievements: The Story of the Extraordinary Hannia) describes the experience of participating in the competition. For the narrator-protagonist, the competition was a way to validate the girls' experiences and to feel like her understanding of life was valid and worthwhile. The narrator states: "Un día la invitaron en su escuela para participar en un concurso escribiendo un cuento, ella muy pero muy feliz, decidió concursar" (One day her school invited her to participate in a story-writing context, she was very happy to compete).[40] In this way, "Triunfos logrados" fictionalizes the author through the character Hannia and her experience of participating in the contest the year before. The narrator describes the personal qualities involved in participating in the story-writing contest, and the narrator explains that it took her a significant period of time: "Se llevó varios días para terminarlo, se esforzó mucho" (It took her a number of days to finish, she worked very hard).[41] Hannia's effort appears to have paid off because the subsequent year, she was able to write for her own enjoyment of writing rather than with the stress she had experienced when she participated in the competition for the first time.[42] The narrator of "Triunfos logrados" explains that she wrote a second story because she wanted to win. Participating in the competition, however, did not give her prizes. Nevertheless, it did give Hannia recognition in her community: "Gracias al concurso logró que publicaran su cuento en el Diario de Xalapa y en un libro ¡wow!, lo que la volvió famosa entre sus amistades y parientes" (Thanks to the contest her story was published in the newspaper in Xalapa and in a book, which made her famous among her friends and relatives).[43] *Historias* and *Historias 2* were later launched at the Feria Internacional del Libro Infantil y Juvenil (International Child and Youth Book Fair), which takes place in Xalapa every year. Girls like Hannia would have become even more famous on a local and perhaps national or international level at the Feria Internacional del Libro Infantil y Juvenil. So even though the protagonist of Laiz García's "Triunfos logrados" did not win she still got her experiences validated because they were published in a public forum—the newspaper—and in a book. Moreover, her family and friends recognized her for her short story. The experience of writing a story and participating in a book fair was a positive experience for the protagonist. Because of the story's close relationship to the author, I extend these observations to apply to the young author's life as well. It is likely that other girls who entered stories in the competition would have had the same experience.

These stories, then, may have offered some sort of psychological validation for the participants. While that is not my area of expertise, it is clear from "Triunfos logrados" that being able to participate in the contest was a meaningful experience for at least one girl. Laiz García's ability to represent her daily life also aligns with Branley's commentary about similar projects in another time period in Ireland. Other stories in *Historias* and *Historias 2* align with the prevailing narratives in children's literature of home as a safe place and children's having only minimal experiences of violence. The short stories show that children experience a range of violence, in both obvious and subtle ways. Children's own writing counters the prevailing notion that adults have the right to choose what children do and do not do. These possibilities exist in tension and in conversation with the various governmental agencies that cooperated with local schools and other organizations to ensure that girls had the opportunity to participate in the competition in honor of International Day of the Girl Child.

The stories in *Historias* and *Historias 2* are about a single topic, girlhood, which furthers a sense of order. The structure is confined by the contest, which solicited stories from and about extraordinary girls. In this way, *Historias* and *Historias 2* could be part of Lauro Zavala's subcategory of a minifiction cycle on a single topic. The stories also deal with topics that range from everyday life in Mexico to life on magical planets.[44] Another way that the short stories' structure aligns with the existing social order is in the way that the graphic design of both collections aligns with a traditional interpretation of girlhood. Both collections have multicolored covers. The first one includes three discernable objects, a sun, a blonde girl, and a cat, and the second, includes a group of pet animals around a boat. These scenes emphasize things that are important to children, and which are also somewhat removed from the reality of Mexico or any place. The text formatting further aligns the collections with a highly feminine vision of girlhood. The table of contents and section headings are in pink and purple in the first collection. The second collection uses black in the table of contents and pink for story titles. These formatting choices create a nonthreatening idea of extraordinary girls. The formatting and graphic design of *Historias* and *Historias 2* as well as the ways that the stories in both collections represent related issues create order and align with an established social order.

In addition to the way that the collections are structured, the stories, when read as a whole, present a nonthreatening idea of who an extraordinary girl is. The fact that each story responds to the prompt about extraordinary girls leads to some level of repetition within and across the collections, as they have titles like Amy Lee Pensado Ortega's "Una buena niña" (A Good Girl), Diana Danae Gómez Callejas's "La niña hada" (The Fairy Girl), and Zulma González García's "La niña que quería cambiar su ciudad" (The Girl Who Wanted to Change Her City). Each of those stories—and every other story in either collection—stars a young female protagonist who experiences girlhood. The protagonist of "Una buena niña," for instance, loves horses.[45] Other stories, like Gómez Callejas's and González García's, allude to issues that children think adults find important. Diana, in "La niña hada," realizes that family is the most important thing, and Vanelope, the protagonist of "La niña que quería cambiar su ciudad," wrote to her mayor to complain about people who throw garbage on the street.[46] The repetition of relatively noncontroversial social issues and continually extraordinary girls creates a sense of flow across both collections.

The artwork in both collections represents condescending social attitudes. People from the Instituto Down de Xalapa, a not-for-profit educational institution for people with Down syndrome, drew pictures for *Historias de niñas extraordinarias,* and adults from the Casa Hogar Mariana Sagayo, a home for older adults, drew pictures for *Historias de niñas extraordinarias 2*.[47] The editors of both collections group together children and people who may experience discrimination because of disability or age. The way that the collections pair these diverse groups of people with children infantilizes the artists. The images are untitled and unattributed to the artists, which further removes the artists' autonomy.

The drawings also lull the reader out of a sense of complacency, and thus prevent the reader from passively accepting patronizing views of older adults or disabled people. The drawings rarely relate to the stories in either collection. Karla Zoé Rebolledo Argueta's "Las salvadoras" (The Saviors) portrays a princess, Stela, and her friends who conquer an evil queen. The page facing the description of her victory, and reconciliation with her abusive father, features a black-and-white image. In the upper-right-hand corner of a black square there is a white, sunlike circle, and at various points along the diagonal line that divided the image, there are white vertical lines, alluding to the contrast between good and evil. The drawing is tenuously connected to the events in Rebolledo Argueta's story, which confuses the reader more than illuminating the plot.[48] Another juxtaposition of a drawing and a story increases the reader's confusion. Marbella Fernández García's "Escribiendo mi futuro" (Writing My Future), for instance, portrays a first-person narrator-protagonist who imagines a better future through writing. A drawing accompanies the story. A grayscale drawing that suggests the outline of a school accompanies Fernández García's story. The square-shaped outline has a border around the edges, like a picture frame.[49] There is a group of stick children in the top left and bottom right inside the frame, as well as a globe or soccer ball, a page full of writing, and squares that appear to be gardens of flowers and vegetables. The sports field, writing, and flowers expand the scope of the story beyond the protagonist's dreams and experiences of school to include elements that are not part of the story, such as gardens. These interruptions lead to a certain amount of confusion and interrupt the flow. They disrupt the order within the text that reduced girls to a simplistic vision of pink flowers. The structure of these collections, then, primarily serves to uphold an existing understanding of the social order. At the same time, the collections celebrate rather than denigrate femininity. Moreover, the somewhat unusual illustrations challenge a total acceptance of the status quo.

Letters to the president are another way that the Mexican people write about the world as it is and the world as it ought to be. Unlike the stories in *Historias* and *Historias 2*, the letters archived in the AGN are written by adults. These letters reflect the forms in their surroundings; that is, they replicate many aspects of the troubling status quo that tacitly accepts violence toward children, and inequality between boys and girls. There is a significant distance between children in the popular imagination and the reality depicted in these letters. Here adults write about the complete breakdown of the idealized version of childhood, hoping that someone higher in the hierarchy might be able to intervene. The letters are from the same *peticiones presidenciales* collection in the AGN examined in Chapter 2. The petitions about violence in children's lives show that children are at risk because of men in positions of power at home, at school, and in other places are violent toward children. Each letter writer hopes that the president can intercede where other institutions, such as the school, or other figures important in a social hierarchy, such as the father, have failed. The letters point to a widespread belief that someone higher in the social hierarchy can fix the problem. The problem is that someone in the hierarchy is acting wrong per his position, because he is not protecting those who are more vulnerable.

Both the letters and the stories uphold some aspects of the status quo and challenge others. Multiple adult letter writers call on the president to enforce the rule of law; several girls' stories also portray court cases that resolve characters' issues. Several stories also present a vision of an ideal family either by direct explanation or by omission. The ideal family is one with two parents of opposite sex, with children. The father would protect mother and children, and they would perform their roles as emotional provider and doer of good behavior, respectively. The stories and letters depict the failure of the ideal family system while the popular imagination tries to shore up the existence of something that does not exist.

The letters to the president illustrate a poignant absence of the ideal father figure. They express the desire that the president intervene as a father figure. The letters are desperate because the domestic relationship has broken down, and yet they are hopeful. They are a type of fantasy, aspiring for a different kind of father in family scenarios, one who would act in a way that befits an ideal paternal role. The letters are the letter writer's only recourse, pushing farther up various hierarchies in an attempt to have the president take control of the situation and make it better. When the president does not do so, he is like a bad father, abdicating his paternal and presidential responsibilities.

To my knowledge, only women wrote letters to the president about children. The letters demonstrate that women do much of the thankless work of political activism, which includes writing letters and petitions. In addition to pointing to broader gendered divisions within activist movements, the letters also suggest that the act of witnessing is gendered. Polit Dueñas's analysis of *crónicas* of social suffering subtly implies that women write more about social issues than men, as her work analyzes only writing by women.[50] At any rate, in the *peticiones presidenciales* collection in the AGN, men do not seem to write letters that testify to violence in children's lives or to advocate for changing children's experiences of violence. These letters, which include a twinned narrative of desperation at the situation and hope that the president will somehow intervene, are especially poignant when they deal with children in vulnerable positions, one because of age and the other because of a disability. The office in charge of responding to citizens responds to some letters but not others. The lack of response to many letters shows that in cases of family-related violence, the state accepts the violent social order in which men can act violently toward women and children without repercussion.

One 2006 account comes from Lidia Salomé Pérez Villavicencio, whose writing movingly describes the challenges facing women and children in

Mexico. The way that she advocates on her son's behalf is incredibly courageous and defies a society that would prefer to hide abuse. At the same time, her letter continually exhibits the faith that the president could somehow convince police to appropriately enforce laws. The lack of response from the Atención a la Ciudadanía program reinforces how Pérez Villavicencio's letter conforms to the existing order. The events Pérez Villavicencio's letter primarily conform to the forces of order, or policing. She testifies to her son's lived experience and is unwilling to make his life seem nicer or more palatable for the sake of her intended audience, the president. She states that her ex-husband had raped their young son and that, after doing so, had tried to convince the boy not to complain by buying him toys. Pérez Villavicencio's letter then outlines the ways she has already tried to use existing channels to report the crime. Her compliance to the existing order is proved when the letter presents her legal case number. It also elaborates on the process through which she was able to report her ex-husband for his crime. As part of the reporting process, Pérez Villavicencio's son had been subjected to physical and psychological examinations. The medical interventions traumatized both her and her son: "Las autoridades . . . no han tenido humanidad ni con mi hijo ni mucho menos conmigo" (The authorities . . . have not been humane toward my child and much less toward me).[51] Police involvement caused problems with her neighbors. It led to further demands for her to give testimony. She fears that appearing in court to testify would further traumatize her son. Pérez Villavicencio pleads, "Por favor ayúdeme a que ni a que las autoridades ya no nos presionen ni a mi hijo ni a mi con más declaraciones" (Please help me so that the authorities do not ask me or my son to make any more statements).[52] She wants the president to intervene so that her child does not have to make further declarations. The burden of proof on the boy is—as in examples from Chapter 2—almost impossible to meet. Their procedures that are supposed to convince them, even though they are primed not to believe, retraumatize the child and his parent rather than bringing about justice. Pérez Villavicencio's short letter illustrates the many problems her son has, particularly his vulnerability to his father. This is compounded by the fact that the police are unwilling to believe Pérez Villavicencio or her child. The letter also implicitly expresses that the system could function better, more than exposing these troubling aspects of the criminal justice system or the life of her son. That Pérez Villavicencio wrote such a letter also reinforces the idea that people are willing to believe that a more elevated position in the hierarchy can intervene and resolve the situation when lower people in the hierarchy have neglected to do so. The lack of response from Atención a la Ciudadanía confirms that hierarchy and bureaucracy are deeply uninterested in intervening in the court case surrounding her abuse allegations and generally uninterested in children's welfare.

A similar letter from 2005 reinforces that Mexican women continue to plead with the political hierarchy to assist their children. Pastora Morales Condado, from the State of Hidalgo, writes seeking presidential intervention in a situation of attempted rape. Her husband raped their fifteen-year-old daughter, Rocío Vásquez Morales, who has a physical disability. Both women sign the letter. The fact that there are two signatures is extremely rare. Indeed, it is the only letter I was able to find in the Mexican archive where a minor, particularly a vulnerable minor, was part of their advocacy in any way.[53] Morales Condado's letter firmly inserts these two women into an almost-colonial system, as neither signature suggests much familiarity with writing. Morales Condado's letter, as with every example in the previous chapter, sheds light on an aspect of society others may prefer to keep hidden. The opening paragraph of the letter reinforces the writers' vulnerable position, explaining that Morales Condado is motivated to do so "por tal acontecimiento tan vergonzoso por parte de mi esposo y padre de mi menor hija" (because of the shameful actions of my husband and father of my youngest daughter).[54] He attempted to rape his fifteen-year-old daughter, who uses crutches to walk, and Morales Condado identifies her as *minosválida* (invalid).[55] Vásquez Morales's dual marginalization, in terms of education and disability, would have made the fifteen-year-old extremely vulnerable to most other people in her life. The letter then continues, turning to explain how the women in question had already attempted to resolve the issue by availing themselves of existing resources. Morales Condado, like Pérez Villavicencio, reported the crime to the police. She does not describe the experience of reporting to the police as traumatic, but simply conveys that reporting was a useless venture, because her ex-husband's lawyer was bullying her into accepting a deal. The information about reporting and a court case shows that Morales Condado had already attempted to resolve the issue with one level of state actors, and when the police and criminal justice system failed her, she was now moving on to engage with the president himself. Morales Condado specifically asked the president to convince her husband's superior in the Mexican Army to intervene on her behalf. As there is no response to Morales Condado in the archives, I conclude that the state did not intervene in this case, simply accepting that men will violate the rights and bodies of vulnerable people. Overall, Morales Condado's pleas are aligned with existing social structures, and when one level does not heed her, she presses on, believing that another level might be able to resolve the issue.

Two other letters women write to the president reiterate confidence in the president that he might be able to intervene where other social structures had failed. The letters are both about cases of fifteen-year-old girls who experience violence outside of the home, and the lack of resolution confirms again the state's disinterest in protecting girls. Fidelia Hernández Juárez's letter describes a girl kidnapped from just outside of her home in the State of Mexico, and María Elena León Pérez states that her daughter was coerced into a sexual relationship with a married man. Hernández Juárez explains that the accused rapist and kidnapper was incarcerated without bail and she simply wanted him to remain incarcerated.[56] Her plea is similar to the petitions about violence in women's lives and I am surprised it received little attention. In León Pérez's case, the judicial system deemed that her daughter was having a consensual relationship with an older man, so she had no legal grounds on which to further her claim of abuse.[57] Both women used existing structures to attempt to seek justice, and when the police gave them unsatisfactory answers, they wrote to the president. Atención a la Ciudadanía did not respond to either woman. The sequence of events in the letters and the lack of return correspondence is part of an established pattern, one that begins when Mexican people like León Pérez and Hernández Juárez believe that a superior force—the president—can resolve problems that occurred at lower levels. It concludes when the bureaucracy neglects them. Bureaucratic neglect is one of many ways that powerful people and institutions act violently and negatively affect ordinary people's lives in Mexico.

Short stories in *Historias* and *Historias 2* also represent characters who depend on structures like legislative action, elections, policing, and the criminal justice system to resolve injustice in their own lives. Some stories offer examples of punishment and escape that involve the police actually upholding the law. For instance, Lucero, the heroine of ten-year-old Diana Laura Osorio Vélez's "¡Ya no más!" (No More!), and her mother, manage to escape an abusive home where her father seeks to confine his daughter and his wife's behavior. Lucero and her mother, though, experience effective policing. The fantasy of effective policing calls to mind the fantasy that the president will somehow step in and change the lives of the people writing him letters. In "¡Ya no más!," after one instance of abuse, the mother immediately leaves. The fictional mother's actions are quite different from most women's lived experiences, as they rarely leave abusive partners in an abrupt fashion. Osorio Vélez's account begins by stating that Lucero "tenía una familia muy feliz" (had a very happy family), a phrase that echoes the beginning of *Anna Karenina*.[58] As the plot of "¡Ya no más!" develops, it becomes clear that the fictional family was probably not happy. The narrator continues, stating that after a week, the man finds his wife and daughter and once he does so, he hits her. The child Lucero tries to intervene in her parents' relationship. In the first case, Lucero rushes to defend her mother, adding, "Qué importa lo que diga la gente con que nosotros seamos felices" (What does it matter what people say about us being happy), and in the second case, she yells at her father to release her mother.[59] Lucero's behavior is very much in keeping with children's experiences of the intimate partner violence their mothers experience, and they feel responsible for protecting them. Eventually, the father finds Lucero and her mother, and they go back to live with him. He continues to act in an abusive way, and so Lucero's mother goes to the police to report her husband's abusive behavior. The narrator does not comment on the mother's experience of reporting to the police, but they get back together, which implies that it was ineffective. But once Lucero's father finds out that her mother has reported him to the police, he hits her mother again. Here the narrator relies on outside forces. The police come and put him in jail. There are no events in the story that would parallel the events represented in the letters to the president, where women report abusive men and those men are arrested or charged. The fictional universe of Osorio Vélez's short story is governed by other institutions as well. The narrator concludes by stating that Lucero and her mother go to therapy, join antiviolence campaigns, and live together happily. Outside interventions from the police and a therapist allow them to live their lives. Osorio Vélez's story is a fictional account that contrasts with the representations of violence in women's lives in the short stories in *¡Basta!* and in some letters to the president. In "¡Ya no más!," the police believe Lucero's mother immediately, act swiftly, and uphold the law. The wishful thinking in the story relies heavily on outside intervention from effective policing, which does align with other letters to the president that imagine that the president can step in and change the lives of the people writing him.

Characters in *Historias* and *Historias 2* also rely on the court system to rectify their problems. Darianna Torres Hernández's "La muerte de la creatividad" (The Death of Creativity) portrays a group of children who mount a legal case against a bad mayor, Sr. Greg Torres. Sr. Greg is a corrupt villain who wins the election only after bribing people to vote for him.[60] As mayor, he is able to exercise significant local power. As the narrator explains, one of his first acts as mayor is to ban creativity. He does not directly abuse his constituents, but he deprives them of the ability to enjoy life. A plucky group of children, Ana, Fátima, Ale, and Miguel, are upset and convinced he is wrong. They attempt to use existing structures to prove that his new laws are wrong. So, the narrator explains that they investigate the situation. Ana finds a library, and Miguel finds a dusty old book that proves that Sr. Greg cannot make such a law. The children learn that it is illegal for Sr. Greg to have banned creativity. After learning that creativity cannot be banned, the children tell the mayor that he has broken the law. The children's fictional actions mirror the actions of the women who write the president about situations of injustice. The group of children in "La muerte de la creatividad" then take the case against Sr. Greg to the Supreme Court,[61] which eventually decides that "a creatividad no se podía anular, eliminar o acabar" (creativity cannot be canceled, banned or ended).[62] This version of legal rhetoric expands the constitutional guarantees to provide for children's basic needs to include a sense of emotional well-being. The fictional court ruling recognizes that a life without creativity would be detrimental to children, as it would deprive them of the ability to enjoy life. The representation of the Supreme Court thus successfully decides a case in favor of a group of children. The fictionalized court system intervenes when a local leader has overstepped his power, and as such, the Supreme Court is part of a just social order. The children's experience represents a sharp departure from the experiences of the desperate people who wrote letters to the president, whose belief in the court system remained unfounded. The system was designed to have such results on only very rare occasions, in order to encourage people to continue to have faith in it.

Other letters and stories deal with questions of education and schooling and shed further light on the promises and failures of constitutional guarantees and of the Children and Adolescents' Rights Law. The Mexican Constitution guarantees that all children have the right to a free, public, secular education. Former president Enrique Peña Nieto emphasized that Articles 3 and 73 promote the right not only to education but also to quality education.[63] Several short stories and educational videos communicate these rights to children in a way that they can understand: a short human rights video on the subject of education explains that all children have the right to happiness and personal growth.[64] The right to growth as it pertains to education means a safe building, in terms of its physical structure, as well as in terms of a classroom where teachers are not abusive and where children do not bully others because of their differences. In addition, education stops people from discriminating against one another. As the narrator of Helena Macario Hernández's "Mi vida y mi sueño" (My Life and My Dream) asserts, a school ensures that students will "respetar a todo ser humano, sin importar el color de la piel, si no fueras pobre o rico" (respect all human beings, regardless of their skin color, or whether they are poor or rich).[65] Macario Hernández emphasizes nondiscrimination, which complements the right to a safe, healthy learning environment. Marbella Fernández García's "Escribiendo mi futuro," discussed earlier, echoes some parts of this and also reflects an ideal school environment. The first-person narrator-protagonist goes to school with her mom, and her mom picks her up at the end of each day. She hands in homework and writes in her journal rather than paying attention in class.[66] Then one day, when she does not leave school with the rest of her class, her teachers and her mom go looking for her. The protagonist is able to access her right to education, her school is in adequate condition, and the adult characters in school and at home protect her when needed. "Escribiendo mi futuro," as well as Macario Hernández's "Mi vida y mi sueño" and the videos, offer a vision of an ideal education.

In spite of the promises in the videos and Fernández García and Macario Hernández's short stories, it is undeniable that most types of education are part of a social structure that upholds unjust patterns in Mexican society—or any society. Children's right to safety is interpreted as a right to have armed guards protecting the educational environment, and the right children have to learn and grow is interpreted as the right to memorize items from textbooks rather than engage in critical thinking about the social structures that govern education. In Mexico, educational structures certainly fall short of the ideals espoused by the Constitution. In spite of constitutional guarantees and former presidential interest, it is difficult for many children to access education, let alone quality education. The physical infrastructure of many schools is deeply inadequate. Many school buildings are out of date or unsafe, without good drainage, or computer equipment.[67] It is also often hard for children to get to schools, particularly in rural areas.[68] Indigenous children have even less access to education, as most Indigenous people in Mexico have completed only primary education, whereas the national average is secondary education.[69] The reality in Mexico is that it is easier for a child of urban middle and upper classes to receive a quality education than it is for other children in the country. The ability to access quality, safe education that promotes a child's growth relates to a number of other social structures, such as a family's literacy level and familiarity with Spanish, internal family dynamics, economics, and ability to have a child who is not working, among other things.

Some of these structural issues relate to a lack of financial investment or corruption at all levels of government when it comes to education. It is widely suspected that the federal Secretary of Education is one of the more corrupt ministries in Mexico. There is also significant corruption in public school administration and the unions that protect teachers' labor rights. Indeed, Mexican public school teachers are all part of a powerful national union, the largest union in Latin America.[70] The union was able to increase wages and influence in a period of economic collapse and de-unionization, which attests to its power. At the same time, there is widespread nepotism and "job inheritance" among teachers in Mexico.[71] Corruption and nepotism in the teachers' union mean that the ideal and the reality are worlds apart.

The archival and literary sources point to the difference between ideals and reality. Letters to the president about sexualized violence illustrate that difference. They exemplify the worst aspects of the educational system, where a teacher or educational administrator abuses power, where there is no system of accountability, and where there is a classroom full of children. Short stories give examples of girls' experiences of violence from their peers and the utter failure of many school leaders to resolve the situation. Girls also offer examples of liberation through schooling in their own stories, which express the consistent belief that education could improve the lives of children, particularly girls, if only it were done correctly. The stories present a belief in reform that strongly echoes remarks elsewhere about policing, yet that belief in reform is misguided at best. Education and policing are structures that order society to maintain the status quo that is profitable for those in power.

Two letters to the president show the depth and breadth of the gap between an ideal education and its reality in Mexico. Silvia Hernández Hernández and Angélica González Quintos write letters that allege that male teachers in Tamaulipas and the Federal District (Mexico City) abused female students. The women's letters point to their marginalized background and express the belief that the president can intervene in a crime that occurred in a local school when other authorities have failed. Atención a la Ciudadanía does not respond to Hernández Hernández or González Quintos, which suggests that reporting does not lead to any kind of change, let alone change that would point to a better future.

These women's letters outline similar cases of rape and abuse. The way the women present their version of events illustrates their vulnerable social positions and misguided belief in presidential intervention. Hernández Hernández, for instance, fills out a web form entirely in uppercase letters, which suggests a lack of familiarity with computers, and, by extension, a lower socioeconomic background or older age. Even so, her account represents familiarity with certain letter-writing conventions. Its single sentence begins by stating "Por medio del presente me permito dirigirme a usted y es un honor poder saludarlo Sr Presidente Vicente Fox, le pido su apoyo para que los responsables de una violación a una menor de 8 años paguen con cárcel" (It is an honor to address you, Mr. President Vicente Fox, and through this letter I am asking for your assistance in ensuring that those responsible for raping an eight-year-old go to jail).[72] In this web form, she tells the president that a group of male teachers raped an eight-year-old girl. She wants him to ensure that the teachers go to jail. Hernández Hernández provides a case number, so it is likely that she has some kind of relationship with the alleged victim. She simply believes the account and would like to see her version of justice served. She believes that the legal system can bring about justice. González Quintos's letter describes a male teacher who sexually abused her niece when she was in the fifth grade. After González Quintos outlines the alleged crime, she refers to law enforcement and a hearing in criminal court.[73] Both letters represent three uncommon events in a situation of child sexual abuse: first, that a child disclosed the abuse to an adult; second, that adults believed them; and third, that the adults reported the crime. The adult women—and the child victims—have faced significant hurdles. They rightly expect a result. González Quintos wonders about the right to a speedy trial.[74] These women's letters rely on a system that is designed not to function and that puts people in such desperate positions that they hope the president will intervene.

Atención a la Ciudadanía bureaucracy never responds to the petition. The cover sheet attached to Hernández Hernández's letter includes an orange sticky note on which a bureaucrat has written the word *urgent*. In González Quintos's case, a bureaucrat underlined the criminal case number. These markings are more common in archival documents from the typewriter era than the computer era. Each bureaucrat, a figurative lower cog in the wheel, likely assumes they are doing the right thing by putting the sticky note in the file, as in Hernández Hernández's file. They may also resolve these cases in an informal way. In this case, the bureaucratic system of Atención a la Ciudadanía is based on the bureaucrats' belief that they are doing the right thing in giving the letter writers the illusion of justice.

Ultimately, both letters represent a misguided reliance on the president to resolve issues in policing and in courts, particularly as they pertain to male teachers abusing female children. Their letters suggest that they thought that the president would be willing to modify the legal system to effectively respond to cases of adult male teachers raping children. Were this president or any other powerful figure to intervene in the situation either González Quintos or Hernández Hernández describes, he would interfere with the powerful teachers' union and upset the violent status quo. The Atención a la Ciudadanía program gives the president the illusion of communicating with the Mexican people and gives desperate people a semblance of hope. The archived letters are part of a system that purports to heed citizens, when in reality Atención a la Ciudadanía merely heeds the status quo.

Several short stories in *Historias* and *Historias 2* also deal with education. As they are written by girls still in school (and not by adults, as is the case with the letters to the president), the short stories primarily focus on the social and academic aspects of schooling. The stories show that relying on education is a social structure that upholds an existing order. Indeed, only Fernández García's "Escribiendo mi futuro" portrays an ideal school environment. The other stories that deal with education confirm that it is a violent social structure that upholds the status quo.

These stories represent violence that girls experience in school. They demonstrate that if girls are able to access education, their lives will still be affected by the status quo that tacitly accepts violence. The fictional representations of violence in *Historias* and *Historias 2*, in which boys and girls abuse other girls, particularly those they perceive to be more vulnerable, and teachers who do not do enough to protect them, conform to research about abuse in the school environment. The fictional stories also show a misplaced belief in hierarchy. In some cases, female protagonists seek their parents' or a teacher's help, which they occasionally receive. These fictional accounts imagine ways for girls to be powerful in their own ways, some of which seems plausible, by winning a sports match against boys, and in other ways that exist only in the realm of dreams.

Several stories that take place at school represent boys who ridicule girls, indicating that schools are rife with unequal gender dynamics. In Tiffany Gutiérrez Acosta and Luz Leylany Trasancos Pérez's "Una cascarita por la igualdad" (A Soccer Match for Equality) a group of boys tells a group of girls that the girls are not worth anything.[75] The boys' sexist statement is detrimental to the girls' sense of self-worth and negatively affects their academic performance. Similarly, in Angela Cruz Morfín's "Bondad sobre ruedas" (Kindness on Wheels), a group of boys tell a girl that she cannot skateboard because she is a girl.[76] Here male characters prey on a female character's athletic ability and bar her from expressing herself in an activity often considered the purview of men and boys. In both stories, male characters insult female characters' athletic ability and senses of self. The male characters' insults are minor in comparison to the more extensive bullying in other short stories. In these cases, the stories explicitly show that boys' bullying of girls has negative effects on girls' schooling; it is not simply insults. For example, in Shaden Jael Valderrábano Velasco's "Entrevista a las niñas extraordinarias" (Interviewing the Extraordinary Girls), a teacher assigns her students a research project.[77] A group of girls wants to do a project about rainbows, and because rainbows are a stereotypically "girly" topic, a group of boys makes fun of the girls. So, the girls heed their bullies and switch topics. They research prehistoric Mexico. The characters' switch from researching rainbows to researching prehistoric Mexico suggests that from an early age, girls are encouraged to rely more on boys than they are on their own ideas. Even though the teacher had encouraged the group to work on a topic that interested them, the group of girls listened to the boys instead. The fact that the girls listen to boys is something that has resonated in science research in the United States, where scientists have noted that children as young as five view boys as smart and girls as nice, regardless of race or socioeconomic status.[78] The group of fictional characters in "Entrevista a las niñas extraordinarias" makes this switch even though the teacher explicitly encouraged them to do a project on a topic that interested them. The female characters thus understand boys' opinions as superior to those of women in a position of authority. The boy characters make fun of all of the girls' choices until the girls decide to research prehistoric Mexico. The group of girls who willingly switch topics to avoid being taunted by boys in their class counters any ideal of nondiscrimination and likely imitates what the children saw at home. The narrator then portrays the consequences of the girls' sexist beliefs, as the group of girls receives a failing grade on their project. In "Una cascarita por la igualdad," "Bondad sobre ruedas," and "Entrevista a las niñas extraordinarias," boys bully girls for their intelligence, for their athleticism, and for the topics that interest them. The way that girls respond shows that these gendered behaviors and relationships begin at a very early age. Moreover, the influence of peers in schooling is so strong that education, as a structure, upholds these gender dynamics rather than transforming them.

In a further fictional example of education upholding a violent status quo, another story gives examples of girls as abusive toward other girls. In Laura Verónica Chávez Andrade's "Las niñas merecemos respeto" (Girls Deserve Respect), three older girls pick on a younger girl, Lizzy. As a younger and smaller girl, Lizzy was vulnerable. The narrator explains: "La molestaban constantemente. La llamaban por un apodo que la hacía sentir mal" (They were constantly bothering her. They used a nickname that made her feel bad).[79] Calling her by a nickname may have been a way for the older girls to make a certain type of claim on Lizzy. One day, the perpetrators' violence worsens and during recess they hit her with a broken chair.[80] School supervision is so lax that during recess they drag a young girl away from other children. The group of girls also managed to acquire a broken chair, and in a secluded location, use it to physically assault the younger and more vulnerable Lizzy. Just as in stories that represented women's experiences of violence at home, the violence Lizzy experiences gets worse over time. The physical structure of the school and the area where the children have recess is such that the girls were able to move from emotional to physical violence. Moreover, the fictionalized bullies likely experienced violence at home and so interact violently with other children.

Children also imitate the patterns of violence in their families by abusing and bullying people with more obvious differences. The authorities in the educational environment, such as teachers or school administrators, allow bullying to occur at school. Teachers or principals may not even notice the beginning of these patterns. Thus, authorities in schools reproduce the violent social order that exists outside of school. Short stories fictionalize children who engage in abusive behavior. Brenda Itzel Castilla Jiménez's "La niña que logró su meta" (The Girl Who Reached Her Goal) portrays Fany, who is in an even more vulnerable position than Lizzy was, since Fany is from a family without enough food, work, or money. She wanted to access education, though, and since there was no school in her community, she walked two hours each way to attend school. The fact that Fany had to walk so far to get to school would have been enough to draw unwanted attention from other children, as it clearly placed her outside of their social norms. Fany's experience of difference from her classmates is magnified by the fact that according to the narrator, when she came home, she worked with the rest of her family to make and sell handicrafts.[81] It is unlikely that she was paid for working in her family business, as most children who work in Mexico are not compensated for their work. The narrator mentions in passing that other children made fun of her.[82] The connection between children making fun of Fany and her economically precarious situation is implied. No one in authority in this account improves Fany's situation at school or ensures that other children in her home community, who may have been less determined to access education, could also be educated there. Castilla Jiménez's representation of inaccessible education, and the lack of effective authority figures, implies that education is intrinsically connected to other unjust social structures and is itself a violent structure.

Another story, Arely Yamileth Rodríguez García's "La lucha de Jovita" (Jovita's Struggle) describes a similar scenario. In this story, the narrator offers more details about the protagonist's experiences in school. "La lucha de Jovita" takes place in the state of Oaxaca, and it portrays a group of Spanish speakers who bully a Zapotec Indigenous girl called Jovita.[83] The narrator explains that Jovita's community only had an elementary school. This means that to continue her education beyond the sixth grade, she would have to attend a school outside of her community. Jovita wishes to go on to secondary school, and so she starts a new school in the seventh grade. As an Indigenous person who speaks a minority language, Jovita occupies a less prestigious linguistic and cultural position than the Spanish-speaking mestizo students. The other kids make fun of how Jovita walks, speaks, and dresses. The fact that the children bully a visibly different child mirrors people's behavior in the world outside of the story. Bullies—in the world and in the story—are especially inclined to act when they know they will face few repercussions. The interactions between characters in these spaces suggest that fictional schools in the stories analyzed here are a violent place for anyone who does not occupy a powerful position.

Children in these short stories try to solve problems in a number of ways. The conclusion of multiple stories in *Historias* and *Historias 2* align with what the critic Perry Nodelman calls the adult expectation of children's literature as being hopeful, optimistic, or utopian.[84] Several represent protagonists who resolve their problems by relying on structures integral to the context of schooling. The first way is through informal athletics during recess. Girls who were told that they could not play soccer soundly trounce a group of boys in "Una cascarita por la igualdad." The girls get mad at the boys who underestimated them, then they get even by winning a soccer game against them.[85] Winning a sports game is a plausible solution to their problem. The second way is through a special performance for the other students in the school. Isabel, the protagonist of "Bondad sobre ruedas" who was told that she could not skateboard, organizes a group of students to dance on skateboard wheels. She even includes a girl who uses a wheelchair in the dance number.[86] Isabel expands her group of friends to include a girl with a physical disability, and by including a new friend, Isabel's dance team wins. In this account, a group of children creatively takes advantage of the existing structure of a talent show to prove that they are worthy. The solutions in "Una cascarita por la igualdad" and "Bondad sobre ruedas" address very real problems. At the same time, the characters' solutions rely on certain aspects of the educational structure, such as informal games at recess or a performance, to fix much larger structural issues within education itself.

The characters also try to simply bear the problems themselves. In two cases, girls do not tell their parents about their mistreatment at school because they think they can solve it themselves. Jovita, for instance, tells her parents that school is going fine.[87] Jovita seems concerned that if she tells her parents about the problems at school, she will no longer be permitted to travel to another town for school. In other words, Jovita fears that if she is honest with her parents, she will have to stop her education. Jovita so desperately wishes to continue her education that she tries to withstand the constant assaults. Lizzy, the protagonist of "Las niñas merecemos respeto," acts in a similar way. After the group of girls attack Lizzy with a broken chair, she does not tell her parents about it. She does tell her mother that she would prefer to stay at home, without elaborating on why.[88] The narrators of both stories tie the girls' reticence to tell their parents about what is happening with their desire to continue learning. In addition to the characters' implied desire to continue learning, they may also wish to protect the people in charge in the schools. They want to continue attending school so badly that they will not mention any reason for their parents to stop sending them.

As these characters are children, they are not able to withstand all the issues inherent to an educational environment. The young protagonists call on characters with more elevated positions in a hierarchy of school or home to intervene. The narrator of "Las niñas merecemos respeto" shows that another authority figure is necessary to right the wrongs of Lizzy's educational experience. Lizzy's mother eventually solves her problems. The narrator explains that the mother likely figured out the situation while bathing her daughter. After seeing her daughter's bruises, the mother's logical next action would be to meet with the authority in Lizzy's school environment. The fictional mother then meets with the school principal. The principal appears to respond to the issue when confronted by other people in a position of power. He suspends the perpetrators. Here the principal acts like a police officer and a judge, although he is marginally more effective than police officers and judges mentioned in the letters to the president. When the girls return, they retaliate against Lizzy with more threats.[89] The educational version of the legal system is no more effective at protecting victims than the criminal justice system. It, too, functions largely to punish enough people to convince the public that it works. Lizzy's parents arrange for her to switch schools. Real change takes place only after Lizzy moves to another educational environment, and only after her parents, who have more powerful social positions, have intervened. Only once they have exhausted the options available to them through the school's version of the legal system do they seek a new educational environment. The story, then, does not disrupt the power and violence embedded in the educational system.

In "Entrevista a las niñas extraordinarias," the characters take a different approach. The group of girls who had mistakenly listened to the group of boys ask an authority figure—their teacher—for a second chance.[90] She agrees. A large group discusses new ideas and the narrator mentions that two of the girls blame themselves for failing the project on the first attempt. The girls' willingness to blame themselves calls to mind both Lizzy and Jovita, who had internalized blame for other children's behavior toward them and were reluctant to discuss the bullying they experienced. In "Entrevista a las niñas extraordinarias," Shaden, one of the girls involved in the rainbow project, reminds her group of friends that it is the boys' fault, not theirs. In spite of Shaden's empowering speech, in the ensuing discussion in the story, the female characters reject each other's ideas for being very "cheesy." The other characters have internalized the idea that boys are smarter, and that any of their own ideas would be too feminine. The narrator adds, as an aside "sin darse cuenta que de nuevo estaban menospreciándose a ellas mismas" (without even realizing that once again they were disempowering themselves).[91] This suggests that these girls have internalized patriarchal ideals, which have destroyed their own belief in themselves at a very early age. Finally, the character Sandy tells the group that they should interview other girls about their own lives. In this way, the characters push back against the constraints that societal gender dynamics had set out for them. The story continues, portraying the group of girls talking to their friends and neighbors. The girls' discussion with other women was a powerful experience for them. They present their project with a unanimous conclusion: "Ya entendemos por qué las niñas somos románticas, tiernas y cursis; porque es nuestro modo de pensar y porque así nos gusta ser, todas nos parecemos y no tenemos que ser iguales a los niños" (Now we know why girls are romantic, kind, and sweet; because it is our way of thinking and because we like to be like this, we are all the same, and we don't have to be like the boys).[92] The girls' new project idea led them to celebrate women and girls rather than denigrate them. Moreover, as they had initially rejected the idea of doing a project on rainbows because it was too feminine, it would have been empowering for these characters to do a project that celebrated all things feminine. Had the girls listened to their own intuition and to their teacher, a female character in a position of authority, they may never have reached this conclusion. The girls' successful project encourages them to celebrate their own accomplishments and to combat harmful gender dynamics. At the same time, the girls' project still supports the misguided notion that teachers or professors can justifiably assign a letter or number grade on a student project. Moreover, it reduces women and girls to typically feminine qualities, and thus reinforces a gender binary, suggesting that in certain spheres, such as education, women can gain power only by expressing their identity through these qualities.

Castilla Jiménez's "La niña que logró su meta" represents connections between education and electoral politics. In that story, the protagonist Fany discovered that whatever she writes in her notebook will come true. She is from an isolated community and has to work after her school day ends, so her dreams rectify some of the issues inherent to her material situation and improve her life and the lives of her family members. Fany does not dream of transforming any of the broader social structures that prevented her—and people like her—from accessing education or other rights and guarantees. She writes in her notebook about issues pertaining to money and work, schooling, and her future participation in the legal profession. First, her dad gets good news at work. Her father's employment would economically benefit him and the rest of the family. Fany also writes about improving schooling for other children by making recess longer and ensuring that her brother gets good grades.[93] Fany's notebook has thus guaranteed positive change in the educational context. It continues to do so throughout her life. The narrator states that Fany continues studying and becomes a lawyer. As a lawyer, she works to create a better world by modifying its electoral system and by ensuring that political parties create more opportunities rather than waste money on propaganda.[94] Fany's notebook ensures that political parties respond to people's needs rather than serving as a way to prove that Mexico is a democracy. The story then moves beyond imagining reforms to social structures to imagining a profoundly different world. The narrator states that the magical notebook also cures cancer, HIV, and violence in women's lives, and it saves people with disabilities.[95] Fany wants to help improve her surroundings. She does so by modifying the forces of order that guarantee systemic violence. Fany improves her father's environment at work and her own environment at school, and ensures that future success in the legal profession will lead to political reforms and fantastically better futures for everyone in Mexico. Fany uses a notebook to modify problematic structures without explaining how she will do so. Thus, the magic notebook is the exception to the status quo that proves the rule.

The fictional and nonfictional representations of daily life for children in school settings take shape in the letters to the president and in the short stories. The short-story format is restricted by length, and the conventions of letter writing constrain the adults who write to the president. The accounts in both genres reflect the idea of constraint in other ways by reinforcing and reproducing patterns that uphold forms that govern a society. The letters to the president in the AGN and the stories in *Historias* and *Historias 2* show that education in Mexico reproduces hierarchical relationships between adults and children, such that authority figures may abuse children or choose to ignore the abuse that children perpetrate against each other. Schooling also reinforces unequal gender relations. Education is a force that upholds the social order, and no outside intervention—parents, school administrators, the president himself—will challenge the fact that it subtly, and violently, reinforces the status quo. The letters and stories offer some ideas for reform or improvement but overall uphold violent social structures.

The stories and letters also exhibit aesthetics that evoke the chaos, disorganization, and disconnection in the Children and Adolescents' Rights Law. Accounts of violence in children's lives, in the collections of short stories, and in letters that ordinary Mexicans write to the president bring to life the statistics I mentioned at the beginning of the chapter. They portray everyday situations of physical, emotional, and sexualized violence. In so doing, they disrupt the violent status quo. The letters and stories demonstrate that those in power accept high levels of everyday violence, be it as seemingly innocuous as bullying or as serious as sexual abuse. In other words, the stories and letters remind us that this violence is integral to the existing social order .

The stories and letters elaborate on various types of violence in children's lives. Divanni Xareli Utrera Amaya's "Una niña fuera de lo común" (An Uncommon Girl) and Matiana Aguilar Juárez's "Sara," represent average lived experiences for girls in Mexico. Their prosaic accounts add to a sense that the collections truthfully portray their context. "Una niña fuera de lo común" exemplifies the routine nature of most people's lives. The first-person plural narrator of "Una niña fuera de lo común" states: "como mujeres nacemos, crecemos, nos casamos, tenemos hijos y morimos como cualquier ser humano de esta tierra" (as women we are born, we grow, we get married, we have kids, and we die like any human on this earth).[96] This expression of the basic life course inadvertently echoes Yuyu/Carmen Castro's story, "Única," in *¡Basta!*. Utrera Amaya's story also illustrates that a woman's life revolves around reproductive work: birth, marriage, children, and death. Her narrator elaborates on what would make a girls' life special, "con poder de elegir su propia vida, de decidir sin culpas, sin apegos, sin dudas, dramas ni ataduras, decide desde el amor propio" (the power to choose her own life, to make decisions without blame, without attachment, without doubt, drama or ties to others, out of self-love).[97] What makes a girl's life distinct is all that pertains to her autonomy over her own body and the ability to make her own decisions. These goals echo constitutional guarantees and remain inaccessible to many women and girls. The narrator concludes by observing, "Una niña extraordinaria sabe que esta vida es una gran oportunidad para fortalecer los principios y valores, para ser exitosa y libre" (An extraordinary girl knows that this life is an opportunity to strengthen her principles and values, to be successful and to be free).[98] "Una niña fuera de lo común" thus emphasizes that there are always opportunities within a normal life, and the rhythms and social patterns that govern the experiences of women and girls can provide them. Utrera Amaya's story completely de-sensationalizes the question of girlhood in Mexico and reinforces a sense of normalcy and routine. The story contrasts sharply with many other fictional accounts of childhood that focus on aspects of a child's life that deviate from the ideal norms and routines.

Aguilar Juárez's short story "Sara" also discusses some common parts of childhood for people in Mexico. The story presents the main character's challenges and good family relationships without idealizing or romanticizing them. The events in Sara's life may validate the lived experience of its author. The relatively prosaic account of everyday life are likely part of the protagonist's experience and the experiences of other children. The narrator describes Sara's fairly idyllic childhood and refers to a precarious economic situation and a life in which a child is separated from her parents. Being separated from her parents makes the protagonist's life more challenging. Sara lives with her grandparents, and on a typical day she goes to school, does homework, and plays with her friends in her neighborhood. She sometimes helps her grandfather in his store, mostly because he will give her popsicles or candy.[99] There are hints of struggle in "Sara," in that the girl lives with her grandparents rather than her parents, and her grandparents are undoubtedly not in the best economic position if their primary income comes from a small store. These challenges are tempered by a school experience that does not appear to be as troubling as many of the accounts in other stories and the fact that she has friends nearby. Moreover, the narrator's adamant defense of childhood in light of absent parents becomes sadder in conjunction with comments that laud Sara for remaining a child rather than being like the other girls who wear makeup or use the newest technology. The story concludes with a simplistic understanding of girlhood. The narrator discloses that Sara knows that being a girl is the most beautiful thing.[100] For the narrator, being a girl is a beautiful time in life, because a girl can "reír, hacer tonterías, caminar descalza por ahí y emocionarse cuando encuentra cinco pesos tirados en la calle" (to laugh, make jokes, walk barefoot and get excited when she finds five pesos on the ground).¹⁰¹ Laughter with friends and finding a small amount of money are relatively commonplace occurrences. The quotidian and idyllic experiences in "Sara," then, contrast with the challenges in the protagonist's life and create a holistic sense of a typical girl's life in Mexico. In this way, "Sara," like "Una niña fuera de lo común," challenges a status quo that romanticizes childhood and glosses over its challenges.

Both collections describe daily life in other stories, and several accounts elaborate on the complexities to which "Sara" alludes. Carmen Pardo Cerecedo's "La lluvia" (Rain), Natalia Shirel Narváez Cadena's "La niña de las manos mágicas" (The Girl with the Magic Hands), Fabiana Pavón Castelán's "La increíble historia de Alondra y Darilé" (Alondra and Darilé's Incredible Adventure), and Rebeca Deydre Jurado Hernández's "El amor de mi vida" (The Love of My Life) touch on poverty and normal family struggles in a way that humanizes the characters rather than pitying or romanticizing them. For example, the protagonist in "La lluvia" collects water in every possible container when it rains, likely because her family does not have easy access to running water, maybe because of infrastructure in their neighborhood or because of cost. Pardo Cerecedo's narrator is proud of herself for collecting water, because it means that she can wash her toys and her younger brother.¹⁰² She may be responsible for her sibling and her belongings because her parents are busy working long hours outside of the family home. Other protagonists have dreams in which access to material objects would improve their situation. An unnamed girl in "La niña de las manos mágicas" imagines playing a piano in a park. She does not have a piano to play on, and the story implies that it is more likely that a piano would appear in a park than that her parents would earn enough money to afford a piano. The luxury of a piano would improve her life.¹⁰³ Other stories allude to families' difficult economic situations in a more direct way. The protagonist of "La increíble historia de Alondra y Darilé," for instance, is Alondra, who simply stopped going to school. When Alondra stops coming to class, her mom is too busy working to notice.¹⁰⁴ Alondra's mother is the head of her household and, like many parents, struggles to economically support her child. Alondra's mother likely had low pay, long hours, or a lengthy commute to meet her family's basic needs. Thus, she could not provide other types of support, and the child found herself in a difficult spot. Still another story portrays the impact of a divorce on the life of a child. Cinthia, the protagonist of "El amor de mi vida," is caught between her fighting parents as they go through a divorce.¹⁰⁵ She is a communication go-between, literally holding the phone as they speak to one another or relaying information from one parent to another, at great personal cost.

"El amor de mi vida" normalizes Cinthia's experience of her parents' divorce, just as the other stories normalize the experiences of children who live in situations of fewer economic resources. All three stories portray girls' lives in a straightforward way and confirm understand what is important for girls. The fictionalized versions of daily life in all these stories also challenge the social structures at home and at school that do not encourage girls to describe their own lives in their own words. *Historias* and *Historias 2* are powerful because they amplify the voices of girls when few other publications offer girls the chance to express their experiences.

Other stories in both collections describe the violence inherent in girls' homes and in their own lived experiences with much the same matter of fact, straightforward tone. They counter the style of representation Alice Driver described as porno-misery and are distinct from children's literature written by adults, as when that literature portrays challenges in children's lives, it, according to Daniel Goldin, in an interview with Emily Hind, focuses on trendy social issues like bullying.[106] The adult authors rely on editors and publishers and so are more likely to uphold norms in children's literature, which portrays homes as safe environments, and violence outside of the home may form a background of children's literature written by adults in Mexico. Children, however, represent events similar to their daily lived experience, and so touch on violence at home and within families.

The presence of inequality and intrafamiliar violence in *Historias* and *Historias 2* also follows what scholars of children's literature written by children have observed. The educational psychologist Janette Habashi, for example, conducted a project with Palestinian children, in which girls portrayed everyday sexism. Habashi's project began as one in which children would journal and eventually included other examples of writing, such as poetry and short stories. In these works, girls "focused on the frustrating challenges of being a female in a world of men. For example, a female co-researcher [Habashi's term for girls involved in the project] became empowered to write about her challenges growing up and the inequality between genders."[107] Male family members were not informed that the girl was involved in the journaling project because they "did not encourage her to take part in community activities under the pretence that they were concerned for her well-being."[108] The family hierarchy affected the experiences of girls writing in Palestine, just as it does in Mexico, as in both cases a father or authority figure would claim to be protecting his daughter while in fact he was preventing her from enjoying a cultural, educational, or social opportunity. The Palestinian girls writing about their own lives included all facets of their experiences, and by describing the positive and negative aspects of their experiences, the girls' journals challenged the existing social hierarchy. The way the Mexican girls write about their experiences of violence in *Historias* and *Historias 2* also challenges the existing social order.

Several stories represent violence in young female characters' homes, which reflects a context in which the stories' authors might experience violence in their own homes. The stories show that intrafamiliar violence is a spectrum. It can begin with an adult male character's desire for his wife to maintain a specific gender role and then, when she refuses to comply, can involve physical violence. Three stories vividly fictionalize the more subtle dynamics of intrafamiliar violence: Diana Laura Osorio Vélez's "¡Ya no más!," Paula Acic Vázquez Hernández's "Yo soy niña" (I'm a Girl), and Laura Cecilia León García's "Lili la guerrera" (Lili the Warrior).

I mentioned "¡Ya no más!" earlier, as it relies on outside forces of policing to solve an unequal family dynamic. It also portrays the dynamics of intrafamiliar violence. Its narrator describes the events that take place after Lucero's mother tells her father that she wants to drive a taxi. Lucero's father is not in favor of his wife seeking employment outside of the home. He tells her mother that it is not an appropriate job for a woman—indeed, in Mexico, driving taxis is a job almost exclusively performed by men. He may not want his wife to work because, if she sought employment, it would mean he could not provide for his family. Should her mother leave the private sphere, where he believes that she belongs, it will reflect badly on him. Lucero's father elaborates, purporting to be worried about her reputation "¿Qué crees que opine la gente sobre esto?" (What will people think about this?).[109] His worry about others' opinion is likely more that he is worried about his own reputation and what people might say about his ability to provide for his family. He wants to confine his wife to the home, and he shouts at her, "¡Mejor dame de comer!" (Better yet, feed me).[110] The way that Osorio Vélez's story introduces an adult woman's desire to work as an interruption of the peaceful family shows that the family was not a peaceful environment prior to him yelling at his wife to feed him. The father begins with probably socially acceptable levels of violence that then eventually become unacceptable later in the story. In this way, the story testifies to the truthful and troubling pattern of escalating violence, much in the way as several of the stories in *¡Basta!* represented violence in women's lives.

"Yo soy niña" also portrays complex family dynamics, including specifically mentioning the subtler ways that men deprive their female partners and their girl children of their rights. I show that the story upends socially accepted silence around men who seek to control their families. The five-year-old's story disrupts the silence around violence that prevents girls from accessing their right to education. "Yo soy niña" opens with a description of what its first-person narrator understands as a normal family: "Soy Luna, una niña como tú, mi familia puede ser como la tuya, tengo a mi papá que piensa que no es bueno que estudie" (I am Luna, a girl like you, my family could be like yours, my dad doesn't think it is good for me to study).[111] The protagonist understands that her father doesn't think girls should be educated and that it is normal to deprive girls of this right. The story implies that Luna is not encouraged to study in part because the family has no money. Her father is clearly depriving her of her right to education, which the Constitution guarantees should be free and accessible to all Mexican children. The narrator adds that another part of a normal family, in addition to the fact that she is not encouraged to study, is that her mother is a housewife.[112] Luna's mother did not have the opportunity to access an education either. "Yo soy niña" adds that her father does not like it if her mom has opinions.[113] In other words, there are consequences if she expresses them. Even if Luna's mother wanted her daughter to attend school, Luna would not be allowed to do so. Depriving girls of education is anticonstitutional and means that they will not get ideas about how the world should be and be more accepting of the world as it is. "Yo soy niña" treats the family dynamic of quiet, unopinionated women and girls as normal, and as a common dynamic, one that is seldom remarked upon in stories written by adults. The short story challenges the social order that would remain quiet about the troubling pattern of men who prevent their female children from seeking education.

"Lili la guerrera" also presents a father who does not believe that girls should not go to school. In addition to breaking silences around the gendered access to education, the story lifts the silence around intrafamiliar violence by vividly portraying physical violence in the protagonist's home. León García's story reiterates that girls have less access to education than boys. Lili's older brothers were able to go to school, but she had to stay at home and help her mother with the housework.[114] The home was the acceptable sphere for the female characters in the story, which places Lili and her mother at greater risk for violence. At one point, she and her mother were making dinner. They began by going to the forest to get firewood and their trip took longer than expected. As a result, supper was not ready on time. The father cannot abide by the fact that his supper is not ready. He does not understand that women who have been confined to their home all day would not necessarily be able to perform their duties to his satisfaction every time. Lili's father acted violently in response to Lili and her mother's violation of his view of the rightful social order. The narrator states that he beat Lili and her mother until there were bruises on their faces.[115] León García's story describes a man who is physically violent toward his wife and daughter with so much detail that it seems likely drawn from the author's experience. The straightforward description of violence and poverty goes a long way toward destigmatizing the experiences of violence women and girls like the characters in this story may have in their lives. Returning to Lili and her mother, the narrator reflects that the father had been physically aggressive toward his family on other occasions as well. The male character's violence in Léon García's story worsens with alcohol addiction, like in Zamudio's short story "Muñeca," in ¡Basta!.[116] Lili's father becomes more violent worsens when he comes home drunk.[117] The narrator reflects one of the many ways that men justify their violence toward women in addition to substance use. At one point, the father explains to his sons, "Las mujeres solo sirven para servir a los hombres y cuando la comida no está, tienen que golpearlas" (Women exist to serve men, and when the food isn't ready, they must be beaten).[118] Male discipline is required when women do not perform their acceptable social role. "Lili la guerrera" goes on to represent a scene in which the mother counters the father's statement in a private conversation with her sons. Even though the story portrays violence against women and girls, the narrator calls it violence against women. The label of violence against women suggests that the Mexican popular imagination is aware of women's rights to a life free of violence and is less familiar with the discourse on children's rights. The eleven-year-old author seems likely all too familiar with men's violence toward women and girls. The account of men's violence is as tragic as it is straightforward, and it defies the status quo that prefers silence about violence that takes place at home.

Diana Laura Osorio Vélez's "¡Ya no más!," Paula Acic Vázquez Hernández's "Yo soy niña," and Laura Cecilia León García's "Lili la guerrera" portray an intimate understanding of violence in the home, particularly the effects of men's violent behavior on family dynamics. The authors also shed light on what letters to the president neglect to mention: when men are abusive toward their own children, they are usually abusive to their partners or spouses as well. They represent violence that confines girls to their homes, performing housework, without the opportunity to attend school or work outside of the home. The stories also defy social expectations by showing exactly how or why men are provoked to be violent. It is clear that their behavior is not at all in proportion to the supposed offense. All these techniques undoubtedly validate the authors' own experiences and challenge the social order that would have them talk about these matters in hushed tones or with trusted friends.

The letters about violence in children's lives archived in the AGN and the short stories in *Historias* and *Historias 2* describe children's lives, including their experiences of violence, in a straightforward way. By giving adults the opportunity to discuss violence that affects different aspects of children's lives, they do not have the same function of validating the children's understanding of their own experiences, but they do break some silence around these events that occur far too frequently. One letter describes violence that affects boys and male teenagers. More girls than boys experience sexualized violence, yet there is more silence around boys and men's experiences, and thus increased stigma and shame.[119] The letters that describe violence and abuse are a powerful way to disrupt the status quo. This destigmatization effort exists in tandem with the fact that when men or boys report violence perpetrated by other men, it disrupts the social order to such an extent that there is a more rapid or forceful response.

Irma Castillo writes a letter after a man sexually assaulted her fifteen-year-old son at his workplace. Castillo's letter sheds light on sexual violence against boys and calls to mind the scholarly accounts, letters, and stories about women and girls who live with sexualized violence to earn an income or attend school. Castillo's letter states that her son had worked for a family member during a school vacation and during that time the family member violently raped her son. The fact that a mother tells the Mexican president that her son was raped by a family member defies so many parts of the acceptable social order. First, Castillo admits that she does not earn sufficient income to provide for her son and so he works on school vacations and holidays. Indeed, as the cover sheet of this archival file notes, Irma Castillo was a housewife, meaning that she did not work outside of the home, or at least that she did not participate in the formal economy.[120] The letter adds that her son specifically wanted to work so he could buy tennis shoes. If he were anything like the male undergraduate students I have taught, sneakers or tennis shoes are an important mark of status at school.[121] Castillo undoubtedly wanted her son to fit in at school and was likely saddened that she could not provide for his every need. Indeed, she was likely happy that her son found enough work to be able to acquire a coveted item. Her letter further defies the social order because it admits that her son was raped and that a family member—not a stranger—was the rapist. Castillo's statements counter the commonly held but misguided belief that rapists are strangers, and that rape is a crime of passion, not a crime of power. It seems that once Castillo decided to believe her son, she was willing to do everything possible to end the silence around his crime. Yet her son's experience of rape could have been avoided if he had had enough money for tennis shoes. That is, if the president had cared about what Castillo's letter calls the welfare of all Mexicans, and actually provided for Mexican people's economic needs, he (and others like him) could have avoided working in a violent place.[122] The president has not protected his people, with state guarantees or a livable minimum wage, and so Mexican people are vulnerable to abuses from others who can exert power over them.

Castillo's letter expresses that the president, the ultimate force of order, might be able to give her son justice even though the legal system has already failed her. The letter outlines the actions she has taken to seek justice: she has gone to the police, who arrested the alleged rapist. However, he was able to pay enough to be released and to then cast doubt on her son's account by paying someone to change her sworn statements about her son being raped. Castillo's letter, as with other letters to the president, implies that she has done everything right after her son became the victim of a crime, so now the system should return the favor.

The response from Atención a la Ciudadanía tragically confirms that the system is not interested in doing everything right for the people it is meant to serve; again, the program does not even respond. The bureaucracy may discriminate against the letter writer because she is from a lower socioeconomic status, she does not have access to a computer, or she has a lower level of education (indicated by certain spelling errors). The bureaucracy may also have accepted that alleged rapists get out of jail by bribing guards and falsifying testimony and so Castillo's pleas are not worth their attention.

Castillo's letter pushes back against significant stigma about violence in the lives of boys and defies the social order that prefers to keep this even more hidden that violence in girls' lives. She and other letter writers are convinced that a man in a higher position in an existing hierarchy can motivate other men in the hierarchy. Castillo was likely motivated to communicate with the president because his office engaged in public messaging around questions of justice. Unfortunately, there is a wide divide between the Mexican people's desire for justice and the response of the president's office. The hierarchy is one of misogyny, so it only protects itself. Atención a la Ciudadanía does not even respond to the letter, and it is clear that from the bureaucracy's point of view, a child from the lower social classes does not deserve protection. It is his fault that he leaves his house to seek work, not the state's fault for failing to provide for its people.

Castillo's letter demonstrated anguish and resignation at the status quo, and hope that the president could offer change. Some fictional accounts in *Historias de niñas extraordinarias* and *Historias de niñas extraordinarias 2* represent changes in children's lives. Marginalized girls portray change in their short stories. The children's social location and portrayal of alternative futures aligns with what Toni Morrison has observed, that utopia is designed by people who are excluded from power.[123] Three stories—"Yo soy niña," "Lili la guerrera," and "El libro mágico"—are situated in early twenty-first-century Mexico and present plausible escapes. "Las salvadoras," "La princesa vengadora" (The Vengeful Princess), and "La extraordinaria Hannia," for their part, transport readers to fantastical universes that include ice kings, vampires, and mermaids, which lead their protagonists to better futures.

"Yo soy niña" represents a girl, Luna, who escapes her family because they would not let her attend school. She moves in with another family member for the promise of future earnings. Luna's father did not want her to attend school or her mother to have any opinions. Her parents solve the dispute by telling her she can go and live with her aunt, who tells Luna that her father "no era malo, solo que no sabía que las niñas podían jugar con carritos y bloques, y trabajar." (he wasn't bad, he just didn't know that girls could play with cars and blocks, or work).[124] The aunt is wasting her breath justifying the abusive behavior of Luna's father. Luna's father knows that girls can do all these things; he just does not want to acknowledge it. The story goes on to state that Luna convinces her father to let her study by telling him that she will earn more money in the future if she has an education. The aunt's comments, Luna's mentioning of finances, and the father's declaration that he loves her facilitate their eventual reconciliation.[125] Reconciliation with a financial motivation is not love, but it might be exactly what a five-year-old like the author of "Yo soy niña" would hear to justify a father's bad behavior. In the story, then, another woman's home provides a safe haven for a young girl to attend school and to reach her dreams. The fact that Luna goes to live with her aunt to avoid her abusive father does not change the abusive man, but it does solve Luna's problems.

Lili, the protagonist of León García's "Lili la guerrera," also escapes her violent family. She had been forced to do chores while her brothers went to school, and when she and her mother did not do them to her father's satisfaction, he beat them. To avoid further conflict, Lili's parents also send her to live with an aunt. León García's narrator states that it was because she was so rebellious rather than putting the blame on her abusive father. The home of Lili's aunt is better than her home of origin but not perfect. Lili's aunt does not have money to send her to school and so Lili works to pay for her school fees. She helps her aunt make and deliver handmade tortillas each morning to earn sufficient income for her education.[126] Lili exercises her right to education, and the right to some sort of equality with her brothers, in a way that goes against her right not to work. She has an extra burden to access education that her brothers do not have. She is eventually able to get an education, and the way she has to work for it underlines the inequalities. Moreover, Lili's escape is profoundly rooted in the material conditions of her existence. The story, then, offers a more realistic notion of escape. "Lili la guerrera" ends on a happy note after Lili's father asks for forgiveness. Lili then meets the love of her life and becomes a lawyer who defends women's rights.[127] "Lili la guerrera" presents limited escapes, both in the initial escape to the aunt's house and the happy ending. The father figure realizes that he will eventually benefit financially from sending his daughter to school and so he allows his daughter to leave his home. Lili's fictional escape may also bolster a feeling of hope for readers in similar circumstances.

Martínez González's "El libro mágico" (The Magic Book) presents a similar account. Its protagonist, Elisa, does not attend school and escapes her circumstances by reading. This fantastical vision of escape is, however, still grounded in material reality. After Elisa learns to read, she uses a book to magically resolve her family's problems. The beginning of the story sheds further light on socially acceptable levels of violence in the lives of girls in Mexico. Elisa was not allowed to attend school and learns to read from a magical book that teaches her what her father will not and opens up a world of intellectual possibility for her.[128] She hides the fact that she can read from her father for some time, until one day a group of strange men come to her home to talk to her father. The men tell Elisa's father that they will take his land because he does not have proof that it is his. The story implies that Elisa has used found her father's property documents while she was forced to clean his house. In the next scene, the narrator states that, because the book taught Elisa to read, she could understand the land title documents and realizes the strange men are thieves.[129] "El libro mágico" concludes by stating that Elisa's heroic acts make her father understand that girls should also go to school. In the story, a girl had to literally save her father's land, and his livelihood, to prove to him that girls should be educated. The story attributes Elisa's father's unlikely but possible change of mind to an unlikely object: a book that teaches someone to read. In this way, the story gestures toward freedom through reading, which can take place even by reading books that are not quite so extraordinary. Education and reading—in this story and anywhere—can be used to teach people how to fit into a certain kind of society, that is, into the existing order, and can simultaneously teach people to claim their rights that can challenge the existing order.

"Yo soy niña" and "Lili la guerrera" represent a father figure who receives an immediate or eventual financial benefit for sending his daughter to school. Only "El libro mágico" offers an example of a girl learning for herself outside of the school environment. The father characters—that is, the characters with power—will never relinquish their power without a fight. Real escape and freedom come from forging new paths that circumvent characters with power.

Three other stories, Rebolledo Argueta's "Las salvadoras," Cruz Morfín's "La princesa vengadora," and Laiz García's "La extraordinaria Hannia," imagine different futures beyond existing hierarchies of power. They refer to events that are, in fact, completely out of the ordinary. Each of these accounts presents a young girl as a savior or rescuer who overcomes evil. As the young female protagonist in the stories overcomes evil, the narrators imply that adult characters will not help them because the adults are often monstrous. These fantastical vampires, evil kings, and other villains likely allude to powerful figures who abuse their power. As in other stories and letters, and even the laws examined here, these bullies and abusers may be fellow students, bad teachers, or fathers who prevent their daughters from attending school.

"Las salvadoras" portrays a young female protagonist in a fairy-tale universe who escapes intrafamiliar violence. The protagonist, Stela, does so in a way that relies in part on schooling and in part on a group of friends and a mentor, a wise older woman. In this way, the story almost completely defies the forces of order that promote admiration of sedate and passive women. "Las salvadoras" relates Stela's experiences in an environment that sounds much like the present.[130] Stela is the odd person out in her family. She has storm powers, while her parents are an ice king and an ice queen, and her sister, Elisa, is an ice princess. The story—perhaps influenced by the immensely popular character Elsa in the movie *Frozen*—represents a hierarchy in the family that leads to abuse and neglect. The narrator states that the ice queen, Stela's mother, questions her husband's dislike of his daughter: "le dijo al rey que por qué tenía que ser tan malo con ella." (she asked the king why he was so mean to her).[131] In response, the king puts Stela in a tower. The king, a man with power, retaliates against his daughter because his wife questions his power. The queen is powerless to stop him and only occasionally glances as the tower. The king does let Stela go to school—in her case, a special school for children with extraordinary powers. He acts differently than other fictionalized fathers, such as those in "Lili la guerrera" or "El libro mágico." His apparent benevolence, moreover, may make his family members more likely to accept his abusive behavior. The father controls his family, and everyone does as he wishes, perhaps to avoid being abused themselves. In this way, "Las salvadoras" evokes many of the accounts of violence in the letters to the president and in other short stories in *Historias* and *Historias 2*.

The story then outlines several ways that Stela escapes her situation. Stela's first escape aligns with existing social structures. Indeed, school provides a significant respite from the abusive family, as it gives her a community with other students. After a few sentences about enjoying school, the narrator describes Stela's graduation ceremony from ninth grade. Stela has thus gained some respite from her family. The graduation ceremony presents a second escape, which is more fantastical than her first escape, which took place via her education. At the ceremony, an old wise woman chooses eight graduating students to protect people, nature, and animals. Stela and her friends have powers over fire and water, and the wise older woman trains the group of girls to fight an evil queen. The story names a female character as evil but does not call a father figure who prevents his daughter from leaving his home abusive. It is easier to identify a woman as evil than a man. The characters accept the wise old woman's challenge and prepare to engage in war. Stela's training experience in a group of female friends gives her the ultimate escape because she finally had the friends she wanted without needing to be a different person.[132] Stela's newfound confidence and acceptance is part of how she, her friends, and her mentor ultimately vanquish the evil queen.

The story concludes with a reconciliation that furthers abusive relationship patterns. After Stela and her friends use their power against another woman, Stela's father tells her that he is sorry he did not accept her as she was, and Stela forgives him. The narrator explains that Stela's father was under the influence of the evil queen.[133] The story further upholds a patriarchal order by placing women in competition with one another. In a further example of the story upholding a patriarchal order, it gives two brief examples of dating abuse. The narrator states that Stela had a boyfriend, Mike, who expressed anxiety about her going into combat. Mike's behavior calls to mind what Habashi's "co-researchers" observed about their own family members' inclination toward protecting the girls, which meant that they could not enjoy cultural, social, or educational activities. Mike's tendency toward protection becomes overtly violent after Stela and her friends vanquish the evil queen. He congratulates her by hugging her so hard that he almost asphyxiates her. Mike justifies his controlling hug by stating that he was just happy.[134] Rather, it seems Mike is expressing control, not happiness. Stela's boyfriend disappears from the story after his hug. His presence demonstrates that girls who grow up in families with abusive male parents often expect similar behavior from their own intimate partners.

Stela conquers an evil woman with her friends and wins the approval of an overbearing father. Ultimately, the story does not directly criticize Mike or offer a triumphant resolution to end the king's intrafamiliar violence. Rebolledo Argueta offers a profound example of the ambivalent attitude toward violence in the home, as is also found across short-story collections and in the text of laws.

"La princesa vengadora" also presents a young girl who vanquishes evil. In Cruz Morfín's short story, an eight-year-old girl forges an unlikely alliance with fantastical figures. Again, the story likely relates strongly to the author's lived experience, given the author's young age. The narrator-protagonist states that her cousins tell her that she cannot do certain things because she is small. But, she explains, she is eight and will soon be nine.[135] It is as if her birthday will decrease her vulnerability. The protagonist, moreover, dreams of gaining power that upends the status quo. She dreams of a magical powder, a vampire, Frankenstein, and *la Dama de negro* (the lady in black). The fantastical vampire becomes the protagonist's unlikely ally, as the vampire only appears horrible on the outside and is actually good. The protagonist enlists him to distribute her magical powder to stop the other two monsters from chasing her in her dreams. A third-person narrator interrupts the first-person account in the final paragraph of the story to observe that "la niña hizo desaparecer la maldad y apareció la bondad, porque sus polvos mágicos eran abrazos de osos y besos" (the girl made evil disappear, and goodness appeared, because her magic powders were bear hugs and kisses).[136] Her escapes are conventional insofar as they involve typical human affection, which makes change seem within a girl's reach. "La princesa vengadora" represents the human desire for a magical powder that could change others, and the protagonist's powder would be something within the realm of possibility. A character dreams of creating a better world that would completely alter the existing social order without relying on social structures of schooling or reading.

Laiz García, whose "Triunfos logrados" reflected on the contest, also wrote about a fantastic universe in "La extraordinaria Hannia." That story is somewhat similar to "La princesa vengadora" in that it imagines girls overcoming evil and completely transforming the existing social order. The first paragraph establishes a social hierarchy. It describes a young girl called Hannia who dreamed of what she wanted to be when she grew up and relates each profession to a way that it could influence other people. A doctor, for instance, can cure sick people; a veterinarian can save animals from the street; a singer can sing about love.[137] All these professions exist within a social order, but as the narrator does not elaborate on how they might act in ways that promote the status quo, I am content to suggest that they leave the story in the realm of dreams. In the next paragraph, the narrator states that Hannia wonders how she could accomplish all these things. After Hannia asks a series of questions to the universe, the narrator provides the answer. The story states that one night, Hannia dreams of a planet called Drul where she could do extraordinary things. On Drul there were "sirenas hermosas, bomberas incansables, maestras cariñosas, cantantes exitosas, astronautas pelirrojas, veterinarias bondadosas" (beautiful mermaids, tireless firewomen, caring teachers, successful singers, red-headed astronauts and generous veterinarians).[138] The fictional planet is the answer to Hannia's rhetorical questions. Moreover, the list of professions mirrors the one in the story's opening, with the exception that a firefighter replaces a doctor. In the imaginary planet, all these professions are in the feminine noun form, and the adjective that accompanies each further qualifies them. Not only are these women in the character Hannia's imaginary world professionally accomplished; they are also tireless, loving, successful, and generous. These women live with a group of beautiful mermaids—not mentioned at the beginning of the story. The most striking description is that the astronauts have red hair. For "La extraordinaria Hannia," red hair is on par with beauty, love, and success. For literary critics, red hair can also be equated with Lilith, and malevolent ideas, such as refusing to obey the patriarchy. According to Laura Turner, some traditions believe that Judas Iscariot, who betrayed Jesus, and Mary Magdalene, the disciple sometimes thought of as a prostitute, both have red hair.[139] It is as if in order to be and to accomplish what was outlined in the opening paragraph, the protagonist would have to go to another universe, or get red hair, which is fairly uncommon in Mexico. Indeed, the narrator concludes that the collective of women in Drul were "mujeres únicas e inigualables [y] le enseñaron a ser todo lo que había soñado" (unique and peerless women who taught her how to be everything she had ever dreamed of).[140] The story dreams of an escape through the new world of Drul even as it maintains that a new world is not required. The narrator and a fairy godmother confirm that if girls try hard enough, they can achieve anything.[141] Hannia learned from the example of women in Drul and temporarily escapes her circumstances. Hannia's escape, together with the alliance with a vampire and magical powder, and Stela's collective of girls who vanquishes an evil queen, present options for escape that occur largely outside of the existing social order.

    *Historias* and *Historias 2*, along with archival letters to the president and the Child and Adolescents' Rights Law, bring to life statistics about child poverty, educational attainment, and inequality between boys and girls. The legal, literary, and archival texts also offer various ideas for how children's lives might change.

The legal text describes an ideal version of society and outlines how the state may use force to protect children. The letters attest to everyday violence in children's lives. Some represent violence against boys and teenagers, which pushes back against the established order that would prefer to ignore than face that men and boys can also be victims of sexualized violence. The fact that girls had the opportunity to validate their lived experiences by participating in a contest and having their stories published in *Historias* and *Historias 2* defies conventions in the genre of children's literature. Multiple stories in both collections also dream of a better world, either reforming or transforming the confines of the current social order. The girls' stories, much like the archival letters, present aspirations for a better future that depend on the existing order of schooling and policing.

The Children and Adolescents' Rights Law, letters to the president, and short stories in *Historias* and *Historias 2* describe the reality for children in Mexico. The genre, form, and content in each type of text gestures toward a better future in ways that both replicate and challenge the existing order. The aspirational aspects of the form, genre, and content of all three types of text remain embedded in existing systems, and careful attention to the desired future in all three encourages readers and critics to develop the texts' lofty goals and put them into practice.

CHAPTER 4

# From Tapachula to Juárez

Migration and Violence

This chapter examines migration in legal and literary texts, comparing Nadia Villafuerte's 2005 short-story collection *Barcos en Houston* (*Ships in Houston*) with the 2011 Ley de Migración. I suggest parallels between the stories' context of production, the way the texts are structured, and the content they represent. I posit that the organizational strategies in Villafuerte's short stories and in the Ley de Migración attempt to confine the information they contain and make their disconnections seem logical. The aesthetics in the legal and literary texts provide context for what the law and short stories describe. The formal constraints of the law structure the ways that the newly created migration authority confines human movement. Villafuerte's short stories, for their part, also confine their characters' movement.

The Ley de Migración arises in a context of increased migration to and through Mexico. Mexico has long been a host country for immigrants, and in the first two decades of the twenty-first century, people have come to Mexico from all over the world. The largest numbers of immigrants are from El Salvador, Guatemala, and Honduras.[1] Indeed, between 2014 and 2018, approximately 250,000–300,000 people from Central America migrated through Mexico each year.[2] They migrated because of gang-related violence, poverty, and lack of economic opportunity, and in many cases, in search of family reunification. In 2019, more than 709,000 people attempted to migrate to the United States from Mexico and Central America.[3] Even when deported by the Mexican or US governments, people are likely to migrate again.[4]

Migration is a treacherous undertaking. People enter Mexico and begin to travel on top of the train known as La Bestia, and then by foot for much of the journey. They often travel at night to evade authorities.[5] The most frequent issues migrants face are extortion, robbery, physical aggression, intimidation and threats, sexual abuse, and detention without being informed of their rights. Mexican authorities, common criminals, and organized crime are responsible for these.[6] Train travel is officially illegal, and so it is more dangerous.[7] Officials patrol the train and raid it regularly. Walking is dangerous because of kidnappers.[8] Migrants face the threat of arrest and detention at almost any time.[9]

Migration is especially dangerous for women. Their experiences of crossing the border almost always involve some sort of sexualized violence. Rape, unintended pregnancies, sexually transmitted infection, and HIV are so common that large posters on the route advertise injectable contraceptives and antiretroviral drugs. Indeed, Amnesty International estimates that about 60 percent of women who migrate experience sexual assault. The journalist Stephanie Nolen interviewed multiple women who migrated from Central America through Mexico and on to the United States. These women reported having heard rumors about places in the State of Chiapas where "old mattresses are piled beside the train tracks—where the 'rape tax' is collected."[10] Women cannot move freely along the typical migrant trail. The police are even more threatening for women than for other migrants. As Nolen goes on to explain, "Many migrants turn temporarily to sex work because they need money to pay off police, or because a night in a hotel room gets them off the street and away from the police."[11] The already-horrifying risks of unauthorized migration are exponentially worse for women.

Migration is also extremely challenging and dangerous for children. Child migrants are also vulnerable to abuses from law enforcement and from organized crime. The number of children who migrate alone has increased dramatically in recent years.[12] They typically travel to be reunited with family members. Mexican border guards and immigration officials apprehend them and deport them back to Guatemala. Sometimes they are released into the care of organized crime.[13] On other occasions, they are piled on buses and, upon arrival, turned out to fend for themselves.[14] The Mexican government deports and detains Central American migrants to curry favor with the US government. By detaining children in Mexico, they solve a problem for US authorities who are theoretically obliged to house them, provide them with access to education, and guarantee other rights. The Mexican government's obligations are not so extensive. Immigrants' rights group show that while people wait in Mexico they do not have access to "family, legal or social support."[15] The increasing numbers of migrants, and the Mexican government's mistreatment of them, will likely continue. The twenty-first-century experience of migration is one where desperate people come to Mexico, from all over the world, and typically cross it in search of a better future elsewhere. As they migrate, they face incredibly high levels of violence, particularly if they are women and children.

The contemporary experiences of migration comes out of Mexico's history of accepting immigrants and the ways that migrants in Mexico have experienced overt violence and more subtle forms of prejudice. Starting in the nineteenth century, Mexican governments focused on attracting immigrants who would improve Mexico's economic standing and aid in its attempts to modernize. The Mexican government sought migrants from Europe and the United States to foster its desire to modernize and develop the country. Over the course of the 1800s, Mexico also experienced significant immigration from the Middle East and Asia. Migrants from these places were considered less desirable migrants, and as a result, Mexican laws and cultural norms permitted them to integrate in only a limited way. Indeed, Mexicans tended to tolerate migrants only insofar as they bring an economic benefit to Mexico.

Violence often resulted when Mexican people thought that the immigrants' integration exceeded the economic benefits they were thought to have brought to Mexico. For example, in 1911, in the city of Torreón, Coahuila, a mob massacred a group of over a hundred Chinese- and Japanese-descendent people. The violence against Asian-descendant Mexicans in Torreón arose after members of those communities had managed to establish themselves and, in the eyes of the middle-class Mexican community, had become a threat. They used common racist tropes to justify they violence. The historian Julian Lim states that middle-class Mexicans blamed Chinese people for being "economic leeches, public health threats, and denizens of vice and crime."[16] These middle-class and elite who expressed anti-Asian views were also suspicious of Jewish immigrants from Europe, North Africa, and the Middle East. Mexican people expressed their anti-Semitic views by equating Jewish people with intellectual ability and science.[17] The Mexican government, then, has sought out some immigrants and tolerated discrimination against others since the nineteenth century. These trends continue in the twenty-first.

In the twentieth century, the Mexican government changed some of its tactics with regard to migrants. In 1947 it passed a law, the Ley General de Población (General Law on Population) to control its population and regulate migration; that law was revised in 1974. The 1947 and 1974 laws had two key features: they categorized people and made legal migration difficult. Both laws categorized people as immigrants, nonimmigrants, and a person who had immigrated.[18] The 1974 revision also criminalized undocumented travel through the country.[19] It practically closed Mexico's door to immigrants.[20] Indeed, the 1974 law was so strict that many people sought solutions outside of the law. For instance, the law threatened unauthorized migrants with such long prison terms that they were willing to pay fees to corrupt immigration officials to avoid incarceration.[21] These laws set up a system whereby it was theoretically possible to immigrate to Mexico and the Mexican government would decide who it wanted to live within its borders.

In the twenty-first century, Mexico changed its population strategy to deter unwanted migration first through improved border security and later through a new immigration law. In 2001, Mexico began to implement its Southern Border Plan. The plan's emphasis on border control was supposed to curb human rights abuses at Mexico's southern border with Guatemala.[22] Border-control checkpoints and staff grew once Mexico began accepting aid from the US Department of Defense for the Mexico-Guatemala-Belize border program.[23] The number of personnel, and the military technology they used, increased further after the Mérida Initiative began. As I mentioned in the introduction, the Mérida Initiative emphasized "a more modern, efficient, prosperous and secure border."[24] Mexico's highly regulated border with Guatemala, however, has not met the Mexican government's stated goals. It has not deterred migration. The securitized border has simply made migration throughout the rest of the country more difficult and more dangerous.

Mexican politicians also attempted to organize migrants already in the country by revising older laws and passing a new one. They revised the 1974 law with changes to the section on immigration so extensive that the Mexican federal government created a separate law. The new Ley de Migración, which punitively and violently imposes order, came into effect on May 25, 2011.[25]

I focus on the 2011 law in this chapter. It is structured to regulate human movement and is at once aspirational, descriptive, and punitive, and the parts of the law that refer to punishment overshadow almost every other part of the legal text. The way the law is organized highlights arrest and detention and overshadows the recognition of migrants' human rights. The law is divided into eight sections, each of which begins by stating that the new law will summarize Mexico's rules and regulations about migration.[26] The law then discusses the rights and obligations of migrants and migration authorities, as well as the administrative procedures that allow the migration authorities to regulate people's movement. Language about punishment is part of each section. The longest and final section is a list of legal sanctions for those who violate the laws and crimes relating to migration.[27] The law's organization, then, emphasizes punishment.

The law also establishes an expanded network of immigration enforcement that further upholds a violent established order. The law recognizes borders without even considering the fictional nature of such territorial divisions. (Although it would be very surprising if it did.) It establishes that borders are divisions on land and water between various countries, and places where government officials have the ability to regulate the traffic of people and goods. The law explains that border officials can arrest and detain anyone who does not comply with the rules. The law also expands the types of officials who can ask questions that relate to immigration and what they are allowed to do when a migrant does not comply with their authority. Indeed, the 2011 law suggests that a vast network of police, border guards, and the military can ask anyone for their documents almost anywhere in Mexico. Moreover, any official in the vast and undefined network of migration authorities can detain a person who does not provide the right documents. In practice, the officials impose more severe consequences for women, queer people, or people with disabilities. The law encourages migration authorities to uphold a misogynist, homophobic, and ableist order.

The migrants, for their part, are forced to cross borders only in certain locations. Regardless of whether these migrants cross in defined locations, they face various types of violent authorities. The authorities are armed forces and range from migration officials to police officers, and other officers who claim state authority to question and detain migrants and remove a migrant's possessions.

The Ley de Migración, together with Villafuerte's short stories, exhibit a tension between expansive and punitive understandings of migration. The tension between expansiveness and punishment calls to mind tensions explored in earlier chapters of this book between politicians who wanted to completely overhaul the criminal justice system and politicians who advocated for smaller reforms, or between guaranteeing the rights of women, children, and adolescents and imposing sanctions on those who would act violently against them. The individuals and broader social forces that effect structural violence in the lives of migrants differ in some ways from structures we have seen in earlier chapters. These include the police and prisons that kept Israel Vallarta incarcerated in *Una novela criminal* and those police officers, politicians, and bureaucrats than ensured that women and children live with high levels of violence at home in letters to the president and in short stories from ¡Basta! and *Historias de niñas extraordinarias*. Yet there are similarities between the ways that police, prisons, politicians, and bureaucrats exert misogynist, hierarchical, bureaucratic, and other forms of violence in the Ley de Migración and in Villafuerte's short stories.

The text of the 2011 Ley de Migración upholds the existing order from its very first article. It states that the law will regulate the "ingreso y salida de mexicanos y extranjeros al territorio de los Estados Unidos Mexicanos y el tránsito y la estancia de los extranjeros en el mismo" (entry and exit of all Mexicans and foreigners in the United Mexican States, and the duration of foreigners' stays in the same).[28] The opening statement expresses a desire for public order and contrasts with the second part of the sentence, where the law adds that public order will be enforced "en un marco de respeto, protección y salvaguarda de los derechos humanos, de contribución al desarrollo nacional, así como de preservación de la soberanía de la seguridad nacionales" (in a framework of respect, protection, and human rights, which will contribute to national development, as well as national security and sovereignty).[29] And yet the fact that the law puts these two ideas together in its very first article shows that the framework of respect for human rights is intimately tied to the state-sanctioned use of force. Other articles offer further guarantees of migrants' rights. Every time the law offers these guarantees, however, they are coupled with its further recognition of violent forces of order. Article 7, for instance, states, "El libre tránsito es un derecho de toda persona y es deber de cualquier autoridad promoverlo y respetarlo. Ninguna persona será requerida de comprobar su nacionalidad y situación migratoria en el territorio nacional" (All people have the right to freedom of movement and it is incumbent on the authorities to promote and respect this right. No one will be required to prove their nationality or immigration status in [Mexican] national territory).[30] In theory, anyone may live in Mexico without needing to produce proof of their right to be there. And yet the migration authorities, who represent the violence forces of order, interrupt the theoretical idea of life without documentation. The very same sentence continues: "más que por la autoridad competente en los casos y bajo las circunstancias establecidos en la presente ley" (except that the corresponding authority [may ask for documents] in certain cases, and under the circumstances, established in the law).[31] Elsewhere, the law adds that migrants have a right to health care, medical attention, and education.[32] The text guarantees health care and education without mentioning migration authorities. The law thus outlines migrants' rights and, at almost every turn, accompanies these statements with some type of threat. The way the law concedes to recognize migrants' rights, however, is partial at best. The migration authorities, well-meaning bureaucrats in charge of migration to and through Mexico, will likely act in ways that are consistent with bureaucratic behavior analyzed in earlier chapters. In other words, migration authorities would act like these other bureaucrats out of a legitimate belief that they were doing the right thing, and in the process, they would harm migrants rather than assisting them. Moreover, in the legal text itself, migration is connected to the legitimate use of force so frequently that it becomes clear that the law's attempts to recognize migrants' rights will eventually lead to regulating the free movement of people, and that, in turn, is always connected to carceral projects.

The Ley de Migración also includes specific protections for women and children. It outlines how it will protect these groups by reducing them to a shared vulnerability. It recognizes that, like Mexican women, many women who migrate to and through Mexico may be victims of crime and require legal assistance. The law goes on to state that, to protect female migrants, it expands the purview of the Instituto National de las Mujeres. The Ley de Migración gives the institute the authority to assist migrating women and Mexican women with their legal issues.[33] Moreover, if women are victims of crime or witnesses to certain types of crime, the law states that they are to be given visas and assistance with permanent residency.[34] The legal text then elaborates on how the Instituto Nacional de Migración will eradicate violence by teaching migration authorities about gender equality, to ensure that migration authorities are better able to protect migrants' human rights.[35] The law's lofty goal of gender equality is, in fact, incompatible with the fact that the law gives migration authorities permission to exercise practically unrestrained force. The incompatibility in the law between gender equality and the use of force, in addition to the way that the legal text consistently emphasizes women's vulnerability, reduces women to a perceived need for protection. This means it is easier for the Instituto Nacional de Migración to impose protection via force. The law's recognition of women's specific challenges thus aligns the law with the existing misogynist order rather than dismantling it.

The legal text also addresses the situation of child migrants and offers special protections for those who travel alone. These statements exist in tension with the way the law also outlines the state's prerogative to decide what is in a child's best interest. It first mentions children in Article 3, when it defines unaccompanied minors as "Niña, niño o adolescente migrante no acompañado: a todo migrante nacional o extranjero niño, niña o adolescente menor de 18 años de edad, que se encuentre en territorio nacional y que no esté acompañado de un familiar consanguíneo o persona que tenga su representación legal" (Unaccompanied girl, boy or adolescent: any child or adolescent migrant, national or foreign, under the age of eighteen, who is in [Mexican] national territory, without a blood relative or legal guardian).[36] The law thus guarantees that a child who migrates will receive assistance from DIF and the CNDH, a government ministry and national human rights commission, respectively. Both agencies, also mentioned in the Children and Adolescents' Rights Law, are charged with assisting non-Mexican children. These two institutions would provide legal assistance on humanitarian grounds, allowing some children to remain in Mexico.[37] The government would then decide on the child's case, either permitting the child to remain beyond the initial humanitarian visa or facilitating the child's deportation. As the Ley de Migración goes on to state, if the courts decide that the child is to return to his or her country of origin, the child is to be accompanied by adults or another responsible party.[38] The law reiterates that the Mexican government must protect children throughout their visa and deportation hearings, and because of its emphasis on protection, the law does not recognize the child's autonomy or decision-making power. This section of the law is another example in which forces of order make a minor concession that in turn increases their powers. In this case, the law allows migration authorities and immigration courts to grant a very minor privilege to migrants, as it authorizes DIF and the CNDH to provide foreign children with various forms of assistance. Immigration authorities, in "thanks" for this benevolence toward children, are allowed to deport children or turn them over to the custody of adults without a clear relationship to the child who has migrated to Mexico. The law's minor concession, of extending protection from CNDH and DIF to include foreign as well as Mexican children, becomes major, because it closely relates to the state's expanding power.

In addition to the ways the law forcefully protects groups it perceives as vulnerable, the law consistently reiterates migrants' need for documentation. The emphasis on documentation in the Ley de Migración further grounds the legal text in the violent status quo. Article 16 outlines that migrants should have identification documents. Two separate fragments of Article 16 explain that the migrant should be able to show these documents whenever migration authorities or other competent authorities require it.[39] The law thus gives an unspecified number of officials the authority to ask any person for identification documents at any time. This expanded ability to ask for identification means that migration authorities could ask Mexican people for their documents, and in this way, migration authorities are allowed to question anyone who appears to be Central American. Migration authorities regularly apprehend Central American, Caribbean, and Mexican people in Chiapas, a state that borders Guatemala, as well as in Veracruz, a state with a large port of entry on the Atlantic Coast.[40] The law limits migration authorities' legitimate use of force when it states that officials review documents, they must return them within four hours.[41] The legally defined time limit is insufficient in terms of its detrimental effect on anyone in Mexico.

The law also creates a new migration authority and gives further permission to other authorities to use force against migrants. The way that the Ley de Migración creates the Instituto Nacional de Migración further aligns the legal text with violent forces that uphold the status quo. As Puar stated in *The Right to Maim*, it is politically advantageous for a government to have a population slowly acquiring injuries and disabilities. Puar reads the work of the French philosophers Gilles Deleuze and Félix Guattari to observe, "Mutilation and amputation are thus no accident but are part of the biopolitical scripting of populations available for injury, whether through laboring or through warring or both."[42] Migrants are not engaging in warfare or consistently engaging in labor during their travels. Nevertheless, they are subject to warlike levels of armed violence, are typically migrating in search of a better labor market, and may work while migrating. The anthropologist Wendy A. Vogt does not refer to Puar's theories but her observations about migrants in Mexico align with the theorist's observations. As Vogt states, Central American migrants are profitable to local and global economies as they are migrating.[43] They are "cargo to smuggle, gendered bodies to sell, labor to exploit, organs to traffic, and lives to exchange for cash."[44] The newly created authority, the Instituto Nacional de Migración (INM), ensures that government ministries align with these interests. The Ley de Migración goes on to state that the INM is a decentralized administrative arm of the Secretaría de Gobernación, or SEGOB.[45] The fact that the INM is decentralized may give its agents more authority, as the law does not provide a clear structure to hold INM agents accountable. The law does note that other undefined authorities must collaborate with the INM.[46] The journalist Stephanie Nolen states that "civilian officers from the National Migration Institute (INM), military police [and] army and navy personnel" monitor the presence of migrants at "layers of checkpoints, on the main roads and lesser ones, some fixed, some mobile, some set up right outside the migrant shelters."[47] The collaboration between INM, military police, and armed forces is a complex network, and officers interpret the law in different ways, which leads to a contradictory and complex system of immigration enforcement in Mexico.[48] Practically anyone in a uniform could assume a position of authority vis-à-vis a person whom the uniformed individual believes is an authorized immigrant in Mexico. In practical terms, anyone who holds himself—a pronoun I use deliberately—in a position of authority or who carries weapons can stop a migrant. The authority figure could take the migrant to an undisclosed location that may or may not be an officially recognized prison, jail, or detention facility. Migrants understand that uniformed officials are dangerous and thus take extreme risks to avoid and evade Mexican migration authorities who are involved in injuring, assaulting, raping, or murdering migrants. Migration authorities and members of Mexico's armed forces are to blame both because they avoid prosecuting those who enact direct harm on migrants and because they are involved in criminal actions themselves. This terrifying situation almost completely overshadows the promises of the Ley de Migración, particularly the fact that it explains that INM staff will be subject to "los principios de legalidad, objetividad, eficiencia, profesionalismo, honradez y respeto a los derechos humanos reconocidos en la Constitución y en la presente Ley" (the principles of legality, objectivity, efficiency, professionalism, honor and respect for human rights, enshrined in the Constitution and in this Law).[49] The fact that the law mentions human rights as a governing philosophy is as senseless as those that described migrant protection.

The final section of the Ley de Migración reinforces the violent status quo of multilayered and overlapping complexes of violence: state actors like the police, others with weapons, and cultural or societally accepted forms of violence against women and children. The forms of violence examined in earlier chapters combine with and are even more forceful against migrants, as migrants are even more vulnerable to these forces of violence in Mexico than Mexican citizens. The law describes and regulates detention centers, which is significant because Latin America's largest migrant detention center is located in the city of Tapachula, Chiapas, a principal entry point into Mexico.[50] The law—which allows migration authorities to detain immigrants without any charge beyond unauthorized immigration—also claims that immigrant detention facilities are different from jails, as the detention facilities are not "centros de encarcelamiento, de reclusión preventiva o de ejecución de sentencias" (detention centers, jails for pretrial detention, or prisons where people go after they are sentenced).[51] The detention centers are, according to the law, remarkably similar to jails or prison. The Ley de Migración explains that the facilities will feed people, house men and women separately, and provide legal representation for authorized immigrants.⁵² The law thus makes a false distinction between an immigrant detention center and a jail, and in this way, it upholds the violent status quo. The text also tempers the section on confinement by limiting the amount of time people can spend in an immigrant detention facility.⁵³ It also states that the "el orden y la disciplina se mantendrán con apego a las disposiciones administrativas que emita la Secretaría y respetando en todo momento sus derechos humanos" (order and discipline will be maintained in accordance with the administrative provisions issued by the Ministry, which in every instance respect their [the migrants'] human rights).⁵⁴ In other words, human rights influence the system through which the Ley de Migración will detail migrants. The law's brief mentions of human rights and limited time in a detention facility are almost completely overshadowed by the description of immigration detention facilities. The form and content of the final section of the Ley de Migración, like other sections of the same text, emphasize containment and uphold the status quo. The aesthetic elements of the legal text—that is, the way that the law's headings and subheadings frame the discussion of migration—suggest that the movement of people arose out of almost nothing, so state authority must regulate it. The description and regulation of migrants, migration authorities, and immigrant detention also emphasizes the state's "legitimate" use of force against migrants. The law develops its framework for regulation migration, from the appropriate registration of migrants to the acceptable conditions of detention centers, in ways that legitimize Mexican officials' violent actions toward migrants in that country. The legal text also creates the conditions for what other scholars have already described as a complex system of enforcement, which, as I have observed, means that migration to and through Mexico is a terrifying prospect at best. The inclusion of the rhetoric of human rights is miniscule in comparison to the portion of the law dedicated to regulating and detaining migrants. The fact that the law even mentions human rights was evidently such a large concession to migration authorities, police, and armed forces that it gave these authorities exponentially larger permission to use force against migrants.

Nadia Villafuerte's 2005 short-story collection *Barcos en Houston* portrays much of the experience of migrants in Mexico. Villafuerte's short stories describe the lives of people at Mexico's southern border, including migrants, people who traffic other people, police officers, migration officials, and politicians.⁵⁵ Villafuerte, from Chiapas's capital city of Tuxtla Gutiérrez, is firmly connected to the broader Mexican cultural sphere. Her published work includes reviews in the cultural magazine *Nexos*, a 2011 novel called *Por el lado salvaje* (*On the Wild Side*), and two collections of short stories. *Barcos en Houston* was her first and came into being after she held a yearlong fellowship at the Fondo Nacional para la Cultura y las Artes' program supporting *jóvenes creadores*, or young creators (2003–2004).[56] It, and her 2008 collection, *¿Te gusta el látex, cielo?* (*Do You Like Latex, Honey?*), portray life at the Mexico-Guatemala border.

Villafuerte's 2008 collection is similar to other works of literature that represent migration in Mexico. It is an early contribution to a growing body of work that represents Mexico's southern border in literature, film, multimedia, and museum exhibits. Multimedia storytelling projects such as *Humanizing Deportation* includes stories of Central American migrants, as do films like *Jaula de oro* (*The Golden Cage*).[57] Literary examples include Alfredo Palacios Espinosa's play about a refugee community in the jungle along the Guatemalan border, *Límites perdidos* (*Lost Borders*; 2005).[58] The portrayals of migrants' travel across Mexico in *Barcos en Houston* also evoke the work of Antonio Ortuño, whose *La fila india* (*Single File*; 2013) describes the dangerous trip on the train many migrants take to cross Mexico and enter the United States.[59] Villafuerte's journalistic approach to fiction, moreover, evokes other portrayals of migration in Mexican literature. These include Julián Herbert's discussion of the 1911 massacre of Chinese and Japanese descendant people in Torreón in his nonfiction novel *La casa del dolor ajeno* (*The House of Other People's Pain*).[60] Another example is Fernanda Melchor's *crónica* "Aquí no es Miami" (This Is Not Miami), which deals with the experiences of migrants from the Dominican Republic who end up in Mexico rather than the United States.[61] Villafuerte's collection further expands those literary understanding of migration, though, to include other borders.

Villafuerte's *Barcos en Houston* attempts to contain and organize migration in a series of short stories. The accounts in Villafuerte's collection confine characters to a story, which is a feature of the genre, according to some theorists. Viorica Pâtea, for instance, states that the short story is a compressed genre.[62] And while that does not necessarily mean confinement, it does in *Barcos en Houston*. Villafuerte's portrayals of migration confine the characters to their experiences of migration. Moreover, and as Pâtea goes on to observe, those experiences are often linked to marginalization.[63] The stories in *Barcos en Houston* represent a brief period in characters' lives, and they include what Pâtea calls an aesthetics of brevity or an aesthetics of economy.[64] That is, they cover important events in a character's lifetime in the span of five to ten pages. "Viernes" (Friday), for instance, covers in eight pages the personal history and current reality of a Central American character, Elena, who crosses Mexico on a bus.[65] The story's limited length further confines Elena—the economy of words necessary to communicate such profound experiences means that some parts of the characters' lives are necessarily excluded from the narrative.

The structure of *Barcos en Houston* further mirrors the social order through several techniques that create a sense of unity or cohesiveness across the collection. *Barcos en Houston* is a more traditional book than *Historias de niñas extraordinarias* and *Historias 2*. After all, it employs a typical font in typical colors (black and white) and like many collections of short stories, there are illustrations. *Barcos en Houston* also aligns with one of Zavala's subcategories of the short story, in this case, a minifiction cycle where each story deals with a similar topic. Villafuerte's collection represents distinct characters in distinct manifestations of the migration experience in a location along the Mexico-Guatemala border, and so I read them as a "whole," where individual stories make sense as part of a broader vision.

Rhetorical strategies also create a sense of unity in *Barcos en Houston*. In an interview, Villafuerte stated that the beginning and end of each story connect with one another.[66] The last story in *Barcos en Houston*, "Ángeles y buitres" (Angels and Vultures) begins and ends with the same phrase, "Para volar es necesario caer" (In order to fly it's necessary to fall), the latter adding, "Definitivamente" (Absolutely).[67] The characters in Villafuerte's collection must fall into migration in order to fly and reach their dreams.

Another rhetorical strategy of containment within the text is the sustained allusion to horizon, sunrise, and sunset. The horizon would seem to bring about expansiveness and possibility beyond a migrant future, yet the characters never arrive there. The horizon always remains elusive. Sunset and sunrise similarly suggest an unreachable possibility. The horizons, sunrises, and sunsets relate the short stories in *Barcos en Houston* to one another. The eighth story in the collection, "Chica cosmo" (Cosmo Girl), for instance, portrays a character called Elena as she crosses Mexico on a bus. Elena—herself an undocumented Central American migrant in Mexico—looks at the horizon as authorities detain other Central American migrants. The narrator states that the bus's lights show the truth about the situation: "El autobús coloca sus luces hacia delante cortando de tajo la noche, rajándole para que aparezca con el sol la vulgaridad las cosas" (The bus's lights advance, cutting a swath in the night, slashing it, revealing, along with the sun, the ordinariness of things).[68] The lights show that Elena has hidden her own identity and pointed authorities to other migrants for her own security. Elena's history of sex work is ordinary, yet the word choice, *vulgaridad*, reiterates that ordinary behavior but in a negative light. After all,

Elena has figuratively thrown her fellow migrants under the bus and to the authorities who can act with complete impunity. In a similar way, the story "120 kilómetros por hora" (120 Kilometers per Hour) represents multiple events alongside mentions of the horizon and sunset. The protagonists, Mira and León, are Mexican teenagers who smuggle Guatemalan migrants. At one point, the narrator states that the two teenagers drive in the following way: "Como si el rojo horizonte fuera la meta final de la carretera, León sume el pie en el acelerador. Prefiere no voltear . . . Frente a ella [Mira] se tiñe apenas la puesta de sol" (León stepped on the gas, as if the red horizon were the end of the highway. [Mira] didn't want to turn around . . . in front of her, the sunset colored the sky).[69] León wants to escape his life so badly that he drives quickly enough that he thinks he can reach the horizon, and so far over the speed limit that it draws the attention of a police officer. The police officer apprehends Mira and León, and arrests both teens and the unnamed migrants they are smuggling in their car. The confining horizon in the story is similar to the vision of the horizon in the next story, "Mala reputación" (Bad Reputation). There, a third-person narrator describes a Honduran migrant Samy who has just been robbed: "Hubieras visto cómo Samy observe por última vez este horizonte" (You should have seen how Samy looked at the horizon for the last time).[70] The horizon alludes to Samy's longing for migration and escape, and the way the thieves have quashed it. Samy's sense of ended dreams reappears with the sunset in the story "Frontera de sal" (Border of Tears). Its narrator tells an unspecified singular you, *tú*: "Has llegado a la hora en que el crepúsculo es el mejor espectáculo. Un atardecer en cualquier mar es lo mismo, piensas" (You have come to the time when sunset is the best show. You think that dusk on any shore is the same).[71] Sunset represents longing for a better future, and each representation of sunset, sunrise, and horizons in Villafuerte's collection builds on those representations that preceded it. In these stories in *Barcos en Houston*, the horizon and sunset are tied to the characters' desire to escape their circumstances and the ways that outside forces thwart it. The sustained metaphors of sunrise, sunset, and horizon is a unifying rhetorical strategy in Villafuerte's collection. The sunsets emphasize the characters' attempts to escape from their situations and from the forces of order (including the extremely flexible narrators) throughout. They, and the horizons, are always receding. The characters never reach the horizons, a liminal space always just beyond their reach.

The narrative strategies disrupt the sense of unity created by sustained imagery and the fact that all of the stories deal with a similar topic: migration at the Mexico-Guatemala border. The narrative strategies in Villafuerte's collection are similar; first- and third-person narrators meander in and out of characters' experiences, physical locations, and times, and they break from the confinement of unreachable horizons. In *Barcos en Houston*, the narrative confusion relates to the context and in some cases helps characters evade violent force; in other cases, even its multiple voices and perspectives are hopeless in the face of overwhelming force. The text seems to escape that order through a kind of derangement and a narrative that communicates a sense of being overwhelmed. The tension between modes of order and confusion mirrors the tension between human rights and immigration detention in the Ley de Migración. In *Barcos en Houston*, the narrative strategies create a sense of confusion that challenges the sense of order created in an individual short story and across the collection. Confusion is a sign of hope, both in the literary text and in the potential for human movement against all odds it represents.

In "Cascarita" (Pickup Game) the narrator moves in time and location, which overwhelms the structure in the text. It portrays two characters, Ima and Carmen, as they attempt to migrate. As they move through time and space, it is unclear whether the experience of migration, of Ima's injury and Carmen's conversations with journalists, are a dream or a lived reality. The story is divided with time marks, which impose a sense of order. They are a countdown with fragments divided by temporal markers (:13, :12, :11, and so on), which calls to mind the divisions in the Ley de Migración, other human rights laws, and the Mexican Constitution. Unlike those legal texts, where the sections begin with 1, Villafuerte's short story goes backward. The countdown moves to the characters' destiny of migration, death, or both, which gives the story's events a sense of urgency and roots them in a specific moment in time. The numerical subdivisions confine the way the story moves through time, space, and imagination, although neither the headings nor the police and migration officials in the story entirely contains the account. The disorder creates a sense of logic and invites the reader's own interpretation of the nonlinear account. In this sense, the numerical order in "Cascarita" functions similarly to the narrator in Volpi's *Una novela criminal*, as it provides a single perspective on the events. The events within each time marker, however, overwhelm the markers' attempt to create a sense of order. Fragment ":12," for instance, is a journalist's description of a woman in a hospital. After describing the hospital, the narrator states, "Pero ella lee la nota" (But she reads the article).[72] Then, the story quotes the journalist, "Yo no dije eso" (I didn't say that).[73] The second half of the same sentence returns to the third-person perspective, "dice indignada. ¿O sí?" (she says, indignant. "Or did I?").[74] These two short sentences contrast the narrator's doubt about what has just appeared on television with the journalist's immediate confirmation of the narrator's point of view, and then the rhetorical question casts doubt on both narrator and journalist. The narrator's doubt, the journalist's confirmation, and the rhetorical question point to the unreliability of the narrator and of television news journalists. As I explored in my analysis of *Una novela criminal*, narrators and journalists can both be extremely unreliable interlocutors. The two sentences of "Cascarita" create so much doubt that it is unclear whether Ima has migrated, whether she has been injured, and whether a journalist ever reported on Ima's injury at all. The other fragments present a similar tension and a profound sense of ambiguity about whether "Cascarita" confines its characters or whether the confining form is what allows for the development of its plot.

"Cascarita" moves expansively between each of its three plotlines, and the way it moves between them mirrors the porous border that maims migrants, which is too profitable for any government to entirely contain. They reinforce the sense of movement. In the first fragment, ":13," Ima looks at water on the border between Mexico and Guatemala: "El otro lado es como ese horizonte de sal que parece casi tocarse pero no se alcanza, porque el agua se mueve, se mueve hacia delante" (The other side is a horizon of salt that looks like [she] could almost touch it, but is always just out of reach, because the water moves, moves ever forward).[75] The narrator's representation of moving water implies that the border is fluid. "Cascarita" continues to emphasize the fluidity of the Mexico-Guatemala border: "Si entra no habrá pisadas sino dos líneas paralelas" (If she gets in, she won't leave footprints, but rather two parallel lines).[76] The life she has is one line and the life she could have is another. These two sentences point to two tensions. The first is between containment by a body of water on the horizon and expansiveness of train tracks and migration, and the second, between a description of Ima's life as it is and the alternatives she imagines for herself. The connection of train tracks, migration, and an alternative future foreshadows the injuries Ima acquires as she attempts to cross the border.

The final fragment of the short story, ":1," returns to Ima's life at the water's edge. In this section, Ima remains on the Guatemalan side and thinks about crossing to Mexico. The narrator reflects Ima's thought pattern with Carmen's belief that nothing ventured, nothing gained.[77] Carmen interrupts Ima's reverie: "Si nos deportan, ni modo. Pero yo no me quedo más aquí" (If they deport us, who cares. But I'm not staying here any longer).[78] It is unclear if they have crossed, or which life Ima and her sister are living, and on which side of the fluid border they reside. The fluid border leaves the reader with a profound sense of ambiguity and mirrors the lack of clarity in "Cascarita": whether the countdown form that structures the account is one that contains the characters or what allows the characters to dream of movement toward a better future.

Villafuerte's interviews about her work make it clear that she is in favor of movement of people, and while an author's professed perspective in interviews is insufficient for developing a literary analysis, her comments lead me to believe that the stories dream of better futures.[79] At the same time, the portrayal of Ima and Carmen alludes to the ways that migrants are detained and arrested in Mexico, and to migrants' painful and sometimes deadly intersections with various people who assume authority over them. The short story's representation of the fluid border intersects with the methods of containment examined in form and content of the Ley de Migración and the fictional borders that they make real.

The second plotline suggests that they have tried to cross the border. It pushes back against the stigma of failing to reach their desired destination. A fictional journalist, Paola López, narrates section ":12" of "Cascarita." López reports that several people made it onto the train, and that one migrant, Ima, never returned to land. López interviews Carmen, who describes Ima's injuries for the reporter. Carmen wants to show the world Ima's injuries, and López's fictional news report illustrates the huge cost human cost of unauthorized migration. The third-person narrator comments on these events, describing how Ima refuses to talk to the reporter: "La mujer mira al suelo. No desea hablar con nadie. Es su hermana quien nos cuenta" (The woman stares at the ground. She refuses to speak with anyone. It's her sister who tells us the story).[80] The fictionalized news does not even name Carmen or Ima. The narrator further dehumanizes Ima when Carmen shames her for being unwilling to talk to narrators: "es que tienes que hablar, tú no eres la primera, pero tampoco la última si siguen haciendo esos operativos" (You've got to talk. You aren't the first, but you won't be the last if they keep doing those stings).[81] Carmen wants to talk about their experience to shed light on her sister's suffering. The representation of Carmen's willingness to discuss dangerous aspects of migration disrupts the order that accepts that migrants' bodies will be maimed as they move toward what they think will be a better future.

Police and other armed characters interact with Ima and Carmen. These characters add to the sense that the story offers a truthful description of the border and attempts to destigmatize those who are injured through migration. The third plotline describes how they came to be detained. The narrator adopts Ima and Carmen's perspective, using the first-person plural:

"Durante dos días nos escondimos, huimos de los policías mexicanos que nos robaron y nos querían abusar" (We hid for two days; we ran from the Mexican police who robbed us and wanted to abuse us).[82] These characters fear the police because they are known for robbing and abusing migrants. Later in the story the narrator returns to the criminal behavior of police officers: "En cada esquina, por mala suerte, o quién sabe por qué, la policía las acosa" (On every corner, for bad luck or who knows why, the police harass them).[83]

The story further likens law enforcement to criminals when an unknown male character tells them, "Ahí esperan los de Migración, policías municipales, hocicos babeantes dispuestos a la caza porque saben que el tren viene lento" (That's where Immigration, local cops are waiting, slobbering snouts ready for the hunt because they know the train's coming in slow).[84] Later, the narrator states that criminals are in charge of the train station.[85] In spite of the way that Ima and Carmen benefit from local knowledge about police and other criminal activity, the narrator goes on to explain that the police detain their group. A police officer tells the group: "Tú y tú, desnúdense . . . Sí, se lo han dicho a los dos hombres, no a ellas, las únicas mujeres del pequeño grupo" (You and you, strip . . . Yes, they said this to the two men, not to them, the only women in the small group).[86] Later on, the narrator reveals that one of the men who was raped says they were not even police.[87] These armed male characters control and confine the experiences Ima and Carmen had of attempting to migrate toward a better future. The way the story leaves room for uncertainty with regard to what had taken place, and what was a dream, suggests that within "Cascarita," the forces of order—be they the countdown or the male characters with guns—do not entirely overshadow the female characters' perspective on their own experience.

"Chica cosmo," mentioned earlier in this chapter, represents a woman leaving the Guatemala-Mexico border for Mexico's northern border. The disjointed narrative moves in time, space, and subject matter, and in this way, defies a sense of chronological time or linear order of events. First, the narrator describes the protagonist Elena's thoughts about her past and relates these thoughts to the experiences of other migrants and to Elena's thoughts about other migrants. The narrator begins by describing a movie playing on the bus and shifts to Elena's past: "Elena por fin ha dejado el Eros, por fin, piensa, incrédula aún de que esté ahí, en la terminal, con un boleto marcándole la salida a la Tapo de México, vientiuna horas, asiento veintinueve" (Elena has finally left Eros, finally, she thinks, still incredulous that she's here, in the station, with a ticket marking her departure to Mexico

City's Tapo station, nine p.m., seat twenty-nine).[88] The reader deduces that the protagonist is on the bus and that she had been a sex worker in a place called el Eros. Her experience, then, was similar to that of many migrants who enter Mexico in hopes of arriving in the United States. The narrator moves from the physical location in her bus seat to Elena's life at Eros, where she had worked for more than a year, in a situation of intense labor exploitation: "apretándose los dientes para no deslumbrarse con créditos que la hicieran adquirir ropa o muebles, por una mensualidad chiquita cuyo precio era en realidad anclarse más a una ciudad en la que se quedó aun cuando Tapachula debía ser de paso" (clenching her teeth to avoid the dazzling offers that would have her buy clothes or furniture for a tiny monthly payment, whose real catch was anchoring her even more firmly in the city where she remained, inexplicably; Tapachula was only supposed to be a stop along the way).[89] She was forced to decorate her space using objects purchased via what amounted to a company store.[90] The same is true for Elena, who works at the cantina and brothel Eros. She had only planned to work there for a short time. Elena, however, was caught up in the economic model designed to keep her in a servile position forever. After touching on Elena's labor exploitation, the narrator returns to the bus and the video that is playing when she gets on: "Sólo una idiota puede creer que siendo latinas se puede correr la suerte de algunas como Jennifer Lo" (Only an idiot could believe that all Latinas could have the good luck of a J-Lo).[91] The opening page of "Chica cosmo," then, connects Elena's past and future to the character sitting in the bus seat watching Jennifer López.

The way the narrator moves in time, space, and imagination expands beyond the status quo represented in the text. One of the allusions to the forces of order is Elena's consideration of her work options at Mexico's northern border: "El trabajo en cualquier bar o burdel estaba garantizado. En ésta como en la otra frontera siempre las preferirían extranjeras. Mejor si no pasaban de los veinte y si ante todo ... se dedicaban a hacer su trabajo" (Work in any bar or bordello was guaranteed. On this border, as on the other, gentlemen preferred them foreign. It was better if they hadn't hit twenty and if, above all, ... they dedicated themselves to their work).[92] At the same time as the story is grounded in reality, and sex work is a dependable source of income for young women, the narrator begins by describing Elena's reality from an omniscient position. The narrator then shifts perspectives, enters Elena's mind, and describes her aspirations: "prefiere ser realista, es ambiciosa, sí, pero también los sueños tienen sus retenes. Además, ni que vivir en una ciudad gringa hiciera la diferencia. Probablemente sí. Prefiere pensar en Juárez. Lo primero, quizá otra vez el teibol, pero por la mañana puede ser una fábrica, un restaurant, recamarera de un hotel" (she prefers to be realistic; she *is* ambitious, but her dreams have guardrails. Besides, it's not like living in a gringo city would make a difference. Probably not, anyway. She prefers to think about Juárez. At first she might dance again, but during the day she could work in a factory, a restaurant, as a hotel maid).[93] The narrator consistently refers to the harsh reality that sex work will remunerate a person better than other employment. At the same time as the events are grounded in the status quo that accepts the necessity of sex work, the narrator enters Elena's minds and shows readers that her dreams expand beyond her immediate reality.

The narrator's meanderings, moreover, allow the protagonist to escape the most brutal imposition of order. When she gets on the bus, as is common in Mexico, she shows her ID. Elena is ready: "Enciende la luz. Saca su credencial de elector. Ésa sí la pagó al contado" (She turns on the light. Takes out her ID. This she paid for in cash).[94] She was willing to comply with the forces of order to move toward what might be a better future. She rehearses her false age and hometown. Later on, a man, only identified as a man or as an official, gets on the bus and walks toward the people behind her, "Tú, tú, tú también" (You, you, you too).[95] He continues to walk on the bus and points at two more women.[96] The migrants go with the unnamed official, and the bus waits for them so long that people become restless. An unspecified passenger goes to the bus driver and reminds him they all want to get to her destination. The bus driver thus continues without them. Elena feels smug that her documents have not attracted any attention and feels resentful toward the undocumented female migrant who is delaying her trip: "La odia. Odia a todas las perras que dan su dinero comprando malas réplicas de credenciales de elector o actas de nacimiento" (She hates her. She hates all the bitches who spend their money on bad replicas of voter IDs or birth certificates).[97] In these parts of the story, the narrator emphasizes that Elena has complied with the appearance of a legal migrant so that she alone can push beyond it. She puts order to the chaotic bus ride by acting in the same way as the immigration authorities. Her actions are reprehensible. In the context of the narrator's representation of Elena's recent past at Eros and her desired future in Juárez, they are also understandable. The movements between the bus ride and the world outside the bus make her actions understandable and ensure that the forces of order do not entirely contain the protagonist and her understanding of the world.

The story "Darse la media vuelta" (Turn Around) reflects women's experiences of migration. The lack of clarity with regard to time and space overshadows the influence of male characters who help her get to the border or prevent her from crossing it. The story is unclear about what is present and what is past. It opens by describing the protagonist's face: "Tenía la cara de alguien que acaba de renunciar al matrimonio... Descorrió la cortina. Estaba en el segundo piso del motel. No era una gran altura pero desde ahí tenía un fragmento de horizonte. Otra vez cerca. Cada vez más cerca" (She has the face of someone who has just sworn off marriage... She drew back the curtain. She was on the third floor of the motel. It wasn't a great height but from there she had a fragment of the horizon. Close again. Closer all the time).[98] The protagonist, whom the narrator later calls Silvia, is a face visible in a hotel window full of longing in a time that seems to be the present day. The narrator then switches tactics to describe the character's past and to give some shape to her lived experience. The narrator explains that she had attempted to migrate to the US on a previous occasion and had gotten as far as a border city in Sonora: "Sólo en una ocasión llegó hasta Nogales. De no haber tenido tantos prejuicios, bien la habría librado. Claro, era apenas una mocosa. Iba intentándolo por la limpia, para eso le había pagado su cuota al coyote. Pero no, bastó que dijera *no* para que la deportaran" (Only on one occasion did she make it as far as Nogales. If it weren't for all of her prejudices, she could have gotten away with it. Of course, she was just a snot-nosed kid. She had been trying to do it the clean way, that's why she had paid her fee to the coyote. But no, saying *no* was enough for them to deport her).[99] The narrator's references to Silvia's past contextualize her appearance in a hotel window and imply that she is somewhere between her home and Nogales. It also reflects on her failed attempts at migration in the past that may have led her to the same hotel and the fact that she attributes her failure to cross the border to having declined something. The narrator's discussion of past and present creates a sense of timelessness and places the narrative outside of the chronological order of events.

The narrator also moves almost seamlessly between different strands of thought, which is starkly different from the rapid shifts in perspective in other short stories, like "Cascarita," in Villafuerte's collection. The final paragraph of "Darse la media vuelta," for instance, begins with Silvia thinking about how she is going to cross the border and dealing with her material reality, her mental state, and the ways she might use her body to facilitate border crossing: "Iba a comprar boleto de autobús ese mismo día, también condones" (She was going to buy a bus ticket that very day, and condoms too).[100] Silvia will materially prepare herself for crossing the border with transportation and prophylactics. The story then goes on to explore the fictional character's mental state: "Cuando llegara no iba a sentir miedo. ¿Desde cuando se había vuelto paranoico? Esa actitud no le dejaría nada, mucho menos si pensaba llegar al otro lado" (When she got there she wouldn't feel any fear. Since when had she become paranoid? This attitude wouldn't get her anywhere, much less if she planned to get to the other side).[101] The narrator suggests that fear and paranoia were not a helpful attitude, although they were certainly part of the fictionalized representation of migration. The paragraph continues, returning to the question of sex work: "De algo tenían que servirle la boca, las tetas y las nalgas" (Her mouth, tits, and ass had to be good for something).[102] The list of body parts reminds us of the reality of migration for women. Many female migrants engage in sex work to earn money and resign themselves to the inevitability of sexual assault and rape. Silvia's reflections continue: "Esta vez sí. Tomó sus cosas, se amarró el cabello y antes de salir alcanzó la inútil huida de una cucaracha" (This time yes. She took her things, tied back her hair and, before leaving, stopped the futile fugue of a cockroach).[103] She is now ready to cross the border because she has a positive attitude and is certain that this time she will be successful. Silvia performs two small actions that express agency: doing her hair and killing a cockroach. The way the narrator rapidly moves between the character's mental state, potential connection with men who impose the violence of systemic misogyny, and precarious economic and social position of women who migrate, as well as the necessary possessions to protect herself, partially challenges the imposition of a misogynist patriarchal order.

Other characters in "Darse la media vuelta" represent forces of order and intrude on the narrator's shifts in time. Two sentences after stating that the protagonist had refused something, the narrator elaborates: "Nada le hubiera costado irse al baño aquella noche, bajarse las pantaletas, dejar que el gringo ese le arrimara la reata" (It wouldn't have cost her anything to go to the bathroom that night, pull down her panties, let that gringo put his cock into her).[104] The narrator berates the character, or presents the character berating herself, because it would have cost nothing to submit to male authority. The character's willingness to stand up for herself is, according to the narrator, stupid and naïve: "Pero no. La muy bruta pensó que ya estaba a unas horas, que esperaría la señal del coyote pa' cruzar. Tuvo miedo" (But no. The idiot thought that she was only a few hours away, that she should wait for the coyote's signal to cross. She was scared).[105] Here a gringo has almost complete ability to control a migrant woman, and the narrator purporting to represent the thoughts of the migrant woman, in turn, berates herself for not accepting. The story also explains how the character gets to the border a second time. She meets a truck driver, Emilio, and goes back to his truck cabin with him and has unprotected sex.[106] He makes her hide at his feet so that the migration authorities do not find her. These men, no matter how benevolent, uphold the social order and ensure that the female protagonist remains in her place—at a man's feet or in her home country.

The fact that "Darse la media vuelta" describes Silvia's experience in such detail emphasizes the precarity of many women who migrate to Mexico or who cross Mexico to attempt to enter the United States. Silvia wants to get there so badly that she accepts a very high level of incursion of the forces of order in her life. Here, as in all the stories, the horizon of the border remains an unrealized goal. In this story, the characters who represent the social order—unspecified male characters who were supposed to help Silvia cross the border—attempt to maintain the status quo of a violent patriarchal order.

"120 kilómetros por hora," for its part, deals with children and migration, specifically children who traffic migrants, in addition to representing the horizon, which I mentioned earlier. The narrator's multifaceted account of migration gives the female protagonist, Mila, some measure of freedom that cannot be overshadowed by the ways that her parents, school, and the criminal justice system confine her.

The first few paragraphs of the story introduce Mila through her interactions with a number of other characters, which presents a complex character with multiple motivations for trafficking migrants across the Mexico-Guatemala border. The narrator initially adopts a third-person perspective and states that Mila's parents argue. After setting the stage of an unhappy family, the mother tells a neighbor that her daughter is hardworking.[107] Mila's good behavior includes flirting with her neighbor, León, whom they hope she will one day marry. After establishing the ways Mila complies with her parents' rules, the narrator gives a third perspective on her, from one of her classmates, called León. Mila is a different person in these interactions than she is at home. The final paragraph of the first page states that León gives her porn magazines and likes that she would prefer to drive than to learn when all the national heroes were born.[108] Mila is fascinated by the idea of driving and León's porn and car begin her double life. Indeed, the first page concludes with the first-person plural narrator stating, "Deberíamos irnos a otro lado, coinciden los dos" (We should go to the other side, the two agree).[109] Their reaction to not liking school, and Mila's additional confrontation with her parents restrictions, is to cross the border. In the span of a page, then, the narrator has presented multiple perspectives on Mila and given us a more complete understanding of her later behavior.

The narrator continues to adopt a variety of perspectives in describing Mila and León's developing relationship and eventual decision to smuggle migrants across the Guatemalan border into Mexico. The scenes that relate the way they smuggle migrants are overshadowed by the threat of detention and then detention itself. At one point, León and Mila go out on a date. Mila tells him they should go to the border. They smuggle two men for four hundred pesos.[110] They are successful on several other occasions, even seeing migration officials as they pick up migrants. Then, one night, as they drive with some women in the back, León drives too fast. A police officer stops them and, here, fiction aligns with the legal text. He asks them for their papers.[111] The officer realizes that Mila and León are smuggling the passengers in the backseat and arrests them and detains the migrants. The forces that uphold the violent status quo contain the youthful characters who wanted to escape their circumstances. The story normalizes the desire of all the characters' for change and a better future and places that desire in a context of economic need, parental expectations, and boredom at school. The expansive understanding of the characters' desire, much like the horizon that is always just one kilometer further away from Mila and León, is insufficient. Police officers—representing the forces of order—apprehend, arrest, and detain the characters. The tension between expansiveness and confinement, and between human desire for a better future and violent imposition of order, has devastating effects for the characters and in every other short story in *Barcos en Houston*. I read this tension together with narrative strategies that defy linear or chronological timelines and other forces that contain characters like Silvia or Elena, and in other cases, as rhetorical strategies of confusion and nonlinear time are no match for characters like migration authorities, who violently enforce the status quo.

Villafuerte's *Barcos en Houston*, as well as the 2011 Ley de Migración, deal with the lived experiences of migrants in Mexico. The legal text aesthetically confines the experience of migration through its formatting: it is divided into eight sections, which are then subdivided into subsections, articles, and fragments of articles. These sections and subsections put migrants back in their place in the existing social order, that is, as a group of people who can be exploited by any official, or, indeed, anyone who would wish to extract something from them. The headings and lists reinforce the understanding of migration as something to be contained and punished. The tension in the Ley de Migración reminds us of the tensions in the formal elements of the constitutional reforms and laws that guaranteed women a life free of violence, and the law that guaranteed children's and adolescents' rights. The structure of the Ley de Migración guides the content in an even more rigid fashion than the Ley General de Acceso de las Mujeres and the Children and Adolescents' Rights Law and constitutional texts. It devotes extensive space to describing the sanctions the government has allowed itself to pursue against migrants who do not follow its desired order. It explains how bureaucrats are allowed to exert force by requiring documentation, and how INM officials and other unspecified groups can participate in procedures for detention and deportation. The law also recognizes migrants' human rights and pays attention to groups vulnerable to the misogynistic violence inherent to the lived reality of migrants. The emphasis on human rights in the Ley de Migración is minor in comparison to the time, attention, and detail it devotes to arrest and detention. Moreover, that the law gives authority to any group that might require it means that almost any group of state or state-adjacent officials can assume authority over migrants. In effect, anyone employed by the Mexican government could act as a type of police. The migration law is even more devoted to punishment than the other laws I have examined, which similarly couple a recognition of human rights with a description of how those who fail to guarantee such rights would be punished. In earlier chapters, I pointed out a sense of unresolved tension in the legal texts, and in the Ley de Migración, too, the sense of punishment and loss outweighs the sense of possibility.

Villafuerte's *Barcos en Houston* also presents various parts of the experience of migration to Mexico, from crossing the border, to detention and sex work, and to most migrants' eventual goal of traveling to the United States. The collection is organized around a central theme and employs sustained images and narrative strategies that create a sense of unity. The collection's narrators mirror the reality of migration with their multiple perspectives and temporal shifts. The characters who represent forces of order contain the characters who attempt to defy their authority. The stories contain the characters' lived experiences of migration and dreams of a better future as on the horizon, always just out of reach. They are organized in such a way that they offer brief snippets of their lives, in line with short-story conventions. In spite of the brief nature of each short story, the narrators contextualize characters' lived experiences and rapidly shift between the context and the individual character's lives. Characters like Elena, Silvia, Ima, and Mila dream of a better future and take every possible step to escape their surroundings. Some characters seem close to realizing their dreams, like Elena, who is on a bus headed toward the US border in "Viernes." Yet she pays a high price to achieve her dream: she effectively cuts all bonds of potential solidarity with other migrants, she repeatedly rehearses the facts of her false life, and she reassures herself that she has purchased good-quality falsified documents. In "Darse la media vuelta," Silvia consents to sex with a truck driver to have a place to sleep and a safer way to cross the country. In "Cascarita," Ima may be permanently injured after a foiled attempt to migrate, and at the end of "120 kilómetros por hora," Mila is in a detention facility. The containment is much bleaker than in other literary texts: it is not just inside of the prison, as in the case of Israel Vallarta in Volpi's *Una novela criminal*. Moreover, in *Barcos en Houston*, there are no entirely hopeful stories as in *¡Basta!*, *Historias* and *Historias 2*, the collections examined elsewhere in this book. Villafuerte's stories are also not written by migrants who could receive some sort of validation about their own experiences, which was similar to the way that the experience of writing stories for *Historias* and *Historias 2* would have validated the children who authored those stories. I read some hope in the narrative strategies that create confusion, and in the descriptions of the rights of migrants in the legal text. Ultimately, I am left with a profound sense of loss as I consider the fictional representations of migration in Villafuerte's collection and the overwhelmingly violent migration rules, regulations, bureaucrats, and law enforcement officials outlined in the Ley de Migración.

# Conclusion

This book has proposed that the site of tension between texts' description of the world as it is and their aspiration for a better world is the location for developing a method of reading for social change. The book looks at how different groups of people in Mexico—from legislators and creative writers to ordinary citizens—have tried to understand the social, political, and historical events in their country and the ways that these same groups of people have made significant efforts to improve the material conditions of their own lives and the lives of those around them.

The method of reading legal, literary, and archival texts that form part of a vast discursive network around violence that circulates in Mexico is based on two core assumptions: One, the texts are descriptive in that they shed light on the historical, political, and social context in which they were produced, and two, they are aspirational in that they point to a better future for the people who live in that historical, political, and social context. It is impossible to dream of a better future without understanding how various groups of people interpret the present.

I combine the consideration of description and aspiration with analysis of genre, form, and content. I show that the genre, form, and content of a given text include descriptive and aspirational components. And when I analyze laws, novels, short stories, and letters, I have used terms like *constraint, confinement*, and *upholding the status quo* or *objective violence* or *structural violence* to talk about the descriptive elements, and words like *openness, possibility, confusion*, and *nonlinear* to talk about the aspirational elements.

No text is entirely descriptive or entirely aspirational. This is in part because many of the authors, especially the women who write letters to the

Mexican president and the girls who author stories in *Historias* and *Historias 2*, are excluded from the halls of power in Mexico. Their writing testifies to the violence done to them by more powerful individuals and social structures, such as police. At the same time, their letters and short stories take advantage of violent structures to testify to their lived experiences of violence. The letters to the president were funneled through the Mexican bureaucracy and often refer to violent structures like the criminal justice system. The stories in *Historias* and *Historias 2* came out of a government-sponsored contest for girls in Xalapa to celebrate the UN-designated International Day of the Girl Child. Allusions to the world as it ought to be are always influenced by the world as it is.

*Unlawful Violence* suggests that genre relates closely to the world as it is, largely in dialogue with the work of Anne Gulick. I use basic vocabulary to classify texts by genre, using words like *legal text, letter, novel*, and *short story*; I subdivide the short-story genre into short-story collection by multiple authors and short-story collection by a single author. The legislative process, for instance, constrains the constitutional amendments and human rights laws. Their existence is deeply connected to the world as it is.

I analyze form using a very broad understanding of the word and propose that form relates closely to the structures of violence and power in the texts' contexts. This approach expands existing ideas about form by thinkers such as Caroline Levine and Anna Kornbluh. When I analyze legal texts, I suggest that the structure of headings, subheadings, and article numbers constrains and organizes vastly different ideas. Formal elements cover up unusual juxtapositions between articles in the Ley General de Acceso and other human rights laws. When I look at archival documents from Atención a la Ciudadanía, I use the terminology of form to examine the communication pattern that surrounds letters to the president and encompass the cover letter that classifies the letter writer, the letter itself, intragovernmental communications about the issue, and the government's eventual response. The formal elements of the legal and archival texts mirror oppression in the context in which the laws and letters were produced.

The same formal elements of a given legal, literary, or archival text that relate to the world as it is also offer space for imagining a better future. Paying attention to the ways that headings and article numbers in the constitution and human rights laws organize disconnected lists of ideas leaves room for interpretation. The space between profoundly different ideas offers space for interpretation and encourages reading the laws and constitution as gestures toward what the world could be.

*Unlawful Violence* also considers how the formal elements of novels and short stories shed light on the Mexican context as it is, even as reading the same formal elements is a way to understand how a text gestures toward alternative futures. I continue to use basic vocabulary for literary analysis, such as intertextuality and narrative strategies such as nonlinear versions of events. When I examine Volpi's *Una novela criminal*, for instance, I showed that the narrator's own reflections on his investigation into Israel Vallarta's criminal case encourage readers to trust his version of injustice in the Mexican criminal justice system. I also showed that metafictional strategies like intertextuality create disjunctions and disconnections in the literary text and offer space for the reader to imagine alternatives.

The third element of my reading method pays attention to the way each text represents the Mexican content, and in many cases, to contrasts between the texts' descriptions of the world as it is and the same texts' allusions to alternative realities and better futures. The fictional accounts in *Historias* and *Historias 2* describe violence in girls' lives in poignant detail—bullying at school, abusive fathers, and lack of access to education. The stories in Villafuerte's *Barcos en Houston*, for their part, portray the violence migrants experience from law enforcement, or as migrants pursue sex work. These literary examples, as well as legal texts, refer to omnipresent prisons, jails, and detention centers. Volpi's *Una novela criminal* concludes by stating that Vallarta has been held in pretrial detention for more than a decade. Legal and literary texts also include elements of openness and possibility. Some short stories in *¡Basta!*, for instance, represent women who murder abusive men. The description of migration in the Ley de Migración establishes a system that attempts to confine migration and movement across borders, which is ultimately impossible as both the law and the world it reflects must grapple with these significant elements of the human experience in the early twenty-first century.

*Unlawful Violence*, then, reads the genre, form, and content of legal, archival, and literary texts to better understand the political, social, and historical context the texts describe and their aspirations for the future. This reading method considers that the texts allude to individual and systemic violence in the carceral system, in women's lives, in children's lives, and in migrants' lives. Violence affects individuals and groups in unique ways, and for this reason, the elements of each text that gesture toward openness, or alterative futures, are also unique. *Unlawful Violence* remains grounded in the specific features of Mexico from 2000 to 2020, but the way I classify archival, literary, and legal texts as descriptive and aspirational, and examine them from the perspective of their genres, forms, and content, could apply to other contexts. The method would yield great understanding of other time periods and other countries and offer visions of other futures.

Imagine what another future could look like if human aspiration were not embedded in violent social structures. I am encouraged to imagine this better world because I have read this minor selection of legal, literary, and archival texts from Mexico in the early twenty-first century. I have focused on the ways that the texts' genre, form, and content relate to the world as it is and gestures toward the world as it could be. In this better world, legal structures bring about justice without revenge. No one—but especially no man—replicates violence experienced as a child. Women reach their potentials because they are free from male insecurity and violence, children learn in conventional and unconventional educational methods, and all people have opportunities to thrive at home, or to move freely across the world.

# Notes

### INTRODUCTION

1. There is a multitude of responses to this time period in literature, art, activism, and so on. For information on feminist activism and art, see, e.g., Amanda L. Petersen and Deborah Shaw, "Mexican Women Aren't Just Fighting for Equality—But Survival," *Globe Post*, March 25, 2020, https://theglobepost.com/2020/03/25/mexico-femicides.
2. Mexico also recognized Afro-Mexicans as a category in its 2020 census. There is not yet new literary fiction that reflects on this change (although historians and anthropologists have conducted excellent work on the role of African descendants in Mexico). See, e.g., Aguirre Beltrán's *Obra antropológica XVI: El negro esclavo en Nueva España* (Mexico City: Fondo de Cultura Económica, 1994); Arce's *México's Nobodies: The Cultural Legacy of the Soldadera and Afro-Mexican Women* (New York: SUNY Press, 2017); and Githiora's *Afro-Mexicans: Discourse of Race and Identity on the African Diaspora* (Trenton, NJ: Africa World Press, 2008). The Mexican federal government and several state governments also passed constitutional amendments that recognize Indigenous autonomy. Films such as *La revolución de los alcatraces*, directed by Luciana Kaplan, and *Las sufragistas*, directed by Ana Cruz, shed light on some of the tensions between existing constitutional guarantees and further recognition of Indigenous autonomy.
3. Jorge Volpi, *Una novela criminal* (Mexico City: Penguin Random House, 2018). All citations come from this version of the novel.
4. This is part of a long tradition in the United States. Stuart Shrader offers an excellent recent summary of US incursion into other countries in "Defund the Global Policeman," *n + 1* 38 (2020), https://nplusonemag.com/issue-38/politics/defund-the-global-policeman.

5. Dawn Paley, *Drug War Capitalism* (Oakland, CA: AK Press, 2014), 32.
6. Clare Ribando Seelke, "Mexico: Evolution of the Mérida Initiative, 2007–2020," *Congressional Research Service: In Focus*, July 20, 2020, https://crsreports.congress.gov/product/pdf/IF/IF10578.
7. "Essential Numbers," in *Mexico Violence Resource Project*, ed. Cecilia Farfán-Méndez and Michael Lettieri (San Diego: UC San Diego Center for US-Mexican Studies, 2020), https://www.mexicoviolence.org.
8. Paley, *Drug War*, 31.
9. Oswaldo Zavala, *Los cárteles no existen: Narcotráfico y cultura en México* (Mexico City: Malpaso, 2018), 9–14.
10. "The Mérida Initiative," *US Embassy and Consulates in Mexico*, 2020, https://mx.usembassy.gov/our-relationship/policy-history/the-Mérida-initiative.
11. William Booth, "Mexico's Crime Wave Has Left about 25,000 Missing, Government Documents Show," *Washington Post*, November 23, 2012, https://www.washingtonpost.com/world/the_americas/mexicos-crime-wave-has-left-upto-25000-missing-government-documents-show/2012/11/29/7ca4ee44-3a6a-11e2-9258-ac7c78d5c680_story.html?noredirect=on&utm_term=.0b136d722485. For more information, see Farfán-Méndez and Lettieri's *Mexico Violence Resource Project*.
12. Molly Molloy, "Homicide in Mexico 2007–March 2018: Continuing Epidemic of Militarized Hyper-Violence," *Small Wars Journal*, April 27, 2018, https://smallwarsjournal.com/jrnl/art/homicide-mexico-2007-march-2018-continuing-epidemic-militarized-hyper-violence; "Mortalidad. Conjunto de datos: Defunciones por homicidios," Instituto Nacional de Estadística y Geografía, October 29, 2020, https://www.inegi.org.mx/sistemas/olap/consulta/general_ver4/MDXQueryDatos.asp?#Regreso&c=.
13. Zavala, *Los cárteles no existen*, 247.
14. Adriana Estévez, "El dispositivo necropolítico de producción y administración de la migración forzada en la frontera Estados Unidos-México," *Estudios Fronterizos* 19 (2018): 4.
15. Matteo Cantarello's compelling article "From Threat to Norm: The Changing Role of Crime in Contemporary Mexican Fiction" argues that the basic condition that underlies much of recent Mexican fiction. Cantarello, *Romance Notes* 60, no. 2 (2020): 395–396.
16. This is not to discount the excellent work on the topic of crime in Mexico (see, e.g., Pablo Piccato's *A History of Infamy* [Berkeley: University of California Press, 2017]), the history of the war on drugs in Mexico (e.g., Anabel Hernández's *Narcoland* [New York: Verso, 2013]), or scholars whose work focuses on women's experiences of violence in Ciudad Juárez (e.g., Julia Monárrez Fragoso's *Trama de una injusticia: Feminicidio sexual sistémico en Ciudad Juárez* [Mexico City: Porrúa; Ciudad Juárez: El Colegio de la Frontera Norte, 2009], and the work of other scholars that examines violence at the Mexico-US border (e.g., Héctor Domínguez-Ruvalcaba and Ignacio Corona's edited

collection *Gender Violence at the US-Mexico Border: Media Representation and Public Response* [Tucson: University of Arizona Press, 2012).
17. Sayak Valencia, *Capitalismo Gore* (Santa Cruz de Tenerife, Spain: Melusina, 2010), 15.
18. Sayak Valencia, "Psicopatía, celebrity culture y el régimen live en la era de Trump," *Norteamérica* 13, no. 2 (2018): 236.
19. Jasbir K. Puar, *The Right to Maim* (Durham, NC: Duke University Press, 2017), 30.
20. Puar, 31.
21. Slavoj Žižek, *Violence: Six Sideways Reflections* (New York: Picador, 2008), 2.
22. Žižek, 2, 12–14.
23. David A. Shirk, "Justice Reform in Mexico: Change and Challenges in the Judicial Sector" (Washington, DC: Woodrow Wilson International Center for Scholars, 2011), https://www.wilsoncenter.org/sites/default/files/media/documents/publication/Chapter%207-%20Justice%20Reform%20in%20Mexico%2C%20Change%20and%20Challenges%20in%20the%20Judicial%20Sector.pdf.
24. For more information about Mexico's legal system, see, for example, Julienne Grant and colleagues' comprehensive survey "Mexican Law and Legal Research," American Association of Law Libraries, 2014, https://lawcommons.luc.edu/facpubs/513.
25. Rita Laura Segato, *La guerra contra las mujeres* (Madrid: Traficantes de Sueños, 2016), 128.
26. "Constitución Política de los Estados Unidos Mexicanos: Texto Vigente," *Cámara de Diputados*, 2020, 17–26. http://www.diputados.gob.mx/LeyesBiblio/pdf/1_080520.pdf.
27. The law that guarantees women a life free of violence was passed in 2007 and revised several times, most recently at the time of writing this manuscript, in April 2020. "Ley General de Acceso de las Mujeres a una Vida Libre de Violencia," Cámara de Diputados del H. Congreso de la Unión, April 13, 2020, http://www.diputados.gob.mx/LeyesBiblio/pdf/LGAMVLV_130420.pdf. The law that guarantees children and adolescents' rights updated a 2000 law that protected children from harm. The text can be found in "Decreto por el que se expide la Ley General de los Derechos de Niñas, Niños y Adolescentes, y se reforman diversas disposiciones de la Ley General de Prestación de Servicios para la Atención, Cuidado y Desarrollo Integral Infantil," *Diario Oficial de la Federación*, December 4, 2014, http://dof.gob.mx/nota_detalle.php?codigo=5374143&fecha=04/12/2014.
28. "Ley de migración," Cámara de Diputados del H. Congreso de la Unión, April 13, 2020, http://www.diputados.gob.mx/LeyesBiblio/pdf/LMigra_130420.pdf.
29. Sergio López-Ayllón and Héctor Fix-Fierro, "'Faraway, So Close!': The Rule of Law and Legal Change in Mexico, 1970–2000," in *Legal Culture in the Age of Globalization: Latin America and Latin Europe*, ed. Lawrence M. Friedman

and Rogelio Pérez-Perdomo (Stanford, CA: Stanford University Press, 2003), 286–287.
30. *¡Basta! Cien mujeres contra la violencia de género* (Mexico City: Universidad Autónoma de México–Xochimilco; Coordinación de Extensión Universitaria, 2014).
31. Nadia Villafuerte, *Barcos en Houston* (Tapachula, Mexico: Gobierno del Estado de Chiapas, 2005).
32. *¡Basta! Cien mujeres.*
33. Guyora Binder and Robert Weisberg, *Literary Criticisms of Law* (Princeton, NJ: Princeton University Press, 2000), 27.
34. Binder and Weisberg, 5.
35. Anna Kornbluh, *The Order of Forms: Realism, Formalism, and Social Space* (Chicago: University of Chicago Press, 2019), 4–5.
36. Ignacio Corona and Beth Jörgensen, introduction to *The Contemporary Mexican Chronicle: Theoretical Perspectives on a Liminal Genre*, ed. Ignacio Corona and Beth Jörgensen (Albany, NY: SUNY Press, 2002), 4. For a more recent study of the genre, see Pablo Calvi's *Latin American Adventures in Literary Journalism* (Pittsburgh, PA: University of Pittsburgh Press, 2019).
37. Gabriela Polit Dueñas, *Unwanted Witnesses: Journalists and Conflict in Contemporary Latin America* (Pittsburgh, PA: University of Pittsburgh Press, 2019), 13, 127n21.
38. Daniel Worden, *Neoliberal Nonfictions: The Documentary Aesthetic from Joan Didion to Jay-Z* (Charlottesville: University of Virginia Press, 2020). See, e.g., his analysis of a comic that portrays the history of hip-hop, and his relation of this comic's aesthetics to social fragmentation (39–46).
39. Cristina Rivera Garza, *Había mucha neblina o humo o no sé qué: Caminar con Juan Rulfo* (Mexico City: Literatura Random House, 2016).
40. Cristina Rivera Garza, *Nadie me verá llorar* (Barcelona: Tusquets, 1999).
41. Julia Érika Negrete Sandoval, "Archivo, memoria y ficción en *Nadie me verá llorar* de Cristina Rivera Garza," *Literatura Mexicana* 24, no. 1 (2013): 100.
42. Joseph R. Slaughter, *Human Rights, Inc.: The World Novel, Narrative Form, and International Law* (New York: Fordham University Press, 2007), 3.
43. Slaughter, 2.
44. Sarah Brouillette, *UNESCO and the Fate of the Literary* (Palo Alto, CA: Stanford University Press, 2019).
45. Anne W. Gulick, *Literature, Law, and Rhetorical Performance in the Anticolonial Atlantic* (Columbus: Ohio State University Press, 2016), 3.
46. Slaughter, *Human Rights*, 45–49; Gulick, *Literature, Law, and Rhetorical Performance*, 16–17.
47. Caroline Levine, *Forms: Whole, Rhythm, Hierarchy, Network* (Princeton, NJ: Princeton University Press, 2015), 3.
48. Levine, 3.
49. Levine, 15.

50. Miguel de Cervantes Saavedra, *Don Quijote de la Mancha* (1605 and 1615), ed. Martín de Riquer (Barcelona: Editorial Juventud, 2000).
51. David Palumbo-Liu, "Fragmented Forms and Shifting Contexts: How Can Social Media Work for Human Rights?," in *The Routledge Companion to Literature and Human Rights*, ed. Sophia A. McClennen and Alexandra Schultheis Moore (New York: Routledge, 2015), 235.
52. Guillermo Melo Guzmán, ed., *Historias de niñas extraordinarias* (Xalapa, Mexico: Instituto Municipal de las Mujeres de Xalapa; Ayuntamiento Constitucional de Xalapa de Enríquez, 2016); Marisol Polanco Mendoza, ed., *Historias de niñas extraordinarias 2* (Xalapa, Mexico: Instituto Municipal de las Mujeres de Xalapa; Ayuntamiento Constitucional de Xalapa de Enríquez, 2017).
53. "Ley General de Acceso de las Mujeres," 3–5.
54. Rosario Gutiérrez, "La delegación," in *¡Basta!*, 102; Rosario Moreno, "SOS ¿Nos ayudamos," in *¡Basta!*, 103.
55. Levine, *Forms*, 18.
56. "Constitución política," 17–26.

## CHAPTER 1

1. Dominique de Courcelles, "El 'affaire Cassez' visto de México," *African Yearbook of Rhetoric* 3, no. 1 (2012): 60.
2. Volpi, *Una novela criminal*, 27–28.
3. Volpi, 250.
4. An *amparo* suit is similar to a *de novo* review in the United States, where a case can be retried if there is significant procedural error. The results of the new case do not create precedent. Pedro Pablo Camargo, "The Claim of 'Amparo' in Mexico's Constitutional Protection of Human Rights," *California Western Law Review* 6 (1969–1970): 202; Julienne Grant et al., "Mexican Law and Legal Research," American Association of Law Libraries, 2014, https://lawecommons.luc.edu/facpubs/513/; Alberto Székely, "Democracy, Judicial Reform, the Rule of Law, and Environmental Justice in Mexico," *Houston Journal of International Law* 21, no. 3 (1999): 411. The most extensive revisions to the concept of *amparo* occurred in 2011, when the concept was expanded to include human rights abuses (see "Constitución política," 89). These reforms were part of a larger project that began with the 2008 reforms, and then in 2011 were reframed as "individual guarantees." There had been some discussion of reframing them as individual rights, and the current constitution uses the language of "human rights." Víctor Manuel Collí Ek, "Improving Human Rights in Mexico: Constitutional Reforms, International Standards, and New Requirements for Judges," *Human Rights Brief* 20, no. 1 (2012): 8.
5. "Se retrasa proceso de Israel Vallarta, ex pareja de Florence Cassez," *YouTube video*, uploaded by Milenio, January 24, 2020, https://www.youtube.com/watch?v=vTtCXf6XLVg.

6. Volpi, *Una novela criminal*, 479. All translations are the author's unless otherwise noted.
7. In November and December 2018, the novel was adapted to a four-episode podcast—"Teatro de marionetas," "Verdades y mentiras," "Las diligencias," and "Una cuestión de poder"—for the Podium Podcast channel (https://www.podium podcast.com/una-novela-criminal/temporada-1/). There are other representations of the case against Cassez and Vallarta, including Anne Vigna, Alain Devalpo, and Jorge M. Mendoza Toyara's *Fábrica de culpables: Florence Cassez y otros casos de la injusticia mexicana* (Mexico City: Random House Mondadori, 2010), José Reveles's *El affair Cassez la indignante invención de culpables en México* (Mexico City: Planeta, 2013), and Emmanuelle Steels's *El teatro del engaño: Buscando a los Zodiaco, la banda de secuestradores que nunca existió* (Mexico City: Grijalbo, 2015).
8. Edward Waters-Hood, review of *Una novela criminal*, *World Literature in Review*, 92, no. 4 (2018): 81.
9. The narrator is a version of the author, and throughout this chapter when the narrator makes himself visible, he does so as an authorial character. For this reason, I also use the masculine pronoun when referring to him.
10. Alberto López, "Cometer fraude electoral en 2006, principal acuerdo entre Calderón y Gordillo: AMLO," *La Jornada*, July 8, 2011, https://www.jornada.com.mx/2011/07/08/politica/009n1pol.
11. Volpi, *Una novela criminal*, 218.
12. Paley, *Drug War*, 18.
13. Paley, 18.
14. Zavala, *Los cárteles no existen*, 119–122.
15. Estévez, "El dispositivo," 4.
16. Volpi, *Una novela criminal*, 218.
17. Volpi, 218.
18. Volpi, 219.
19. Volpi, 219.
20. "Reformas constitucionales," by the *Instituto de Investigaciones Jurídicas*, provides a chronological list of these reforms, as well as a list of reforms by article (see https://www.juridicas.unam.mx/legislacion). In other years (e.g., 1928, 1934, 1947–1948) reforms to multiple articles took place in multiple installments.
21. Volpi, *Una novela criminal*, 151–152.
22. Dawn Paley, "Legal Battles in Mexico," *Upside Down World*, December 12, 2011, http://upsidedownworld.org/archives/mexico/legal-battles-in-mexico.
23. "Seminario 'La Constitución: análisis rumbo a su centenario,'" *Senado de la República*, April 15, 2015, https://www.senado.gob.mx/comisiones/puntos_constitucionales/docs/Seminario_Constitucion/SC_conclusiones.pdf.
24. Levine, *Forms*, 16–17.
25. Gulick, *Literature, Law, and Rhetorical Performance*, 2.

26. "Constitución política," 1.
27. "Constitución política," 1.
28. Toni Morrison, "Conversation: Toni Morrison," interview by Elizabeth Farnsworth, *PBS NewsHour*, March 9, 1998, https://www.pbs.org/newshour/show/toni-morrison.
29. "Constitución política," 1–47.
30. "Constitución política," 48–58.
31. "Constitución política," 58–107.
32. "Constitución política," 107–112, 112–130.
33. "Constitución política," 130–141, 141–145.
34. "Constitución política," 145–146.
35. Raymond Williams, *Television: Technology and Cultural Form*, ed. Ederyn Williams (New York: Taylor and Francis, 2005), 86–87.
36. Fredric Jameson, *Postmodernism, or, The Cultural Logic of Late Capitalism*, 1991 (Durham, NC: Duke University Press, 2003), 70.
37. Valencia, "Psicopatía," 236.
38. "Constitución política," 5.
39. "Constitución política," 5.
40. "Constitución política," 5–6.
41. "Constitución política," 9.
42. William Hine-Ramsberger, "Drug Violence and Constitutional Revisions: Mexico's 2008 Criminal Justice Reform and the Formation of Rule of Law," *Brooklyn Journal of International Law* 37, no. 1 (2011): 291–292.
43. Volpi, *Una novela criminal*, 151.
44. Volpi, 151.
45. Volpi, 151.
46. Volpi, 151.
47. Volpi, 481.
48. Louisiana employs the civil law system and is a notable exception to the prevalence of the common law system in the United States.
49. Volpi, *Una novela*, 151.
50. Volpi, 151.
51. Volpi, 151.
52. For more information on how courtroom dramas influence US perceptions of the criminal justice system, see, for example, Jacqui Shine's "What Perry Mason Taught American Audiences about the Criminal Justice System," *Smithsonian Magazine*, June 19, 2020, https://www.smithsonianmag.com/arts-culture/moral-order-perry-masons-universe-180975140.
53. "Constitución política," 18.
54. "Constitución política," 19.
55. "Constitución política," 19–20.
56. "Constitución política," 21–24.
57. "Constitución política," 69, 116.

58. Hine-Ramsberger, "Drug Violence," 293.
59. Volpi, *Una novela criminal*, 152.
60. Volpi, 152.
61. Volpi, 152.
62. Beatriz Magaloni and Luis Rodriguez, "Institutionalized Police Brutality: Torture, the Militarization of Security, and the Reform of Inquisitorial Criminal Justice in Mexico," *American Political Science Review* 114, no. 4 (2020): 1014.
63. Volpi, *Una novela criminal*, 9.
64. Julio Cortázar, *Rayuela* (1963; Buenos Aires: Sudamericana, 1966); Macedio Fernández, *Museo de la novela de la Eterna* (1967), ed. Ana María Camblong and Adolfo de Obieta (Madrid: Allca XX, FCE, 1996).
65. They wanted to counter "light" literature, best sellers written by female authors such as Ángeles Mastretta and Laura Esquivel. See Burkhard Pohl, "'Ruptura y continuidad': Jorge Volpi, el 'Crack' y la herencia del 68," *Revista de Crítica Literaria Latinoamericana* 30, no. 59 (2004): 58–59. This corresponded with the rise of other literary movements in Latin America, including the McOndo literary movement in Colombia. Pablo Brescia and Oswaldo Estrada, introduction to *McCrack: McOndo, el Crack y los destinos de la literatura latinoamericana*, ed. Pablo Brescia and Oswaldo Estrada (Madrid: Albatrós, 2018), 11.
66. Pohl, "Ruptura y continuidad," 57; Tomás Regalado López, "El crack vs. la crítica: Encuentros, mediaciones, contrastes," in Brescia and Estrada, *McCrack*, 95.
67. Pedro Ángel Palou, "The Poetics of Crack," in *The Mexican Crack Writers: History and Criticism*, ed. Héctor Jaimes (New York: Palgrave-Macmillan, 2017), 198.
68. Sergio Gutiérrez Negrón, "Ética cosmopolita en *El jardín devastado* y *Oscuro bosque oscuro* de Jorge Volpi," *Confluencia* 28, no. 2 (2013): 109; Pohl, "Ruptura y continuidad," 55.
69. Ignacio Padilla, "The New Pocket Septenary," in Jaimes, *The Mexican Crack Writers*, 200.
70. "About *Una novela criminal*," *Penguin Random House*, 2018, https://www.penguinrandomhouse.com/books/594913/una-novela-criminal-premio-alfaguara-de-novela-2018--a-crime-novel-by-jorge-volpi/
71. Waters-Hood, review of *Una novela criminal*, 81–82.
72. Seymour Menton, *La nueva novela histórica de la América Latina, 1979–1992* (Mexico City: Fondo de Cultura Económica, 1993), 42–46.
73. H. Rosi Song, "En torno al género negro: ¿La disolución de una conciencia ética o la recuperación de un nuevo compromiso político?" *Revista Iberoamericana* 76, no. 321 (2010): 461.
74. Volpi, *Una novela criminal*, 64.
75. Daniel Calleros Villareal, in "Corales y espejos rotos: Articulación y fractalidad narrativa en *Las rémoras* de Eloy Urroz," *Chasqui* 48, no. 2 (2019): 176–189, describes magic realism in relation to another author in the Crack literary

movement. For general information about the marvelous real, see, for example, Edmundo Paz Soldán's "Alejo Carpentier: Teoría y práctica de lo real maravilloso," *Anales de Literatura Hispanoamericana* 37 (2008): 35–42.
76. Marcie Paul, "The Search for Identity: The Return to Analytic Detective Fiction in Mexico," in *Hispanic and Luso-Brazilian Detective Fiction: Essays on the Género Negro Tradition*, ed. Renée W. Craig-Odders, Jacky Collins, and Glen S. Close (New York: McFarland, 2006), 198.
77. Volpi, *Una novela criminal*, 38; Volpi also narrated a podcast episode that dealt with similar events. Uncertainty was a hallmark of that work as well ("Teatro de marionetas").
78. Volpi, 479.
79. Volpi, 477–478.
80. Volpi, 478.
81. "About *Una novela criminal*," https://www.penguinrandomhouse.com/books/594913/una-novela-criminal-premio-alfaguara-de-novela-2018--a-crime-novel-by-jorge-volpi.
82. Irmgard Emmelhainz, *La tiranía del sentido común: La reconversion neoliberal de México* (Mexico City: Paradiso, 2016), 22.
83. Volpi, *Una novela criminal*, 27.
84. Brian T. Chandler, "The Scale of History in Jorge Volpi's *En busca de Klingsor*," *Hispania* 101, no. 3 (2018): 424.
85. Roberto Ángel G., "Narratología en la novela híbrida *No será la tierra* de Jorge Volpi," *Alpha* 36 (2013): 43.
86. Volpi, *Una novela criminal*, 212.
87. Volpi, 212.
88. Volpi, 212–213.
89. Volpi, 213–214.
90. Volpi, 481.
91. Volpi, 61. *Primero Noticias* is a news show every morning on the Televisa cannel, and *Hechos AM* was a similar show on TV Azteca. These are the two largest television channels in Mexico, controlling more than 60 percent of all television in the country. Raúl Trejo Delabre, "Bajo el imperio de la televisión," *Infoamérica* 6 (2011): 77. The Agencia Federal de Investigaciones was created in 2001 to restructure the Policía Judicial Federal (1908–2002). In 2009, it was reformed and is now the Policía Federal Ministerial, tasked with fighting corruption and organized crime. Both entities work under the Attorney General's Office, which was called the Procuraduría General de la República at the time the novel was written.
92. Volpi, *Una novela criminal*, 62.
93. Volpi, 61.
94. Volpi, 61–62.
95. Pablo Ordaz, "Literatura para liberar la verdad," *El País*, March 26, 2018, https://elpais.com/cultura/2018/03/23/babelia/1521803125_386534.html.

96. Volpi, *Una novela criminal*, 61 (original emphasis).
97. Volpi, 479.
98. Volpi, 458.
99. Daniel Ruiz, director, *Duda razonable* (Mexico City: Fluxus Comunicaciones, 2014).
100. Yuli García reflects on her own experience of investigation in an interview with Carmen Aristegui in March 2012. "Yuli García y Héctor de Mauleón con Aristegui Caso Cassez," *Aristegui Noticias*, YouTube video, March 16, 2012, https://www.youtube.com/watch?v=0_NaG7Jqs3U.
101. Paley, *Drug War*, 18,
102. Volpi, *Una novela criminal*, 62.
103. Volpi, 63.
104. Volpi, 64.
105. Volpi, 64.
106. This entity (1974–2018) was essentially a government ministry. It is now called the Fiscalía General de la República, in an attempt to make the courts more autonomous and separate from other branches of government. Melissa Galván, "¡Adiós, PGR! México 'da a luz' a la Fiscalía General de la República," December 20, 2018, https://politica.expansion.mx/mexico/2018/12/20/adios-pgr-mexico-da-a-luz-a-la-fiscalia-general-de-la-republica).
107. Volpi, *Una novela criminal*, 66.
108. Volpi, 66.
109. Volpi, 64.
110. Volpi, 64.
111. Volpi, 64.
112. Volpi, 65.
113. Volpi, 65.
114. Volpi, 377.
115. D. A. Miller, *The Novel and the Police* (Berkeley: University of California Press, 1988), 24–25.
116. Volpi, *Una novela criminal*, 61–62.
117. Volpi, 61.
118. Volpi, 482.
119. Volpi, 482.
120. Volpi, 482.
121. Volpi, 479.
122. Roberto Gómez Beltrán, "El que la hace, ¿la paga? *Dos crímenes* de Jorge Ibargüengoitia," in *Escena del crimen: Estudios sobre narrativa policíaca mexicana*, ed. Miguel G. Rodríguez Lozano (Mexico City: UNAM Press, 2009), 42–43; Rubén Varona, "*No habrá final feliz*, de Paco Ignacio Taibo II: Una mirada a la (in)justicia del detective Héctor Belascoarán Shayne," *Chasqui: Revista de Literatura Latinoamericana* 49, no. 1 (2020): 28.

123. Alberto Vital, "La novela policíaca mexicana reciente, ¿propuesta de un nuevo realismo? Apropiación de realidad en *La bicicleta de Leonardo*, de Paco Ignacio Taibo II," *América: Cahiers du CRICCAL* 25, no. 2 (2000): 180, https://doi.org/10.3406/ameri.2000.1489.
124. Clemens A. Franken K(urzen), "En busca de Klingsor de Jorge Volpi: Una novela con formato policial híbrido, posmoderno y poscolonial," *Acta Literaria* 44 (2012): 71.
125. Juan Carlos Ramírez-Pimienta and José Pablo Villalobos, "Detección pública/detección privada: El periodista como detective en la narrativa policíaca norfronteriza," *Revista Iberoamericana* 75, no. 231 (2010): 389.
126. Worden, *Neoliberal Nonfictions*, 88.
127. Worden, 96.
128. Clemens Franken Kurzen and Magda Sepúlveda, *Tinta de sangre: Narrativa policíaca chilena en el siglo XX* (Santiago de Chile: Ediciones UCSH, 2009), 48. These general remarks belie divisions within the genre, such as hard-boiled fiction and noir novels, as well as the *novela policíaca* and *novela negra* in Spanish-language literatures. For more information on these genres and on the relationship between *novela negra* and *noir fiction* in English, see William J. Nichols's "A los márgenes: Hacia una definición de 'negra,' " *Revista Iberoamericana* 76, no. 231 (2010): 295–303. Recent work on noir fiction includes Christopher Breu and Elizabeth A. Hatmaker's edited collection *Noir Affect* (New York: Fordham University Press, 2020).
129. Volpi, *Una novela criminal*, 38.
130. Gianna M. Martella and Jacky Collins, "Theme Issue: Hispanic Detective Fiction: Introduction," *Clues: A Journal of Detection* 24, no. 3 (2006): 3.
131. Martella and Collins, 3.
132. Ainhoa Vásquez Mejías, "Un detective tras la pista de feminicidios: *El leve aliento de la verdad* de Ramón Díaz Eterovic," *Acta Literaria* 52 (2016): 54.
133. Volpi, *Una novela criminal*, 61.
134. Worden, *Neoliberal Nonfictions*, 9.
135. Worden, 9.
136. Volpi, *Una novela criminal*, 207.
137. Volpi, 207.
138. Volpi, 209.
139. Volpi, 210.
140. Jei Alanis Bello Ramírez and Germán Parra Gallego, "Cárceles de la muerte: Necropolítica y sistema carcelario en Colombia," *Universitas Humanística* 82 (2016): 389, https://doi.org/10.11144/Javeriana.uh82.cmns.
141. Volpi, *Una novela criminal*, 124.
142. Volpi, 125.
143. Volpi, 207.
144. Volpi, 207.

145. Volpi, 208.
146. David Graeber, *The Utopia of Rules: On Technology, Stupidity, and the Secret Joys of Bureaucracy* (Hoboken, NJ: Melville House, 2015), 9.
147. Volpi, *Una novela criminal*, 208.
148. Volpi, 208.
149. Volpi, 209.
150. Volpi, 209.
151. Volpi, 209.
152. Volpi, 209.
153. Volpi, 211.
154. Volpi, 211.
155. Volpi, 210.
156. Volpi, 479.
157. Volpi, 377.
158. Volpi, 377.
159. Volpi, 378.
160. Volpi, 378.
161. Volpi, 462.
162. Volpi, 475.
163. Volpi, 475.

**CHAPTER 2**

1. "Tres preguntas sobre el incremento de la violencia en 2020," *México Evalúa*, July 19, 2020, https://www.mexicoevalua.org/tres-preguntas-sobre-el-incremento-de-la-violencia-en-2020.
2. Alan López and Max Holst, "Cómo usar el 911 para salvar vidas de mujeres," *México Evalúa*, August 13, 2020, https://www.mexicoevalua.org/como-usar-el-911-para-salvar-vidas-de-mujeres.
3. Teresa Incháustegi Romero and María de la Paz López Barajas, eds., with Carlos Echarri Cánovas and Karla Ramírez Ducoing, *Feminicidio en México: Aproximaciones, tendencias y cambios 1985–2009* (Mexico City: ONU Mujeres, Colegio de México, Instituto Nacional de las Mujeres, 2011), 79.
4. Petersen and Shaw, "Mexican Women."
5. Petersen and Shaw.
6. "Quiénes somos," *Nuestras Hijas de Regreso a Casa*, September 4, 2020, https://nuestrashijasderegresoacasa.blogspot.com/p/quienes-somos.html.
7. These terms may be less familiar to English-language readers. *Feminicide* means genocide of women, that is, epidemic levels of women being killed because they are women. *Feminicide* is different from *femicide*. Alice Driver explains that the term *femicide* was coined in England in 1801, and then popularized by Diana E. H. Russell in 1975, to mean women killed by men because of misogyny. Driver, *More or Less Dead: Feminicide, Haunting, and the Ethics of Representation in Mexico* (Tucson: University of Arizona Press, 2015),

32. Some researchers prefer the term *feminicide* because it refers to a global system. It "acknowledges the contributions made in the Global South to a concept originating in the Global North." Dana A. Meredith and Luis Alberto Rodríguez Cortés, "Feminicide: Expanding Outrage: Representations of Gendered Violence and Feminicide in Mexico," in *Modern Mexican Culture: Critical Foundations*, ed. Stuart A. Day (Tucson: University of Arizona Press, 2017), 254n1.
8. "Ley General de Acceso de las Mujeres," 8.
9. "Código penal federal," *Justia Mexico*, January 1, 2020, 313–314, https://mexico.justia.com/federales/codigos/codigo-penal-federal/libro-segundo/titulo-decimonoveno/capitulo-v.
10. Kathleen Staudt, *Violence and Activism at the Border: Gender, Fear, and Everyday Life in Ciudad Juárez* (Austin: University of Texas Press, 2008), 20.
11. Julia Monárrez Fragoso, Pedro Díaz de la Vega García, and Patricia Morales Castro, *Sistema socioeconómico y geo-referencial sobre la violencia de género en Ciudad Juárez. Análisis de la violencia de género en Ciudad Juárez, Chihuahua: Propuestas para su prevención* (Ciudad Juárez, Mexico: Comisión para Prevenir y Erradicar la Violencia contra las Mujeres and El Colegio de la Frontera Norte, 2006), 44.
12. Rosa-Linda Fregoso and Cynthia Bejarano, "Introduction: A Cartography of Feminicide in the Americas," in *Terrorizing Women: Feminicide in the Americas*, ed. Rosa-Linda Fregoso and Cynthia Bejarano (Durham, NC: Duke University Press, 2010), 1–42.
13. Monárrez Fragoso, *Trama de una injusticia*, 86.
14. Sergio González Rodríguez, *The Femicide Machine*, trans. Michael Parker-Stainback (Los Angeles: Semiotext(e), 2012), 9. *The Femicide Machine* expands on González Rodríguez's 2002 work *Huesos en el desierto* (Barcelona: Anagrama, 2010).
15. González Rodríguez, *Femicide Machine*, 11.
16. Brenna Bhandar and Fareef Ziadah's edited collection *Revolutionary Feminisms* (New York: Verso, 2020) is a recent example of this vein.
17. Driver, *More or Less Dead*, 81.
18. There are many theories behind the high number of murders in Ciudad Juárez. Alicia Gaspar de Alba debunks many of them, including serial killers like Abdel Latif Sharif and David Meza, satanic cults, and human trafficking, as well as cases against groups of bus drivers (Los Choferes) and against the small gang Los Rebeldes. Gaspar de Alba, "Poor Brown Female: The Miller's Compensation for 'Free' Trade," in *Making a Killing*, 67–69, 84–85.
19. For more information about the history of feminism's interactions with the law, see, for example, Katharine T. Bartlett "Feminist Legal Methods," *Harvard Law Review* 103, no. 4 (1990): 829–888; Mary Joe Frug, "A Postmodern Feminist Legal Manifesto (An Unfinished Draft)," *Harvard Law Review* 105, no. 5 (1992): 1045–1075.

20. Gloria Luz Alejandre Ramírez and Eduardo Torres Alonso, "El primer congreso feminista de Yucatán 1916: El camino a la legislación del sufragio y reconocimiento de ciudadanía a las mujeres. Construcción y tropiezos," *Estudios Politicos* 39 (2016): 60–61.
21. Alejandre Ramírez and Torres Alonso, 60.
22. "Constitución política," 4.
23. "Ley General para la Igualdad entre Mujeres y Hombres," Cámara de Diputados del H. Congreso de la Unión, June 14, 2018, http://www.diputados.gob.mx/LeyesBiblio/pdf/LGIMH_140618.pdf.
24. For discussion of Marcela Lagarde's advocacy in congress, see her "Acuerdo del Pleno de la Cámara de Diputados para hacer seguimiento de los feminicidios," March 2005, http://www.mujeresenred.net/spip.php?article120.
25. Alberto López Rojas, "Estado de México," *Diario de los Debates: Órgano oficial de la Cámara de Diputados del Congreso de los Estados Unidos Mexicanos*, 60th Legislature, Year 1, 1st Period, Session 21, October 30, 2006, 64.
26. Mónica Arriola, "Ley General para la Igualdad entre Mujeres y Hombres," *Diario de los Debates: Órgano oficial de la Cámara de Diputados del Congreso de los Estados Unidos Mexicanos*, 60th Legislature, Year 1, 1st Period, Session 25, November 14, 2006, 60.
27. Ludivina Menchaca Castellanos, "Fiscalía especial de delitos contra las mujeres," *Diario de los Debates: Órgano oficial de la Cámara de Diputados del Congreso de los Estados Unidos Mexicanos*. 60th Legislature, Year 1, 1st Period, Session 27, November 21, 2006, 44.
28. Menchaca Castellanos, 44.
29. Jorge Godoy Cárdenas, "Ley General de Acceso a las Mujeres a una Vida Libre de Violencia." *Diario de los Debates: Órgano oficial de la Cámara de Diputados del Congreso de los Estados Unidos Mexicanos*, 60th Legislature, Year 1, 1st Recess, Session 5, January 24, 2007, 173.
30. Godoy Cárdenas, 174.
31. "Ley General de Acceso de las Mujeres," 1.
32. "Ley General de Acceso de las Mujeres," 1.
33. I would submit that the end of the patriarchal social order would also improve the lives of men and nonbinary people.
34. "Ley General de Acceso de las Mujeres," 3.
35. "Ley General de Acceso de las Mujeres," 4–10.
36. "Ley General de Acceso de las Mujeres," 3.
37. "Ley General de Acceso de las Mujeres," 3.
38. "Ley General de Acceso de las Mujeres," 3.
39. See, e.g., sentencing in Article 9 and reporting in Article 17, found in "Ley General de Acceso de las Mujeres," 4, 6.
40. "Ley General de Acceso de las Mujeres," 10.
41. "Ley General de Acceso de las Mujeres," 13–14.
42. "Ley General de Acceso de las Mujeres," 13.

43. "Ley General de Acceso de las Mujeres," 15, 22–23. These centers typically work in several areas, one, in providing legal and psychological assistance to women; two, in relating to efforts other parts of the government made in promoting women's equality; three, future planning; and four, promoting their work to the community at large. María Inés Canto, email to the author, November 22, 2019.
44. "Ley General de Acceso de las Mujeres," 17–18.
45. According to the National Archive, the petitions began under Cárdenas because his presidency had "una politica [sic] de atención de los problemas de cada ciudadano, es por ello que a lo largo de todo un proceso histórico se genera primeramente un órgano capaz de regular y ventilar los problemas surgidos, dándoles paso a un primer momento a la Secretaría Particular de la Presidencia." "Descripción de Fondo 'Unidad de Atención a la Ciudadanía,'" Carlos Salinas de Gortari Collection, 1988–1994, Archivo General de la Nación, Mexico City. The program underwent several name changes. Under the presidency of Carlos Salinas de Gortari (1988–1994), it become what it is today, the Unidad de Atención a la Ciudadanía ("Descripción de Fondo"). There were more than 1041 meters of petitions for Vicente Fox, not numbered in boxes. The previous president, Ernesto Zedillo (1994–2000), had 1,951 boxes of petitions, and Carlos Salinas de Gortari had 2,530 boxes. Buscador AGN (Archivo General de la Nación database), Mexico City, 2018.
46. During Vicente Fox's term, Mexican people wrote 456,188 letters that were later cataloged in the archives. During the author's archival research, letters to presidents Felipe Calderón and Enrique Peña Nieto were not yet available to the public.
47. For more information about the history of women short-story writers, see Liliana Pedroza's *Historia secreta del cuento mexicano, 1910–2017* (Monterrey, Mexico: Universidad Autónoma de Nuevo León, 2018). For more information about flash fiction, see Lauro Zavala's *La minificción bajo el microscopio* (Mexico City: Universidad Nacional Autónoma de México, 2006).
48. Linda Arnold, *Bureaucracy and Bureaucrats in Mexico City, 1742–1835* (Tucson: University of Arizona Press, 1988), 56. Today, individuals do not have the same opportunity to meet in person with the president as they did during *audiencias*, and surely it is much easier to write a letter, send an email, or fill out an online form than to petition during an *audiencia*. Yet accessibility is one of the ways that these requests get buried under the weight of bureaucracy. The fact that Mexican people can ask the president for help, and that the Atención a la Ciudadanía (Service to Citizens) program in the Secretaría de Gobernación (Secretary of State) facilitates a response, evokes the relationship between the vice-regal representative and the people in colonial New Spain.
49. As scholars in multiple disciplines have noted, archives tend to preserve the interests of the powerful. Melissa Adler has critically interrogated library classification systems, and her observations apply here: "The tools and techniques

involved in determining where books are to be placed on library shelves and naming them in authorized terms are classificatory mechanisms that reduce texts and their readings to disciplined subjects." Melissa Adler, *Cruising the Library: Perversities in the Organization of Knowledge* (New York: Fordham University Press, 2017), 2.

50. For more information about masculinity, gender performance, policing and courts, see Angela P. Harris's "Heteropatriarchy Kills: Challenging Gender Violence in a Prison Nation," *Washington University Journal of Law & Policy* 37 (2011): 13–65.
51. Departamento de Seguimiento de Peticiones Ciudadanas, "María Antonia Márquez Hernández," Memorandum, May 8, 2006, Archivo General de la Nación, Vicente Fox Quesada II Collection, Coordinación General de Administración, Red Federal de Servicio a la Ciudadanía, 2002–2006.
52. María Antonia Márquez Hernández to Vicente Fox Quesada, December 13, 2005, Vicente Fox Quesada II Collection, Coordinación General de Administración, Red Federal de Servicio a la Ciudadanía, 2002–2006, Archivo General de la Nación.
53. Márquez Hernández to Fox Quesada.
54. Márquez Hernández to Fox Quesada.
55. Márquez Hernández to Fox Quesada (original emphasis).
56. Márquez Hernández to Fox Quesada.
57. Márquez Hernández to Fox Quesada.
58. Pablo Zavala, "La producción antifeminicidista mexicana: Autoría, representación y feminismo en la frontera juarense," *Chasqui* 45, no. 2 (2016): 67. For a complete listing of these works, pp. 59–60 of Zavala's article.
59. Márquez Hernández to Fox Quesada.
60. Arturo Cruz Noyola, "Coordinación de la red federal de servicio a la ciudadanía, Ficha de validación de seguimientos," September 19, 2006, Vicente Fox Quesada II Collection, Coordinación General de Administración, Red Federal de Servicio a la Ciudadanía, 2002–2006, Archivo General de la Nación.
61. Adriana Cabrera Santana to C. Lic. Gabriel Ruiz Martínez, March 14, 2006, Vicente Fox Quesada II Collection, Coordinación General de Administración, Red Federal de Servicio a la Ciudadanía, 2002–2006, Archivo General de la Nación.
62. Cabrera Santana to Ruiz Martínez.
63. Cabrera Santana to Ruiz Martínez.
64. Cabrera Santana to Ruiz Martínez.
65. Departamento de Seguimiento de Peticiones Ciudadanas, "María Antonia Márquez Hernández."
66. Pía Barros and Martha Manier, ¡*Basta! + de 100 mujeres contra la violencia de género* (Santiago de Chile: Asterión, 2012).
67. Amanda L. Petersen, "Breaking Silences and Revealing Ghosts: Spectral Moments of Gender Violence in Mexico," *iMex: Interdisciplinary Mexico* 8, no. 2 (2019): 30.

68. Lauro Zavala, "The Boundaries of Serial Narrative," in *Short Story Theories: A Twenty-First Century Perspective*, ed. Viorica Pâtea (New York: Rodopi, 2007), 283.
69. Adaliz Patricia Estrada Torres, "Ojos ciegos a oídos sordos," in *¡Basta!*, 15.
70. Yuyu/Carmen Castro, "Única," in *¡Basta!*, 114
71. Perla Cristal Hermosillo Núñez, "'Ni una más': Microrrelatos contra la violencia de género," review of *¡Basta! Cien mujeres contra la violencia de género, edición mexicana*, *Revista de Estudios de Género: La Ventana* 46 (2017): 348.
72. Martha Bátiz Zuk, "Tragedia doméstica," *in ¡Basta!*, 81.
73. Emma Irene L. Martínez, "Sumisión: Enseñanza mortal," in *¡Basta!*, 50; Rebeca Monroy Nasr, "Presencia y ausencia," in *¡Basta!*, 97; Laura Edith Saavedra Hernández, "¿Por qué las leyes son así?," in *¡Basta!*, 67.
74. Driver, *More or Less Dead*, 78.
75. Driver, 73.
76. Segato, *La guerra*, 51.
77. Carmen Nozal, "Ciudad Juárez," in *¡Basta!*, 38.
78. Nozal, 38.
79. Nozal, 38.
80. Rosas Pineda, "Desde aquel día," in *¡Basta!*, 61.
81. Rosas Pineda, 61.
82. Rosas Pineda, 61.
83. Rosas Pineda, 61 (ellipses in original).
84. Gabriela Morales Ríos, "Duelo eterno . . . ," in *¡Basta!*, 54.
85. Michael Hobbes and Sarah Marshall, "Murder," *You're Wrong About* (podcast), July 27, 2020. https://podcasts.apple.com/us/podcast/murder/id1380008439.
86. Gloria León Hernández to Vicente Fox Quesada (email), "Petición para esclarecer un crimen," May 15, 2006, Vicente Fox Quesada II Collection, Coordinación General de Administración, Red Federal de Servicio a la Ciudadanía, 2002–2006, Archivo General de la Nación.
87. León Hernández to Fox Quesada.
88. Adriana Cabrera Santana to C. Lic. Gabriel Ruiz Martínez, June 22, 2006, Vicente Fox Quesada II Collection, Coordinación General de Administración, Red Federal de Servicio a la Ciudadanía, 2002–2006, Archivo General de la Nación.
89. Guadalupe Campos Villa to President Vicente Fox, "Tema: Asesinato de jóvenes mujeres en Cd. Juárez," February 22, 2003, Vicente Fox Quesada I Collection, Coordinación General de Administración, Red Federal de Servicio a la Ciudadanía, 2002–2005, Archivo General de la Nación.
90. Diana Washington Valdez, *The Killing Fields: Harvest of Women* (Los Angeles: Peace at the Border, 2006), 301.
91. Driver, *More or Less Dead*, 61.
92. Campos Villa to Fox.
93. Campos Villa to Fox.

94. Adriana Laura Romo Fregoso to President Vicente Fox, August 9, 2004, Vicente Fox Quesada II Collection, Coordinación General de Administración, Red Federal de Servicio a la Ciudadanía, 2002–2006, Archivo General de la Nación.
95. David Graeber, *Bullshit Jobs: A Theory* (New York: Simon and Schuster, 2018).
96. Graeber, 155.
97. Jorge Leonel Sánchez Ruiz to C. Lic. Benigno Aladro Fernández, October 25, 2004, Vicente Fox Quesada II Collection, Coordinación General de Administración, Red Federal de Servicio a la Ciudadanía, 2002–2006, Archivo General de la Nación.
98. Fernando Blumenkron Escobar to María López Urbina, November 4, 2004, Vicente Fox Quesada II Collection, Coordinación General de Administración, Red Federal de Servicio a la Ciudadanía, 2002–2006, Archivo General de la Nación.
99. María López Urbina to Adriana Romo Fregoso, November 22, 2004, Vicente Fox Quesada II Collection, Coordinación General de Administración, Red Federal de Servicio a la Ciudadanía, 2002–2006, Archivo General de la Nación.
100. Miriam Ruiz, "Aún no responde Fox a invitación para visitar Ciudad Juárez," *Cimac Noticias* 25 (2003), https://www.cimacnoticias.com.mx/node/29389.
101. Coordinadora de Organismos no Gubernamentales en Pro de la Mujer to Vicente Fox Quesada, February 28, 2003, Vicente Fox Quesada II Collection, Coordinación General de Administración, Red Federal de Servicio a la Ciudadanía, 2002–2006, Archivo General de la Nación.
102. Coordinadora de Organismos no Gubernamentales en Pro de la Mujer to Fox Quesada.
103. Coordinadora de Organismos no Gubernamentales en Pro de la Mujer to Fox Quesada.
104. Coordinadora de Organismos no Gubernamentales en Pro de la Mujer to Fox Quesada.
105. Laura Carrera Lugo to Santiago Creel Miranda, July 17, 2003, Vicente Fox Quesada II Collection, Coordinación General de Administración, Red Federal de Servicio a la Ciudadanía, 2002–2006, Archivo General de la Nación.
106. "Nombra Calderón subsecretarios en Segob," January 2, 2008, https://archivo.eluniversal.com.mx/notas/477399.html.
107. Ricardo J. Sepúlveda Iguíniz to Integrantes de Organismos no Gubernamentales en Pro de la Mujer, July 30, 2003, Vicente Fox Quesada II Collection, Coordinación General de Administración, Red Federal de Servicio a la Ciudadanía, 2002–2006, Archivo General de la Nación.
108. Sepúlveda Iguíniz to Integrantes de Organismos no Gubernamentales en Pro de la Mujer.
109. Sepúlveda Iguíniz to Integrantes de Organismos no Gubernamentales en Pro de la Mujer.
110. Ricardo J. Sepúlveda Iguíniz to Coordinadora de Organismos no Gubernamentales en Pro de la Mujer, August 12, 2003, Vicente Fox Quesada II Collec-

tion, Coordinación General de Administración, Red Federal de Servicio a la Ciudadanía, 2002–2006, Archivo General de la Nación.

111. Teresa Gómez Ibarra to Vicente Fox Quesada, March 25, 2004, Vicente Fox Quesada II Collection, Coordinación General de Administración, Red Federal de Servicio a la Ciudadanía, 2002–2006, Archivo General de la Nación.
112. Gómez Ibarra to Fox Quesada.
113. Gómez Ibarra to Fox Quesada.
114. There is also significant grassroots organizing in Mexico. For a recent article on this, see Petersen and Shaw, "Mexican Women."
115. Laura Carrera Lugo to Sra. Gómez Ibarra y firmantes, April 5, 2004, Vicente Fox Quesada II Collection, Coordinación General de Administración, Red Federal de Servicio a la Ciudadanía, 2002–2006, Archivo General de la Nación.
116. Carrera Lugo to Sra. Gómez Ibarra y firmantes.
117. Carrera Lugo to Sra. Gómez Ibarra y firmantes.
118. Staudt, *Violence and Activism*, 20.
119. See, e.g., Claudia Esthela Espinoza Cid and Gabriela García Figueroa's "Significados de género y sexualidad en la violencia de pareja: Víctimas, agresores y policías en Hermosillo, Sonora," *Estudios Sociológicos* 36, no. 108 (2018): 571–594, https://doi.org/10.24201/es.2018v36n108.1602. See Rosalva Aída Hernández Castillo's "Violencia de Estado y violencia de género," *Trace* 57 (June 2010): 86–98, http://trace.org.mx/index.php/trace/article/view/386/360, for more detail about these issues.
120. Accurate studies of intimate partner violence are difficult to find. Anita S. Anderson and Celia C. Lo's "Intimate Partner Violence within Law Enforcement Families," *Journal of Interpersonal Violence* 26.6 (2011): 1176–1193, discusses these tendencies based on data from the police department in Baltimore, Maryland. In 2013, Sarah Cohen, Rebecca R. Ruiz, and Sarah Childress reported on this issue in "Departments Are Slow to Police Their Own Abusers," *New York Times*, November 23, 2013. http://www.nytimes.com/projects/2013/police-domestic-abuse/index.html.
121. Melissa W. Wright, "Public Women, Profit, and Femicide in Northern Mexico," *South Atlantic Quarterly* 105, no. 4 (2006): 686.
122. Gutiérrez, "La delegación," 102.
123. Gutiérrez, 102.
124. Wright, "Public Women," 686.
125. Saavedra Hernández, "Por qué las leyes," 67.
126. Monárrez Fragoso, *Trama de una injusticia*, 155.
127. Saavedra Hernández, "Por qué las leyes," 67.
128. Saavedra Hernández, 67.
129. Saavedra Hernández, 67.
130. Celia González, "Amor, miedo y costumbre," in *¡Basta!*, 39.
131. González, 39.
132. González, 39.

133. Candida Leigh Saunders, "Rape as 'One Person's Word against Another's': Challenging the Conventional Wisdom," *International Journal of Evidence and Proof* 22, no. 2 (2018): 162.
134. González, "Amor," 39.
135. Patricia Karina Vergara Sánchez, "Violación," in *¡Basta!*, 93.
136. Debra A. Castillo, María Gudelia Rangel Gómez, and Armando Rosas Solís, "Violence and Transvestite/Transgender Sex Workers in Tijuana," in *Gender Violence at the US-Mexico Border: Media Representation and Public Response*, ed. Héctor Domínguez-Ruvalcaba and Ignacio Corona (Tucson: University of Arizona Press), 27.
137. Claire M. Renzetti, *Violent Betrayal: Partner Abuse in Lesbian Relationships* (Newbury Park, CA: Sage, 1992), 105.
138. Hermosillo Núñez, "Ni una más," 350.
139. Juana Leticia Herrera Ale, "Ley Federal de Acciones Compensatorias a Favor de las Mujeres," *Diario de los Debates: Órgano oficial de la Cámara de Diputados del Congreso de los Estados Unidos Mexicanos*, 60th Legislature, Yeaer 1, 1st Period, Session 27, December 14, 2006, 87.
140. Margarita Pulido Navarro, "Manipulación," in *¡Basta!*, 76; Carla Patricia González Canseco, "Cortina," in *¡Basta!*, 35.
141. Adela Margarita Lucero Hernández, "Carne de edecán," in *¡Basta!*, 16.
142. Cynthia Menchaca, "Fibonacci," in *¡Basta!*, 42; Leticia Romero Chumacero, "Despierta," in *¡Basta!*, 69.
143. Petersen, "Breaking Silences," 36.
144. Fabiola Morales Gasca, "Modelo," in *¡Basta!*, 52 (Mexico City: Universidad Autónoma de México-Xochimilco; Coordinación de Extensión Universitaria, 2014).
145. Teresa Isabel Ruvalcaba Rodríguez, "Más de tres motivos," in *¡Basta!*, 111.
146. Angelina Zamudio, "Muñeca," in *¡Basta!*, 24.
147. Zamudio, 24.
148. Elodia Corona Meneses, "El curso de inglés," in *¡Basta!*, 49.
149. Ruvalcaba Rodríguez, "Más de tres motivos," 111.
150. Martínez, "Sumisión," 50.
151. Paulina Calderón Ramos, "Frente al destino," in *¡Basta!*, 91.
152. Sergio de la Mora, *Cinemachismo: Masculinities and Sexuality in Mexican Film* (Austin: University of Texas Press, 2006), 110.
153. de la Mora, 1–5.
154. Calderón Ramos, "Frente al destino," 91.
155. Calderón Ramos, 91.
156. Jessica Kelliher Rabon, Jameson K. Hirsch, and Edward C. Chang, "Positive Psychology and Suicide Prevention: An Introduction and Overview of the Literature," in *A Positive Psychological Approach to Suicide*, ed. Jameson K. Hirsch, Edward C. Chang, and Jessica Kelliher Rabon (Cham, Switzerland: Springer, 2018), 1–2.

157. Ninfa Adriana Estrada Orozco, "La decisión," in ¡Basta!, 88.
158. Ileana Rodríguez, *Gender Violence in Failed and Democratic States: Besieging Perverse Masculinities* (New York: Palgrave-Macmillan, 2016), 170.
159. For more information about Jael, see Judges 4–5; see also Tamar Kadari, "Jael Wife of Heber the Kenite: Midrash and Aggadah," *Jewish Women: A Comprehensive Historical Encyclopedia*, February 2, 2009, Jewish Women's Archive, https://jwa.org/encyclopedia/article/jael-wife-of-heber-kenite-midrash-and-aggadah.
160. Bobby Allyn, "Cyntoia Brown Released after 15 Years in Prison for Murder," *NPR*, August 7, 2019, https://www.npr.org/2019/08/07/749025458/cyntoia-brown-released-after-15-years-in-prison-for-murder.
161. María Eugenia Merina, "En la cocina," in ¡Basta!, 76.
162. Deborah K. Anderson and Daniel G. Saunders, "An Empirical Review of Predictors, the Process of Leaving, and Psychological Well-Being," *Trauma, Violence, & Abuse* 4, no. 2 (2003): 164.
163. Lenore Walker, *The Battered Woman Syndrome*, 3rd ed. (New York: Springer, 2007), 4.
164. Merino, "En la cocina," 76.
165. Romero Chumacero, "Despierta," 69.
166. Romero Chumacero, 69.
167. Romero Chumacero, 69.
168. Anderson and Saunders, "Empirical Review," 180.
169. Norma Pinal," Palabras," in ¡Basta!, 89.
170. Pinal, 89.
171. Tressie McMillan Cottom, "Twitter / @tressiemcphd: If you don't have get out money . . ." thread, August 17, 2020, 9:53 a.m., https://twitter.com/tressiemcphd/status/1295358138384818176.
172. Elizabeth Vivero, "Más allá del vacío," in ¡Basta!, 48.
173. Vivero, 48.
174. Menchaca, "Fibonacci," 41.
175. Eglé Margarita Hernández Grijalva, "Mariposa," in ¡Basta!, 45.
176. Hernández Grijalva, 45.

## CHAPTER 3

1. UNICEF México and Mauricio Ramos, "La agenda de la niñez y la adolescencia 2019–2024," *Fondo de las Naciones Unidas para la Infancia/UNICEF*, 4–5, https://www.unicef.org/mexico/media/306/file/agenda%20de%20la%20infancia%20y%20la%20adolescencia%202019–2024.pdf.
2. "La niñez en México: Datos duros," *Universia Mx*, April 29, 2013, https://www.universia.net/mx/actualidad/orientacion-academica/ninez-mexico-datos-duros-1020651.html.
3. UNICEF México and Ramos, "La agenda," 5.
4. *11 de octubre: Día internacional de la niña* (Mexico City: Comisión Nacional de los Derechos Humanos, 2017).

5. *¿Qué es la violencia familiar y cómo contrarrestarla? Todos los seres humanos nacemos libres e iguales en dignidad y en derechos* (Mexico City: Comisión Nacional de los Derechos Humanos, Prográfico, 2017), 2–3.
6. 11 de octubre.
7. 11 de octubre.
8. For more information, see, e.g., Krista McQueeney and Alicia A. Girgenti-Malone, eds., *Girls, Aggression, and Intersectionality: Transforming the Discourse of "Mean Girls" in the United States* (New York: Routledge, 2018). Several chapters in this volume explore the way that girls of different races face different repercussions for the same behavior, attitudes or forms of dress. Alyssa Pavlakis and Rachel Roegman specifically address the question of clothing in "How Dress Codes Criminalize Males and Sexualize Females of Color," *Phi Delta Kappan* (2018): 54–58.
9. Clark Butler, "Children's Rights: An Historical and Conceptual Analysis," in *Child Rights: The Movement, International Law, and Opposition*, ed. Clark Butler (West Lafayette, IN: Purdue University Press, 2014), 15.
10. For more information on the development of children's rights on a global scale, see Courtney Farrell, *Children's Rights* (Edina, MN: Abdo, 2010).
11. "Derechos de los niños, niñas y adolescentes," *Secretaría de Relaciones Exteriores*, July 5, 2012, https://www.gob.mx/sre/acciones-y-programas/derechos-de-los-ninos-ninas-y-adolescentes.
12. Ricardo Ruiz Carbonell, *Análisis jurídico de la nueva Ley General de los Derechos de Niñas, Niños y Adolescentes* (Mexico City: Comisión Ejecutiva de Atención A Víctimas, 2016), 22–23; "Constitución política" 10.
13. The Ley Federal del Trabajo has provided daycare for state workers since 1963. Comisión de la Infancia de la Unión Nacional de Mujeres Mexicanas, Unión Nacional de Mujeres Mexicanas, et al., "Proyecto de Modificaciones a la Ley de Guarderías Infantiles," July 1968, Archivo Histórico de la Universidad Iberoamericana, Ana Victoria Jiménez Collection, Mexico City. For information on the legal provision for daycare, see "Decreto por el que se expide la Ley General de Prestación de Servicios Atención, Cuidado y Desarrollo Integral Infantil," *Diario Oficial de la Federación,* October 24, 2011, 107.
14. "Decreto por el que se expide la Ley General de los Derechos de Niñas, Niños y Adolescentes, y se reforman diversas disposiciones de la Ley General de Prestación de Servicios para la Atención, Cuidado y Desarrollo Integral Infantil," *Diario Oficial de la Federación*, December 4, 2014, http://dof.gob.mx/nota_detalle.php?codigo=5374143&fecha=04/12/2014.
15. Gustavo Guerra, "Mexico: Children's Rights," in *Children's Rights: Laws and Practices in Sixteen Nations*, ed. Brooke Dabney and Michael Eldridge (New York: Nova Publishers, 2013), 165.
16. "Decreto por el que se expide la Ley General de los Derechos."
17. "Decreto por el que se expide la Ley General de los Derechos."
18. "Decreto por el que se expide la Ley General de los Derechos."

19. "Decreto por el que se expide la Ley General de los Derechos."
20. "Decreto por el que se expide la Ley General de Prestación."
21. Guerra, "Mexico," 169.
22. Martin Guggenheim, *What's Wrong with Children's Rights* (Cambridge, MA: Harvard University Press, 2005), 211–212.
23. The CNDH is a government-funded institution that advocates for human rights in Mexico's courts and in mediation programs. It also provides workshops to schools, nonprofit organizations and the public sector. In December 2019 alone, its workshops reached more than 75,000 people working in the Mexican ministry of health, the prison system, and federal, state and local prosecutors' offices. Comisión Nacional de los Derechos Humanos, "CNDH México. Presentación gráfica. Diciembre 2019," December 2019, 24, https://www.cndh.org.mx/sites/default/files/doc/informes/Actividades/2019_dic_PG.pdf.
24. Yadira Hidalgo González, "Presentación," in *Historias de niñas extraordinarias 2*, 15.
25. A total of 147 girls participated in the short-story competition that led to *Historias de niñas extraordinarias*, which published thirty stories. See Hidalgo González "Presentación," in *Historias de niñas extraordinarias,* 14. Most authors were seven years old (seven girls), eight (nine girls), and nine (five girls); there were no twelve-year-olds. For the second publication, 206 girls participated in the competition for *Historias de niñas extraordinarias 2, which* published thirty-three stories. Most authors were eight years old (seven girls) and nine (ten).
26. Hidalgo González, "Presentación," in *Historias de niñas extraordinarias 2, 14.*
27. A third installment of the series, published in 2018, was launched at a children's book fair in the fall of 2019.
28. Perry Nodelman, *The Hidden Adult: Defining Children's Literature* (Baltimore, MD: Johns Hopkins University Press, 2008), 242.
29. Nodelman, 78–80.
30. Socorro Venegas, interviewed in Emily Hind, ed., *Literatura infantil y juvenil mexicana: Entrevistas* (New York: Peter Lang, 2020), 18–21.
31. Daniel Goldin, interviewed in Emily Hind, ed., *Literatura infantil y juvenil mexicana: entrevistas* (New York: Peter Lang, 2020), 14.
32. Emily Hind, introduction to *Literatura infantil y juvenil mexicana: entrevistas*, ed. Emily Hind (New York: Peter Lang, 2020), 1–2.
33. Hind, 3–4.
34. Mary Branley, "Writing with Children: From Teacher to Writer," *Bookbird: A Journal of International Children's Literature* 55, no. 2 (2017): 65–67.
35. Branley's article does not say how many children were involved; the information on the publisher's website states that it was a "team of 11 and 12 year old children in Scoil Ursula Primary School." "Rebellion in the Village: NEW Adventure Novel," *Kids' Own Publishing Partnership* (Sligo: Kids' Own, 2013).
36. Branley, "Writing with Children," 66.

37. Branley, 65.
38. Yadira Hidalgo González, interview by Francia Bautista, Feria Nacional del Libro Infantil y Juvenil, Xalapa, Veracruz, *Cosas Olvidadas-Eureka Medios*, July 28, 2017, video, 2:22, https://www.facebook.com/cosasolvidadasxalapa/videos/1305057219603511/UzpfSTYzNTQwNzQ5NDoxMDE1NjQxMTI4OTE4MjQ5NQ/?filters_rp_author=stories-feed-friends.
39. Helen Bradford and Dominic Wyse, "Writing and Writers: The Perceptions of Young Children and Their Parents," *Early Years* 33, no. 3 (2013): 252, 257.
40. Hannia Laiz García, "Triunfos logrados: La historia de la extraordinaria niña Hannia," in *Historias de niñas extraordinarias* 2, 65.
41. Laiz García, 65.
42. Laiz García, 67.
43. Laiz García, 65.
44. Zavala, "Boundaries of Serial Narrative," 283.
45. Amy Lee Pensado Ortega, "Una buena niña," in *Historias de niñas extraordinarias*, 120–121.
46. Diana Danae Gómez Callejas, "La niña hada," in *Historias de niñas extraordinarias*, 146; Zulma González García, "La niña que quería cambiar su ciudad," in *Historias de niñas extraordinarias*, 39.
47. Hidalgo González, "Presentación," in *Historias de niñas extraordinarias*, 14; Hidalgo González, "Presentación," in *Historias de niñas extraordinarias* 2, 15.
48. Karla Zoé Rebolledo Argueta, "Las salvadoras," in *Historias de niñas extraordinarias*, 63.
49. Marbella Fernández García, "Escribiendo mi futuro," in *Historias de niñas extraordinarias*, 99.
50. Polit Dueñas's *Unwanted Witnesses* examines the work of Marcela Turati, Daniela Rea, Sandra Rodríguez, Patricia Nieto, and María Eugenia Ludueña—which subtly suggests that the narrative journalists who best chronicle social suffering are women.
51. Lidia Salomé Pérez Villavicencio to Vicente Fox, February 13, 2006, Vicente Fox Quesada I Collection, Coordinación General de Administración, Red Federal de Servicio a la Ciudadanía, 2002–2005, Archivo General de la Nación.
52. Pérez Villavicencio to Fox.
53. There are other examples of children writing letters to the president, but they do not relate to questions of human rights, violence, or injustice.
54. Pastora Morales Condado and Rocio Vasquez Morales to President of the United Mexican States, received June 10, 2005, Vicente Fox Quesada I Collection, Coordinación General de Administración, Red Federal de Servicio a la Ciudadanía, 2002–2005, Archivo General de la Nación.
55. Morales Condado and Vasquez Morales to President.
56. Fidelia Hernández Juárez to Vicente Fox Quesada, February 27, 2002, Vicente Fox Quesada I Collection, Coordinación General de Administración, Red Federal de Servicio a la Ciudadanía, 2002–2005, Archivo General de la Nación.

57. Arturo Jiménez Salazar to Martín Orenday Barrones and María Elena León Pérez, January 25, 2001, Vicente Fox Quesada I Collection, Coordinación General de Administración, Red Federal de Servicio a la Ciudadanía, 2001–2002, Archivo General de la Nación.
58. Diana Laura Osorio Vélez, "¡Ya no más!," in *Historias de niñas extraordinarias* 2, 135.
59. Osorio Vélez, 135–136.
60. Darianny Torres Hernández, "La muerte de la creatividad," in *Historias de niñas extraordinarias*, 138.
61. Torres Hernández, 139.
62. Torres Hernández, 141.
63. Alejandro Márquez Jiménez, editorial in *Perfiles Educativos* 37, no. 150 (2015): 4.
64. Márquez Jiménez, 4.
65. Helena Macario Hernández, "Mi vida y mi sueño," in *Historias de niñas extraordinarias*, 156.
66. Fernández García, "Escribiendo mi futuro," 96–97.
67. Alejandra Delgado Santoveña, ed., *Directrices para mejorar la atención educativa de niñas, niños y adolescentes indígenas* (Mexico City: Instituto Nacional para la Evaluación de la Educación, 2017), 8–9.
68. Delgado Santoveña, 10.
69. Delgado Santoveña, 8, 11.
70. Clive Glaser, "Champions of the Poor or 'Militant Fighters for a Better Pay Cheque?' Teacher Unionism in Mexico and South Africa, 1979–2013," *Safundi: The Journal of South African and American Studies* 17, no. 1 (2016): 43.
71. Glaser, 45–46.
72. Silvia Hernández Hernández, web form, Re: Apoyo para imponer justicia, May 30, 2006, Vicente Fox Quesada I Collection, Coordinación General de Administración, Red Federal de Servicio a la Ciudadanía, 2002–2005, Archivo General de la Nación.
73. Angélica González Quintos, web form, Re: Queja enviada hace 5 años abuso sexual, April 8, 2006, Vicente Fox Quesada I Collection, Coordinación General de Administración, Red Federal de Servicio a la Ciudadanía, 2002–2005, Archivo General de la Nación.
74. Hernández Hernández web form.
75. Tiffany Gutiérrez Acosta and Luz Leylany Trasancos Pérez, "Una cascarita por la igualdad," in *Historias de niñas extraordinarias*, 170.
76. Angelina Cruz Morfín, "Bondad sobre ruedas," in *Historias de niñas extraordinarias* 2, 56.
77. Shaden Jael Valderrábano Velasco, "Entrevista a las niñas extraordinarias," in *Historias de niñas extraordinarias* 2, 25–30.
78. Lin Bian, Sarah-Jane Leslie, and Andrei Cimpian, "Supplementary Materials for Gender Stereotypes about Intellectual Ability Emerge Early and Influence Children's Interests," *Science* 355, 389 (2017): 2–4.

79. Laura Verónica Chávez Andrade, "Las niñas merecemos respeto," in *Historias de niñas extraordinarias 2*, 82.
80. Chávez Andrade, 82.
81. Brenda Itzel Castilla Jiménez, "La niña que logró su meta," in *Historias de niñas extraordinarias 2*, 85.
82. Castilla Jiménez, 86.
83. Arely Yamileth Rodríguez García, "La lucha de Jovita," in *Historias de niñas extraordinarias 2*, 127.
84. Nodelman, *Hidden Adult*, 14.
85. Gutiérrez Acosta and Trasancos Pérez, "Una cascarita por la igualdad," 170–172.
86. Cruz Morfín, "Bondad sobre ruedas," 56.
87. Rodríguez García, "La lucha de Jovita," 129.
88. Chávez Andrade, "Las niñas merecemos respeto," 81.
89. Chávez Andrade, 82.
90. Valderrábano Velasco, "Entrevista a las niñas extraordinarias," 27.
91. Valderrábano Velasco, 28.
92. Valderrábano Velasco, 30.
93. Fernández García, "Escribiendo mi futuro," 101.
94. Castilla Jiménez, "La niña que logró su meta," 86, 88.
95. Fernández García, "Escribiendo mi futuro," 103.
96. Divanni Xareli Utrera Amaya, "Una niña fuera de lo común," in *Historias de niñas extraordinarias 2*, 73.
97. Utrera Amaya, 73.
98. Utrera Amaya, 74.
99. Matiana Aguilar Juárez, "Sara," in *Historias de niñas extraordinarias 2*, 93.
100. Aguilar Juárez, 95.
101. Aguilar Juárez, 95–96.
102. Carmen Pardo Cerecedo, "La lluvia," in *Historias de niñas extraordinarias*, 73.
103. Natalia Shirel Narváez Cadena, "La niña de las manos mágicas," in *Historias de niñas extraordinarias*, 52.
104. Fabiana Pavón Castelán, "La increíble historia de Alondra y Darilé," in *Historias de niñas extraordinarias*, 87.
105. Rebeca Deydre Jurado Hernández, "El amor de mi vida," in *Historias de niñas extraordinarias*, 166.
106. The editor Daniel Goldin mentioned that he acquired books that dealt with bullying. See Hind, *Literatura infantil*, 14.
107. Janette Habashi, "Children Writers: Methodology of the Rights-Based Approach," *International Journal of Children's Rights* 21 (2013): 19.
108. Habashi, 19. This example of men controlling women is as present or absent in Palestine as in other contexts. Habashi discusses other girls involved in the project who were recognized community youth leaders and were able to use their place in the community to further the project.
109. Osorio Vélez, "¡Ya no más!" 135.

110. Osorio Vélez, 135.
111. Paula Acic Vázquez Hernández, "Yo soy niña," in *Historias de niñas extraordinarias*, 76.
112. Vázquez Hernández, 76.
113. Vázquez Hernández, 76.
114. Laura Cecilia León García, "Lili la guerrera," in *Historias de niñas extraordinarias 2*, 75.
115. León García, 75.
116. Angelina Zamudio, "Muñeca," 24.
117. León García, "Lili la guerrera," 75–76.
118. León García, 75.
119. Heather R. Hlavka, "Speaking of Stigma and the Silence of Shame: Young Men and Sexual Victimization," *Men and Masculinities* 20, no. 4 (2017): 483–484.
120. Irma Castillo to Lic. Vicente Fox Quesada, June 21, 2006, Vicente Fox Quesada I Collection, Coordinación General de Administración, Red Federal de Servicio a la Ciudadanía, 2002–2005, Archivo General de la Nación.
121. Iain Denny, "The Sneaker—Marketplace Icon," *Consumption Markets & Culture* (2020): 1–12, https://doi.org/10.1080/10253866.2020.1741357.
122. Castillo to Fox Quesada.
123. Morrison, "Conversation: Toni Morrison."
124. Vázquez Hernández, "Yo soy niña," 76.
125. Vázquez Hernández, 78.
126. León García, "Lili la guerrera," 76
127. León García, 78.
128. Patricia Anaís Martínez González, "El libro mágico," in *Historias de niñas extraordinarias*, 21.
129. Martínez González, 23–24.
130. Rebolledo Argueta, "Las salvadoras," 56.
131. Rebolledo Argueta, 56.
132. Rebolledo Argueta, 62.
133. Rebolledo Argueta, 59.
134. Rebolledo Argueta, 61.
135. Angelina Cruz Morfín, "La princesa vengadora," in *Historias de niñas extraordinarias*, 128.
136. Cruz Morfín, 131.
137. Hannia Laiz García, "La extraordinaria Hannia," in *Historias de niñas extraordinarias*, 152.
138. Laiz García, 154.
139. Laura Turner's "Redheads: A Personal History" contextualizes misconceptions about red hair in the United States in the ideas of Catholic thinkers and ideas about biblical characters, and is thus appropriate for my study.
140. Laiz García, "La extraordinaria Hannia," 154.
141. Laiz García, 154.

## CHAPTER 4

1. Muzaffar Chishti and Faye Hipsman, "Increased Central American Migration to the United States May Prove an Enduring Phenomenon," *Migration Information Source*, February 18, 2016, https://www.migrationpolicy.org/article/increased-central-american-migration-united-states-may-prove-enduring-phenomenon; Astrid Galvin, "By the Numbers: Migration to the US-Mexico Border," *AP News*, July 25, 2019.
2. Stephanie Leutert and Sarah Spalding, "How Many Central Americans Are Traveling North?," *Lawfare*, March 14, 2019, https://www.lawfareblog.com/how-many-central-americans-are-traveling-north. Leutert and Spalding developed a model to estimate numbers of migrants, using data from US Customs and Border Protection (CBP) of apprehended adults, families, and unaccompanied minors who seek out CBP officials and CBP's estimates for the percentage of migrants apprehended each year. The data are useful, as they recognize that the number of apprehensions is not the same as numbers of individuals who attempt to migrate; they also compare findings to estimates from the Mexican government, think tanks, and nonprofits.
3. Stephanie Leutert and Sarah Spalding, "Central America Migration Model," August 11, 2020, https://docs.google.com/spreadsheets/d/1Rp8Zhwtul-WUNr3mlI-kO5rnBpFYaQRTf8aFXZ_MflY/edit#gid=172439985; Stephanie Leutert and Sarah Spalding, "How Many Central Americans Are Traveling North: An Update," *Lawfare*, August 12, 2019, https://www.lawfareblog.com/how-many-central-americans-are-traveling-north-update.
4. Stephanie Nolen, "Southern Exposure: The Costly Border Plan Mexico Won't Discuss," *Globe and Mail*, January 5, 2017, https://www.theglobeandmail.com/news/world/the-costly-border-mexico-wont-discuss-migration/article30397720.
5. Vladimir González Roblero, "La construcción de una región histórica: Representaciones de la frontera de México en la literatura chiapaneca," in *Memorias del XXV Coloquio Internacional de Literatura Mexicana e Hispanoamericana* 1 (2015): 81–82.
6. Claudia Yadira Perales Garza, "Ley de migración: 'Reforma a cuentagotas,'" *Boletín Mexicano de Derecho Comparado* 46, no. 137 (2013): 752.
7. Nolen, "Southern Exposure."
8. Adam Isacson, Maureen Meyer, and Gabriela Morales, *Mexico's Other Border: Security, Migration, and the Humanitarian Crisis at the Line with Central America* (Washington, DC: Washington Office on Latin America, 2014), 2, https://www.wola.org/files/mxgt/report.
9. The Migration Data Portal recognizes that it is almost impossible to provide accurate data on the topic of deaths and disappearances of migrants. In the data that pertain to Central America and Mexico, the portal relies on information from the Honduran and Mexican governments, as well as data from US county medical examiners and sheriffs' offices, particularly the Humane

Borders organization, which uses data from Pima County, Arizona. "Migrant Deaths and Disappearances," *Migration Data Portal,* March 17, 2020, https://migrationdataportal.org/themes/migrant-deaths-and-disappearances.
10. Nolen, "Southern Exposure."
11. Nolen.
12. "Child Migrants in Central America, Mexico and the US," *UNICEF USA,* 2020, https://www.unicefusa.org/mission/emergencies/child-refugees-and-migrants/child-migrants-central-america-mexico-and-us; "Rising Child Migration to the United States," *Migration Policy Institute,* 2020, https://www.migrationpolicy.org/programs/us-immigration-policy-program/rising-child-migration-united-states. Two famous examples of migrant children's experiences in literature are Valeria Luiselli's *Lost Children Archive* and *Tell Me How It Ends: An Essay in Forty Questions.*
13. Chishti and Hipsman, "Increased Central American Migration."
14. Nolen, "Southern Exposure."
15. "Frequently Asked Questions 'Remain in Mexico' Policy," *Justice for Immigrants,* February 2019, https://justiceforimmigrants.org/wp-content/uploads/2019/02/Remain-in-Mexico_en.pdf.
16. Julian Lim, *Porous Borders Multiracial Migrations and the Law in the US-Mexico Borderlands* (Chapel Hill: University of North Carolina Press, 2017), 144.
17. Claudio Lomnitz, "Anti-Semitism and the Ideology of the Mexican Revolution," *Representations* 110, no. 1. (Spring 2010): 1–2.
18. Luisa Gabriela Morales Vega, "Categorías migratorias en México: Análisis a la Ley de Migración," *Anuario Mexicano de Derecho Internacional* 12 (2012): 952.
19. Wendy A. Vogt, "Crossing Mexico: Structural Violence and the Commodification of Undocumented Central American Migrants," *American Ethnologist* 40 (2013): 771.
20. Laura González-Murphy and Ray Koslowski, "Understanding Mexico's Changing Immigration Laws" (Washington, DC: Woodrow Wilson International Center for Scholars, Mexico Institute, March 2011), 5, https://www.wilsoncenter.org/sites/default/files/media/documents/publication/GONZALEZ%20%2526%20KOSLOWSKI.pdf.
21. González Murphy and Koslowski, 2.
22. González Murphy and Koslowski, 10.
23. Isacson, Meyer, and Morales, *Mexico's Other Border,* 5.
24. Nolen, "Southern Exposure."
25. "Ley de Migración," 2.
26. Morales Vega, "Categorías migratorias en México," 933.
27. Morales Vega, 934–936.
28. "Ley de Migración," 1.
29. "Ley de Migración," 1.
30. "Ley de Migración," 6.
31. "Ley de Migración," 6.

32. "Ley de Migración," 6.
33. "Ley de Migración," 12.
34. "Ley de Migración," 34.
35. "Ley de Migración," 34.
36. "Ley de Migración," 3.
37. "Ley de Migración," 18.
38. "Ley de Migración," 17.
39. "Ley de Migración," 7.
40. Isacson, Meyer, and Morales, *Mexico's Other Border*, 4.
41. "Ley de Migración," 13.
42. Puar, *Right to Maim*, 64.
43. Vogt, "Crossing Mexico," 765.
44. Vogt, 765.
45. "Ley de Migración," 8.
46. "Ley de Migración," 28.
47. Nolen, "Southern Exposure."
48. Isacson, Meyer, and Morales, *Mexico's Other Border*, 2.
49. "Ley de Migración," 9.
50. Isacson, Meyer, and Morales, *Mexico's Other Border*, 6; "Ley de Migración," 7.
51. "Ley de Migración," 29.
52. "Ley de Migración," 30.
53. "Ley de Migración," 31.
54. "Ley de Migración," 30.
55. Julie Ward, "The Other Southern Border: Mexico's Forgotten Frontier in Nadia Villafuerte's *Barcos en Houston* (2005)," *Revista de Estudios Hispánicos* 53, no. 1 (2019): 68.
56. Nadia Villafuerte's reviews include "Blanco sobre blanco," review of Ximena Sánchez Echenique's *El ombligo del dragón*, *Nexos* 29, no. 359 (2007): 97–98, and "Sacrificio de doncellas, sin doncellas," review of Vicente Alfonso's *Partitura para mujer muerta*, *Nexos* 30, no. 360 (2008): 101–102. For Villafuerte's biography, see Elizabeth Villalobos, "Cartografías corporales: La violencia travesti como recodificación de la masculinidad en la frontera sur de México en '¿Te gusta el látex, cielo?' de Nadia Villafuerte," *Chasqui: Revista de Literatura Latinoamericana* 45, no. 2 (2019): 55.
57. "About the Project," *Humanizing Deportation/Humanizando la deportación*, 2020, http://humanizandoladeportacion.ucdavis.edu/en/about-the-project/; Diego Quemado-Díez, director, *La jaula de oro* (Mexico City: CONACULTA, Estudios Churubusco, and IMCINE, 2013).
58. González Roblero, "La construcción de una región histórica," 84.
59. González Roblero, 84.
60. Julián Herbert, *La casa del dolor ajeno* (Mexico City: Literatura Random House, 2015).
61. Fernanda Melchor, *Aquí no es Miami*, rev. ed. (New York: Random House, 2018).

62. Viorica Pâtea, "The Short Story: An Overview of the History and Evolution of the Genre," in *Short Story Theories: A Twenty-First Century Perspective*, ed. Viorica Pâtea (New York: Rodopi, 2007). 3.
63. Pâtea, 7.
64. Pâtea, 12.
65. Nadia Villafuerte, *Barcos en Houston* (Tapachula, Mexico: Gobierno del Estado de Chiapas, 2005), 57–66.
66. Arthur Dixon, "'An Immigrant Never Really Arrives': An Interview of Nadia Villafuerte," *Latin American Literature Today* 1 (January 2017), http://www.latinamericanliteraturetoday.org/en/2017/january/immigrant-never-really-arrives-interview-nadia-villafuerte-arthur-dixon.
67. Villafuerte, *Barcos*, 135, 146.
68. Villafuerte, 73. English translation from Nadia Villafuerte, "Cosmo Girl," trans. Julie Ann Ward, *World Literature Today* 91, no. 1 (2017): https://www.worldliteraturetoday.org/2017/january/cosmo-girl-nadia-villafuerte.
69. Villafuerte, *Barcos*, 88.
70. Villafuerte, 95.
71. Villafuerte, 125.
72. Villafuerte, 76. English translation from Nadia Villafuerte, *Ships in Houston*, trans. Julie Ann Ward (unpublished manuscript), 20.
73. Villafuerte, 76 (*Ships in Houston*, 20).
74. Villafuerte, 76 (*Ships in Houston*, 20).
75. Villafuerte, 75 (*Ships in Houston*, 19).
76. Villafuerte, 75 (*Ships in Houston*, 19).
77. Villafuerte, 81.
78. Villafuerte, 81 (*Ships in Houston*, 26).
79. Dixon, "Immigrant Never Really Arrives"; Julie Ward, "An Interview with Nadia Villafuerte," *World Literature Today,* January 2017, https://www.worldliteraturetoday.org/2017/january/interview-nadia-villafuerte-julie-ann-ward.
80. Villafuerte, *Barcos*, 76 (*Ships in Houston*, 20).
81. Villafuerte, 76 (*Ships in Houston*, 21).
82. Villafuerte, 76 (*Ships in Houston*, 21).
83. Villafuerte, 79 (*Ships in Houston*, 23).
84. Villafuerte, 78 (*Ships in Houston*, 23).
85. Villafuerte, 79.
86. Villafuerte, 79 (*Ships in Houston*, 24).
87. Villafuerte, 81.
88. Villafuerte, 67 ("Cosmo Girl")
89. Villafuerte, 67 ("Cosmo Girl").
90. As an employee of a company store, the individual receives pay in "company scrip," a form of currency that can be used only in employer-owned stores. The company store model is a closed economic system in which workers are completely subordinate to employers, confined in a circular system of debt

and repayment. This type of economic system is well documented in the history of primary resource extraction industries such as logging and mining. Linda Carlson, *Company Towns of the Pacific Northwest* (Seattle: University of Washington Press, 2003), 101–103, provides a comprehensive explanation as it pertains to mining in the Pacific Northwest of the United States.

91. Villafuerte, *Barcos*, 67 ("Cosmo Girl").
92. Villafuerte, 68 ("Cosmo Girl").
93. Villafuerte, 71 ("Cosmo Girl").
94. Villafuerte, 69 ("Cosmo Girl").
95. Villafuerte, 72 ("Cosmo Girl").
96. Villafuerte, 72 ("Cosmo Girl").
97. Villafuerte, 72–73 ("Cosmo Girl").
98. Villafuerte, 43. English translation from Nadia Villafuerte, "Turn Around?", trans. Julie Ann Ward, *Latin American Literature Today* 1, no. 1 (2017), http://www.latinamericanliteraturetoday.org/en/2017/january/turn-around-nadia-villafuerte.
99. Villafuerte, *Barcos*, 43 ("Turn Around?").
100. Villafuerte, 48 ("Turn Around?").
101. Villafuerte, 48 ("Turn Around?").
102. Villafuerte, 48 ("Turn Around?").
103. Villafuerte, 48 ("Turn Around?").
104. Villafuerte, 43 ("Turn Around?").
105. Villafuerte, 43 ("Turn Around?").
106. Villafuerte, 44.
107. Villafuerte, 83.
108. Villafuerte, 83.
109. Villafuerte, 83.
110. Villafuerte, 87.
111. Villafuerte, 91.

# References

Adler, Melissa. *Cruising the Library: Perversities in the Organization of Knowledge.* New York: Fordham University Press, 2017.
Aguirre Beltrán, Gonzalo. *Obra antropológica XVI: El negro esclavo en Nueva España.* Mexico City: Fondo de Cultura Económica, 1994.
Albarrán, Elena Jackson. *Seen and Heard in Mexico: Children and Revolutionary Cultural Nationalism.* Lincoln: University of Nebraska Press, 2014.
Alejandre Ramírez, Gloria Luz, and Eduardo Torres Alonso. "El primer congreso feminista de Yucatán 1916: El camino a la legislación del sufragio y reconocimiento de ciudadanía a las mujeres, Construcción y tropiezos." *Estudios Políticos* 39 (2016): 59–89.
Allyn, Bobby. "Cyntoia Brown Released after 15 Years in Prison for Murder." *NPR*, August 7, 2019. https://www.npr.org/2019/08/07/749025458/cyntoia-brown-released-after-15-years-in-prison-for-murder.
Anderson, Anita S., and Celia C. Lo. "Intimate Partner Violence within Law Enforcement Families." *Journal of Interpersonal Violence* 26, no. 6 (2011): 1176–1193.
Anderson, Deborah K., and Daniel G. Saunders. "An Empirical Review of Predictors, the Process of Leaving, and Psychological Well-Being." *Trauma, Violence, & Abuse* 4, no. 2 (2003): 163–191.
Ángel G., Roberto. "Narratología en la novela híbrida *No será la tierra* de Jorge Volpi." *Alpha* 36 (2013): 41–54.
Arce, B. Christine. *México's Nobodies: The Cultural Legacy of the Soldadera and Afro-Mexican Women.* New York: SUNY Press, 2017.
Arnold, Linda. *Bureaucracy and Bureaucrats in Mexico City, 1742–1835.* Tucson: University of Arizona Press, 1988.
Arriola, Mónica. "Ley para la Protección de los Derechos de Niñas, Niños y Adolescentes." *Diario de los Debates: Órgano oficial de la Cámara de*

Diputados del Congreso de los Estados Unidos Mexicanos, 60th Legislature, Year 1, Session 7, September 19, 2006, 29–33.

———. "Ley General para la Igualdad entre Mujeres y Hombres." *Diario de los Debates: Órgano oficial de la Cámara de Diputados del Congreso de los Estados Unidos Mexicanos*, 60th Legislature, Year 1, 1st Period, Session 25, November 14, 2006, 60–65.

Barros, Pía, and Martha Manier, eds. *¡Basta! + de cien mujeres contra la violencia de género*. Santiago de Chile: Asterión, 2012.

Bartlett, Katharine T. "Feminist Legal Methods." *Harvard Law Review* 103, no. 4 (1990): 829–888.

*¡Basta! Cien mujeres contra la violencia de género*. Mexico City: Universidad Autónoma de México–Xochimilco; Coordinación de Extensión Universitaria, 2014.

Bátiz Zuk, Martha. "Tragedia doméstica." In *¡Basta! Cien mujeres contra la violencia de género*, 81. Mexico City: Universidad Autónoma de México–Xochimilco; Coordinación de Extensión Universitaria, 2014.

Bello Ramírez, Jei Alanis, and Germán Parra Gallego. "Cárceles de la muerte: Necropolítica y sistema carcelario en Colombia." *Universitas Humanística* 82 (2016): 365–391. https://doi.org/10.11144/Javeriana.uh82.cmns.

Bhandar, Brenna, and Fareef Ziadah, eds. *Revolutionary Feminisms*. New York: Verso, 2020.

Bian, Lin, Sarah-Jane Leslie, and Andrei Cimpian. "Supplementary Materials for Gender Stereotypes about Intellectual Ability Emerge Early and Influence Children's Interests." *Science* 355, no. 6323 (2017): 389–391. https://doi.org/10.1126/science.aah6524.

Binder, Guyora, and Robert Weisberg. *Literary Criticisms of Law*. Princeton, NJ: Princeton University Press, 2000.

Booth, William. "Mexico's Crime Wave Has Left about 25,000 Missing, Government Documents Show." *Washington Post*, November 23, 2012, https://www.washingtonpost.com/world/the_americas/mexicos-crime-wave-has-left-upto-25000-missing-government-documents-show/2012/11/29/7ca4ee44-3a6a-11e2-9258-ac7c78d5c680_story.html?noredirect=on&utm_term=.0b136d722485.

Bradford, Helen, and Dominic Wyse. "Writing and Writers: The Perceptions of Young Children and Their Parents." *Early Years* 33, no. 3 (2013): 252–265. https://doi.org/10.1080/09575146.2012.744957.

Branley, Mary. "Writing with Children: From Teacher to Writer." *Bookbird: A Journal of International Children's Literature* 55, no. 2 (2017): 64–67. https://doi.org/10.1353/bkb.2017.0026.

Brescia, Pablo, and Oswaldo Estrada, eds. *McCrack: McOndo, el Crack y los destinos de la literatura latinoamericana*. Madrid: Albatrós, 2018.

———. Introduction to *McCrack: McOndo, el Crack y los destinos de la literatura latinoamericana*, 11–19. Madrid: Albatrós, 2018.

Breu, Christopher, and Elizabeth A. Hatmaker, eds. *Noir Affect*. New York: Fordham University Press, 2020.

Brouillette, Sara. *UNESCO and the Fate of the Literary*. Palo Alto, CA: Stanford University Press, 2019.

Brooks, Peter. "Clues, Evidence, Detection: Law Stories." *Narrative* 25, no. 1 (2017): 1–28.

Butler, Clark. "Children's Rights: An Historical and Conceptual Analysis." In *Child Rights: The Movement, International Law, and Opposition*, edited by Clark Butler, 13–37. West Lafayette, IN: Purdue University Press, 2014.

Calderón Ramos, Paulina. "Frente al destino." In *¡Basta! Cien mujeres contra la violencia de género*, 91. Mexico City: Universidad Autónoma de México-Xochimilco; Coordinación de Extensión Universitaria, 2014.

Calleros Villareal, Daniel. "Corales y espejos rotos: Articulación y fractalidad narrativa en *Las rémoras* de Eloy Urroz." *Chasqui* 48, no. 2 (2019): 176–189.

Calvi, Pablo. *Latin American Adventures in Literary Journalism*. Pittsburgh, PA: University of Pittsburgh Press, 2019.

Camargo, Pedro Pablo. "The Claim of 'Amparo' in Mexico's Constitutional Protection of Human Rights." *California Western Law Review* 6 (1969–1970): 201–217.

Cantarello, Matteo. "From Threat to Norm: The Changing Role of Crime in Contemporary Mexican Fiction." *Romance Notes* 60, no. 2 (2020): 395–407.

Carlson, Laura. *Company Towns of the Pacific Northwest*. Seattle: University of Washington Press, 2003.

Castilla Jiménez, Brenda Itzel. "La niña que logró su meta." In *Historias de niñas extraordinarias 2*, edited by Marisol Polanco Mendoza, 85–88. Xalapa, Mexico: Instituto Municipal de las Mujeres de Xalapa; Ayuntamiento Constitucional de Xalapa de Enríquez, 2017.

Castillo, Debra A., María Gudelia Rangel Gómez, and Armando Rosas Solís. "Violence and Transvestite/Transgender Sex Workers in Tijuana." In *Gender Violence at the US-Mexico Border: Media Representation and Public Response*, edited by Héctor Domínguez-Ruvalcaba and Ignacio Corona, 14–34. Tucson: University of Arizona Press.

Castro, Yuyu/Carmen. "Única." In *¡Basta! Cien mujeres contra la violencia de género*, 114. Mexico City: Universidad Autónoma de México–Xochimilco; Coordinación de Extensión Universitaria, 2014.

Cervantes Saavedra, Miguel de. *Don Quijote de la Mancha*. 1605 and 1615. Edited by Martín de Riquer. Barcelona: Editorial Juventud, 2000.

Chandler, Brian T. "The Scale of History in Jorge Volpi's *En busca de Klingsor*." *Hispania* 101, no. 3 (2018): 422–432. https://doi.org/10.1353/hpn.2018.0148.

Chávez Andrade, Laura Verónica. "Las niñas merecemos respeto." In *Historias de niñas extraordinarias 2*, edited by Marisol Polanco Mendoza, 79–84. Xalapa, Mexico: Instituto Municipal de las Mujeres de Xalapa; Ayuntamiento Constitucional de Xalapa de Enríquez, 2017.

Chávez Castañeda, Ricardo, Ignacio Padilla, Pedro Ángel Palou, Eloy Urroz, and Jorge Volpi. *Manifiesto del Crack (1996)/Postmanifiesto del Crack (1996–2006)*. Miami: La Pereza, 2017.

———. "Crack Manifesto." Translated by Cecilia Bartolin and Scott Miller. In *The Mexican Crack Writers: History and Criticism*, edited by Héctor Jaimes, 177–190. New York: Palgrave Macmillan, 2017.

———. "Crack Postmanifiesto (1996–2016)." Translated by Ezra Fitz. In *The Mexican Crack Writers: History and Criticism*, edited by Héctor Jaimes, 191–203. New York: Palgrave Macmillan, 2017.

Chishti, Muzaffar, and Faye Hipsman. "Increased Central American Migration to the United States May Prove an Enduring Phenomenon." *Migration Information Source*, February 18, 2016. https://www.migrationpolicy.org/article/increased-central-american-migration-united-states-may-prove-enduring-phenomenon.

Cohen, Sarah, Rebecca R. Ruiz and Sarah Childress. "Departments Are Slow to Police Their Own Abusers." *New York Times*, November 23, 2013. http://www.nytimes.com/projects/2013/police-domestic-abuse/index.html.

Collado Campos, Alejandra Nallely. "Los efectos y las imposibilidades." In *¡Basta! Cien mujeres contra la violencia de género*, 18. Mexico City: Universidad Autónoma de México–Xochimilco; Coordinación de Extensión Universitaria, 2014.

Collí Ek, Víctor Manuel. "Improving Human Rights in Mexico: Constitutional Reforms, International Standards, and New Requirements for Judges." *Human Rights Brief* 20, no. 1 (2012): 7–14.

Comisión Nacional de los Derechos Humanos. "CNDH México. Presentación gráfica. Diciembre 2019." December 2019. https://www.cndh.org.mx/sites/default/files/doc/informes/Actividades/2019_dic_PG.pdf.

———. "Consejo Consultivo. Informe mensual. Septiembre 2020." September 2020. https://www.cndh.org.mx/informe-mensual-consejo-consultivo.

———. *11 de octubre: Día internacional de la niña*. Mexico City: Comisión Nacional de los Derechos Humanos, 2017.

Comisión Nacional de los Derechos Humanos, ed. *¿Qué es la violencia familiar y cómo contrarrestarla? Todos los seres humanos nacemos libres e iguales en dignidad y en derechos*. Mexico City: Comisión Nacional de los Derechos Humanos, Prográfico, 2017.

"Constitución Política de los Estados Unidos Mexicanos: Texto Vigente." *Cámara de Diputados*, 2020. http://www.diputados.gob.mx/LeyesBiblio/pdf/1_080520.pdf.

Corona Meneses, Elodia. "El curso de inglés." In *¡Basta! Cien mujeres contra la violencia de género*, 49. Mexico City: Universidad Autónoma de México-Xochimilco; Coordinación de Extensión Universitaria, 2014.

Corona, Ignacio, and Beth Jörgensen, eds. *The Contemporary Mexican Chronicle: Theoretical Perspectives on a Liminal Genre*. Albany, NY: SUNY Press, 2002.

Corona, Ignacio, and Beth Jörgensen. Introduction to *The Contemporary Mexican Chronicle: Theoretical Perspectives on a Liminal Genre*, 1–21. Albany, NY: SUNY Press, 2002.

Coulon, Ana Luisa. "Sobre la extrema violencia en la vida cotidiana: Por el lado salvaje, de Nadia Villafuerte." *Romance Notes* 54 (2014): 85–92.

Cortázar, Julio. *Rayuela*. 1963. Buenos Aires: Sudamericana, 1966.

Craig-Odders, Renée W., Jacky Collins, and Glen S. Close, eds. *Hispanic and Luso-Brazilian Detective Fiction: Essays on the* Género Negro *Tradition*. New York: McFarland, 2006.

Cruz, Ana, dir. *Las sufragistas/The Suffragists*. Mexico City: Instituto Mexicano de Cinematografía, 2012.

Cruz Morfín, Angelina. "Bondad sobre ruedas." In *Historias de niñas extraordinarias* 2, edited by Marisol Polanco Mendoza, 55–59. Xalapa, Mexico: Instituto Municipal de las Mujeres de Xalapa; Ayuntamiento Constitucional de Xalapa de Enríquez, 2017.

———. "La princesa vengadora." In *Historias de niñas extraordinarias*, edited by Guillermo Melo Guzmán, 128–131. Xalapa, Mexico: Instituto Municipal de las Mujeres de Xalapa; Ayuntamiento Constitucional de Xalapa de Enríquez, 2016.

Cruz Salazar, Tania. "Lucinda." *¡Basta! Cien mujeres contra la violencia de género*, 110. Mexico City: Universidad Autónoma de México-Xochimilco; Coordinación de Extensión Universitaria, 2014.

de Courcelles, Dominique. "El 'affaire Cassez' visto de México." *African Yearbook of Rhetoric* 3, no. 1 (2012): 59–67.

de la Mora, Sergio. *Cinemachismo: Masculinities and Sexuality in Mexican Film*. Austin: University of Texas Press, 2006.

"Decreto por el que se adiciona un quinto párrafo al Artículo 18 de la Constitución Política de los Estados Unidos Mexicanos." *Diario Oficial de la Federación*, February 4, 1977. https://archivos.juridicas.unam.mx/www/legislacion/federal/reformas/rc085.pdf.

"Decreto por el que se expide la Ley General de los Derechos de Niñas, Niños y Adolescentes, y se reforman diversas disposiciones de la Ley General de Prestación de Servicios para la Atención, Cuidado y Desarrollo Integral Infantil." *Diario oficial de la federación*, December 4, 2014. http://dof.gob.mx/nota_detalle.php?codigo=5374143&fecha=04/12/2014.

"Decreto por el que se expide la Ley General de Prestación de Servicios para la Atención, Cuidado y Desarrollo Integral Infantil." *Diario Oficial de la Federación*, October 24, 2011, 107–122.

"Decreto por el que se reforman diversas disposiciones de la Ley General de Acceso de las Mujeres a una Vida Libre de Violencia." *Diario Oficial de la Federación*, January 20, 2009.

"Decreto por el que se reforman y adicionan diversas disposiciones de la Constitución Política de los Estados Unidos Mexicanos." *Diario Oficial de la Federación* June 18, 2008, 3–11. https://archivos.juridicas.unam.mx/www/legislacion/federal/reformas/18062008.pdf.

Delgado Santoveña, Alejandra, ed. *Directrices para mejorar la atención educativa de niñas, niños y adolescentes indígenas*. Mexico City: Instituto Nacional para la Evaluación de la Educación, 2017.

Denny, Iain. "The Sneaker—Marketplace Icon." *Consumption Markets & Culture* (2020): 1–12. https://doi.org/10.1080/10253866.2020.1741357.

Diéguez Caballero, Ileana. "Encarnaciones poéticas. Cuerpo, arte y necropolítica." *Athenea Digital* 18, no. 1 (2018): 203–219. https://doi.org/10.5565/rev/athenea.2250.

Dixon, Arthur. "'An Immigrant Never Really Arrives': An Interview of Nadia Villafuerte." *Latin American Literature Today* 1 (2017). http://www.latinamericanliteraturetoday.org/en/2017/january/immigrant-never-really-arrives-interview-nadia-villafuerte-arthur-dixon.

Doane, Bethany, Kaitlin McCormick, and Giuliana Sorce. "Changing Methods for Feminist Public Scholarship: Lessons from Sarah Koenig's Podcast *Serial*." *Feminist Media Studies* 17, no. 1 (2016): 119–121. https://doi.org/10.1080/14680777.2017.1261465.

Domínguez-Ruvalcaba, Héctor, and Ignacio Corona, eds. *Gender Violence at the US-Mexico Border: Media Representation and Public Response*. Tucson: University of Arizona Press, 2012.

Domínguez-Ruvalcaba, Héctor, and Ignacio Corona. "Gender Violence: An Introduction." In *Gender Violence at the U. S.-Mexico Border: Media Representation and Public Response*, edited by Héctor Domínguez-Ruvalcaba and Ignacio Corona, 1–13. Tucson: University of Arizona Press, 2012.

Driver, Alice. *More or Less Dead: Feminicide, Haunting, and the Ethics of Representation in Mexico*. Tucson: University of Arizona Press, 2015.

Ruiz, Daniel, director. *Duda razonable*. Mexico City: Fluxus Comunicaciones, 2014.

Emmelhainz, Irmgard. *La tiranía del sentido común: La reconversion neoliberal de México*. Mexico City: Paradiso, 2016.

Espinoza Cid, Claudia Esthela, and Gabriela García Figueroa. "Significados de género y sexualidad en la violencia de pareja: Víctimas, agresores y policías en Hermosillo, Sonora." *Estudios Sociológicos* 36, no. 108 (2018): 571–594. https://doi.org/10.24201/es.2018v36n108.1602.

"Essential Numbers." In *Mexico Violence Resource Project*, edited by Cecilia Farfán-Méndez and Michael Lettieri. San Diego: UC San Diego Center for US-Mexican Studies, 2020. https://www.mexicoviolence.org.

Estévez, Ariadna. "El dispositivo necropolítico de producción y administración de la migración forzada en la frontera Estados Unidos-México." *Estudios Fronterizos* 19 (2018): 1–18. https://doi.org/10.21670/ref.1810010.

Estrada Orozco, Ninfa Adriana. "La decisión." In *¡Basta! Cien mujeres contra la violencia de género*, 88. Mexico City: Universidad Autónoma de México-Xochimilco; Coordinación de Extensión Universitaria, 2014.

Estrada Torres, Adaliz Patricia. "Ojos ciegos a oídos sordos." In ¡Basta! Cien mujeres contra la violencia de género, 15. Mexico City: Universidad Autónoma de México-Xochimilco; Coordinación de Extensión Universitaria, 2014.

Farrell, Courtney. *Children's Rights*. Edina, MN: Abdo, 2010.

Fernández, Macedonio. *Museo de la novela de la Eterna*. 1967. Edited by Ana María Camblong and Adolfo de Obieta. Madrid: Allca XX, Fondo de Cultura Económica, 1996.

Fernández García, Marbella. "Escribiendo mi futuro." In *Historias de niñas extraordinarias*, edited by Guillermo Melo Guzmán, 96–103. Xalapa, Mexico: Instituto Municipal de las Mujeres de Xalapa; Ayuntamiento Constitucional de Xalapa de Enríquez, 2016.

Franken K[urzen], Clemens A. "*En busca de Klingsor* de Jorge Volpi: Una novela con formato policial híbrido, posmoderno y poscolonial." *Acta Literaria* 44 (2012): 53–72.

Franken Kurzen, Clemens, and Magda Sepúlveda. *Tinta de sangre: Narrativa policíaca chilena en el siglo XX*. Santiago de Chile: Ediciones UCSH, 2009.

Franks, Mary Anne. "Men, Women, and Optimal Violence." *University of Illinois Law Review* 2016, no. 3 (2016): 929–968.

Fregoso, Rosa-Linda and Cynthia Bejarano. "Introduction: A Cartography of Feminicide in the Americas." In *Terrorizing Women: Feminicide in the Americas*, edited by Rosa-Linda Fregoso and Cynthia Bejarano, 1–42. Durham, NC: Duke University Press, 2010.

Frug, Mary Joe. "A Postmodern Feminist Legal Manifesto (An Unfinished Draft)." *Harvard Law Review* 105, no. 5 (1992): 1045–1075.

Galván, Melissa. "¡Adiós, PGR! México 'da a luz' a la Fiscalía General de la República." December 20, 2018. https://politica.expansion.mx/mexico/2018/12/20/adios-pgr-mexico-da-a-luz-a-la-fiscalia-general-de-la-republica.

Galvin, Astrid. "By the Numbers: Migration to the US-Mexico Border." *AP News*. July 25, 2019.

Gaspar de Alba, Alicia, with Georgina Guzmán, eds. *Making a Killing: Femicide, Free Trade, and La Frontera*. Austin: University of Texas Press, 2010.

Gaspar de Alba, Alicia. "Poor Brown Female: The Miller's Compensation for 'Free' Trade." In *Making a Killing: Femicide, Free Trade, and La Frontera*, edited by Alicia Gaspar de Alba and Georgina Guzmán. 63–93. Austin: University of Texas Press, 2010.

Githiora, Chege J. *Afro-Mexicans: Discourse of Race and Identity on the African Diaspora*. Trenton, NJ: Africa World Press, 2008.

Glaser, Clive. "Champions of the Poor or 'Militant Fighters for a Better Pay Cheque?' Teacher Unionism in Mexico and South Africa, 1979–2013." *Safundi: The Journal of South African and American Studies* 17, no. 1 (2016): 40–62. https://doi.org/10.1080/17533171.2015.1118868.

Godoy Cárdenas, Jorge. "Ley General de Acceso a las Mujeres a una Vida Libre de Violencia." *Diario de los Debates: Órgano oficial de la Cámara de Diputados del Congreso de los Estados Unidos Mexicanos*, 60th Legislature, Year 1, 1st Recess, Session 5, January 24, 2007, 173–175.

Gómez Beltrán, Roberto. "El que la hace, ¿la paga? *Dos crímenes* de Jorge Ibargüengoitia." In *Escena del crimen: Estudios sobre narrativa policíaca mexicana*, edited by Miguel G. Rodríguez Lozano, 37–51. Mexico City: UNAM Press, 2009.

Gómez Callejas, Diana Danae. "La niña hada." In *Historias de niñas extraordinarias*, edited by Guillermo Melo Guzmán, 146–147. Xalapa, Mexico: Instituto Municipal de las Mujeres de Xalapa; Ayuntamiento Constitucional de Xalapa de Enríquez, 2016.

González Canseco, Carla Patricia. "Cortina." In *¡Basta! Cien mujeres contra la violencia de género*, 35. Mexico City: Universidad Autónoma de México-Xochimilco; Coordinación de Extensión Universitaria, 2014.

González García, Zulma. "La niña que quería cambiar su ciudad." In *Historias de niñas extraordinarias 2*, edited by Marisol Polanco Mendoza, 39–42. Xalapa, Mexico: Instituto Municipal de las Mujeres de Xalapa; Ayuntamiento Constitucional de Xalapa de Enríquez, 2017.

González Roblero, Vladimir. "La construcción de una región histórica: Representaciones de la frontera de México en la literatura chiapaneca." *Memorias del XXV Coloquio Internacional de Literatura Mexicana e Hispanoamericana* 1 (2015): 77–88.

González Rodríguez, Sergio. *The Femicide Machine*. Translated by Michael Parker-Stainback. Los Angeles: Semiotext(e), 2012.

———. *Huesos en el desierto*. 2002. Barcelona: Anagrama, 2010.

González-Murphy, Laura, and Ray Koslowski. *Understanding Mexico's Changing Immigration Laws*. Washington, DC: Woodrow Wilson International Center for Scholars, Mexico Institute. March 2011. https://www.wilsoncenter.org/sites/default/files/media/documents/publication/GONZALEZ%20%2526%20KOSLOWSKI.pdf.

González, Cecilia. "Amor, miedo y costumbre." In *¡Basta! Cien mujeres contra la violencia de género*, 39. Mexico City: Universidad Autónoma de México-Xochimilco; Coordinación de Extensión Universitaria, 2014.

Graeber, David. *Bullshit Jobs: A Theory*. New York: Simon and Schuster, 2018.

Graeber, David. *The Utopia of Rules: On Technology, Stupidity, and the Secret Joys of Bureaucracy*. Hoboken, NJ: Melville House, 2015.

Grant, Julienne, Jonathan Pratter, Bianca Anderson, Marisol Floren-Romero, Jootaek Lee, Lyonette Louis-Jacques, Teresa Miguel-Stearns and Sergio Stone l. "Mexican Law and Legal Research." American Association of Law Libraries, 2014. https://lawecommons.luc.edu/facpubs/513.

Guerra, Gustavo. "Mexico: Children's Rights." In *Children's Rights: Laws and Practices in Sixteen Nations*, edited by Brooke Dabney and Michael Eldridge, 165–172. New York: Nova Publishers, 2013.

Guggenheim, Martin. *What's Wrong with Children's Rights*. Cambridge, MA: Harvard University Press, 2005.

Gulick, Anne W. *Literature, Law, and Rhetorical Performance in the Anticolonial Atlantic*. Columbus: Ohio State University Press, 2016.

Gutiérrez Acosta, Tiffany, and Luz Leylany Trasancos Pérez. "Una cascarita por la igualdad." In *Historias de niñas extraordinarias*, edited by Guillermo Melo Guzmán, 170–173. Xalapa, Mexico: Instituto Municipal de las Mujeres de Xalapa; Ayuntamiento Constitucional de Xalapa de Enríquez, 2016.

Gutiérrez Negrón, Sergio. "Ética cosmopolita en *El jardín devastado* y *Oscuro bosque oscuro* de Jorge Volpi." *Confluencia* 28, no. 2 (2013): 107–120.

Gutiérrez, Rosario. "La delegación." In *¡Basta! Cien mujeres contra la violencia de género*, 102. Mexico City: Universidad Autónoma de México–Xochimilco; Coordinación de Extensión Universitaria, 2014.

Habashi, Janette. "Children Writers: Methodology of the Rights-Based Approach." *International Journal of Children's Rights* 21(2013): 12–24. https://doi.org/10.1163/157181812X634229

Harris, Angela P. "Heteropatriarchy Kills: Challenging Gender Violence in a Prison Nation." *Washington University Journal of Law & Policy* 37 (2011): 13–65.

Herbert, Julián. *La casa del dolor ajeno*. Mexico City: Literatura Random House, 2015.

Hermosillo Núñez, Perla Cristal. "'Ni una más': Microrrelatos contra la violencia de género." Review of *¡Basta! Cien mujeres contra la violencia de género, edición mexicana*. *Revista de Estudios de Género: La Ventana* 46 (2017): 347–350.

Hernández Castillo, Rosalva Aída. "Violencia de Estado y violencia de género." *Trace* 57 (June 2010): 86–98. http://trace.org.mx/index.php/trace/article/view/386/360.

Hernández Grijalva, Eglé Margarita. "Mariposa." In *¡Basta! Cien mujeres contra la violencia de género*, 45. Mexico City: Universidad Autónoma de México–Xochimilco; Coordinación de Extensión Universitaria, 2014.

Hernández, Anabel. *Narcoland: The Mexican Druglords and Their Godfathers*. New York: Verso, 2013.

Herrera Ale, Juana Leticia. "Ley Federal de Acciones Compensatorias a Favor de las Mujeres." *Diario de los Debates: Órgano oficial de la Cámara de Diputados del Congreso de los Estados Unidos Mexicanos*. 60th Legislature, Yeaer 1, 1st Period, Session 27, December 14, 2006, 84–102.

Hesford, Wendy S. "Contingent Vulnerabilities: Child Soldiers as Human Rights Subjects." In *The Routledge Companion to Literature and Human Rights*, edited by Alexandra Schultheis Moore and Sophia A. McClennen, 69–77. New York: Routledge, 2015.

———. "Presentación." In *Historias de niñas extraordinarias*, edited by Guillermo Melo Guzmán, 13–15. Xalapa, Mexico: Instituto Municipal de las Mujeres de Xalapa; Ayuntamiento Constitucional de Xalapa de Enríquez, 2016.

———. "Presentación." In *Historias de niñas extraordinarias 2*, edited by Marisol Polanco Mendoza, 15–16. Xalapa, Mexico: Instituto Municipal de las Mujeres de Xalapa; Ayuntamiento Constitucional de Xalapa de Enríquez, 2017.

Hind, Emily. Introduction to *Literatura infantil y juvenil mexicana: Entrevistas*, edited by Emily Hind, 1–4. New York: Peter Lang, 2020.

Hind, Emily, ed. *Literatura infantil y juvenil mexicana: entrevistas*. New York: Peter Lang, 2020.

Hine-Ramsberger, William. "Drug Violence and Constitutional Revisions: Mexico's 2008 Criminal Justice Reform and the Formation of Rule of Law." *Brooklyn Journal of International Law* 37, no. 1 (2011): 291–316.

Hlavka, Heather R. "Speaking of Stigma and the Silence of Shame: Young Men and Sexual Victimization." *Men and Masculinities* 20, no. 4 (2017): 482–505.

Hobbes, Michael, and Sarah Marshall. "Murder." *You're Wrong About* (podcast). July 27, 2020. https://podcasts.apple.com/us/podcast/murder/id1380008439.

Incháustegi Romero, Teresa and María de la Paz López Barajas, eds., with Carlos Echarri Cánovas and Karla Ramírez Ducoing. *Feminicidio en México: Aproximaciones, tendencias y cambios 1985–2009*. Mexico City: ONU Mujeres, Colegio de México, Instituto Nacional de las Mujeres, 2011.

Isacson, Adam, Maureen Meyer, and Gabriela Morales. *Mexico's Other Border: Security, Migration, and the Humanitarian Crisis at the Line with Central America*. Washington, DC: Washington Office on Latin America, 2014. https://www.wola.org/files/mxgt/report.

Jaimes, Héctor, ed. *The Mexican Crack Writers: History and Criticism*. New York: Palgrave Macmillan, 2017.

Jameson, Fredric. *Postmodernism; or, The Cultural Logic of Late Capitalism*. 1991. Durham, NC: Duke University Press, 2003.

Jurado Hernández, Rebeca Deydre. "El amor de mi vida." In Melo Guzmán, *Historias de niñas extraordinarias*, 166–169.

Kadari, Tamar. "Jael Wife of Heber the Kenite: Midrash and Aggadah." *Jewish Women: A Comprehensive Historical Encyclopedia*. February 2, 2009. Jewish Women's Archive. https://jwa.org/encyclopedia/article/jael-wife-of-heber-kenite-midrash-and-aggadah.

Kaplan, Luciana, dir. *La revolución de los alcatraces/Eufrosina's Revolution*. Mexico City: Centro de Capacitación Cinematográfica; Fondo para la Producción Cinematográfica de Calidad; Instituto Mexicano de Cinematografía, 2013.

Kelliher Rabon, Jessica, Jameson K. Hirsch, and Edward C. Chang. "Positive Psychology and Suicide Prevention: An Introduction and Overview of the Literature." In *A Positive Psychological Approach to Suicide*, edited by Jessica Kelliher Rabon, Jameson K. Hirsch, and Edward C. Chang. 1–16. Cham, Switzerland: Springer, 2018.

Kitzmann, Katherine M., Noni K. Gaylord, Aimee R. Holt, and Erin D. Kenny. "Child Witnesses to Domestic Violence: A Meta-Analytic Review." *Journal of Consulting and Clinical Psychology* 1, no. 2 (2003–2004): 339–352.

Kornbluh, Anna. *The Order of Forms: Realism, Formalism, and Social Space.* Chicago: University of Chicago Press, 2019.

"La niñez en México: Datos duros." *Universia Mx,* April 29, 2013. https://www.universia.net/mx/actualidad/orientacion-academica/ninez-mexico-datos-duros-1020651.html.

Lagarde (y de los Ríos), Marcela. "Acuerdo del Pleno de la Cámara de Diputados para hacer seguimiento de los feminicidios." March 2005. http://www.mujeresenred.net/spip.php?article120.

Laiz García, Hannia. "La extraordinaria Hannia." In *Historias de niñas extraordinarias,* edited by Guillermo Melo Guzmán, 152–155. Xalapa, Mexico: Instituto Municipal de las Mujeres de Xalapa; Ayuntamiento Constitucional de Xalapa de Enríquez, 2016.

——. "Triunfos logrados: La historia de la extraordinaria niña Hannia." In *Historias de niñas extraordinarias* 2, edited by Marisol Polanco Mendoza, 65–68. Xalapa, Mexico: Instituto Municipal de las Mujeres de Xalapa; Ayuntamiento Constitucional de Xalapa de Enríquez, 2017.

"Las diligencias." *Una novela criminal* (Podium Podcast), December 14, 2018. https://www.podiumpodcast.com/una-novela-criminal/temporada-1.

León García, Laura Cecilia. "Lili la guerrera." In *Historias de niñas extraordinarias* 2, coordinated by Marisol Polanco Mendoza, 75–78. Xalapa, Mexico: Instituto Municipal de las Mujeres de Xalapa; Ayuntamiento Constitucional de Xalapa de Enríquez, 2017.

Leutert, Stephanie, and Sarah Spalding. "Central America Migration Model." August 11, 2020. https://docs.google.com/spreadsheets/d/1Rp8Zhwtul-WUNr3mlI-kO5rnBpFYaQRTf8aFXZ_MflY/edit#gid=172439985.

——. "How Many Central Americans Are Traveling North: An Update." *Lawfare,* August 12, 2019. https://www.lawfareblog.com/how-many-central-americans-are-traveling-north-update.

——. "How Many Central Americans are Traveling North?" *Lawfare,* March 14, 2019. https://www.lawfareblog.com/how-many-central-americans-are-traveling-north.

Levine, Caroline. *Forms: Whole, Rhythm, Hierarchy, Network.* Princeton, NJ: Princeton University Press, 2015.

"Ley de Migración." Cámara de Diputados del H. Congreso de la Unión, April 13, 2020. http://www.diputados.gob.mx/LeyesBiblio/pdf/LMigra_130420.pdf.

"Ley General de Acceso de las Mujeres a una Vida Libre de Violencia." Cámara de Diputados del H. Congreso de la Unión. April 13, 2020. http://www.diputados.gob.mx/LeyesBiblio/pdf/LGAMVLV_130420.pdf.

"Ley General para la Igualdad entre Mujeres y Hombres." Cámara de Diputados del H. Congreso de la Unión. June 14, 2018. http://www.diputados.gob.mx/LeyesBiblio/pdf/LGIMH_140618.pdf.

Lim, Julian. *Porous Borders: Multiracial Migrations and the Law in the US-Mexico Borderlands.* Chapel Hill: University of North Carolina Press, 2017.

Lomnitz, Claudio. "Anti-Semitism and the Ideology of the Mexican Revolution." *Representations* 110, no. 1 (2010): 1–28.

López Rojas, Alberto. "Estado de México." *Diario de los Debates: Órgano oficial de la Cámara de Diputados del Congreso de los Estados Unidos Mexicanos.* 60th Legislature, Year 1, 1st Period, Session 21, October 30, 2006, 63–65.

López-Ayllón, Sergio, and Héctor Fix-Fierro. "'Faraway, So Close!': The Rule of Law and Legal Change in Mexico, 1970–2000." In *Legal Culture in the Age of Globalization: Latin America and Latin Europe*, edited by Lawrence M. Friedman and Rogelio Pérez-Perdomo, 285–351. Palo Alto, CA: Stanford University Press, 2003.

López, Alan, and Max Holst. "Cómo usar el 911 para salvar vidas de mujeres." *México Evalúa*, August 13, 2020. https://www.mexicoevalua.org/como-usar-el-911-para-salvar-vidas-de-mujeres.

López, Alberto. "Cometer fraude electoral en 2006, principal acuerdo entre Calderón y Gordillo: AMLO." *La Jornada*, July 8, 2011. https://www.jornada.com.mx/2011/07/08/politica/009n1pol.

Lucero Hernández, Adela Margarita. "Carne de edecán." In *¡Basta! Cien mujeres contra la violencia de género*, 16. Mexico City: Universidad Autónoma de México–Xochimilco; Coordinación de Extensión Universitaria, 2014.

Luiselli, Valeria. *Lost Children Archive.* New York: Vintage Books, 2019.

———. *Tell Me How It Ends: An Essay in Forty Questions.* Minneapolis, MN: Coffee House Press, 2017.

Macario Hernández, Helena. "Mi vida y mi sueño." In *Historias de niñas extraordinarias*, coordinated by Guillermo Melo Guzmán, 156–159. Xalapa, Mexico: Instituto Municipal de las Mujeres de Xalapa; Ayuntamiento Constitucional de Xalapa de Enríquez, 2016.

Magaloni, Beatriz, and Luis Rodriguez. "Institutionalized Police Brutality: Torture, the Militarization of Security, and the Reform of Inquisitorial Criminal Justice in Mexico." *American Political Science Review* 114, no. 4 (2020): 1013–1034.

Márquez Jiménez, Alejandro. "Editorial." *Perfiles Educativos* 37, no. 150 (2015): 3–17.

Martella, Gianna M., and Jacky Collins. "Theme Issue: Hispanic Detective Fiction: Introduction." *Clues: A Journal of Detection* 24, no. 3 (2006): 3–5.

Martínez González, Patricia Anaís. "El libro mágico." In *Historias de niñas extraordinarias*, coordinated by Guillermo Melo Guzmán, 18–25. Xalapa, Mexico: Instituto Municipal de las Mujeres de Xalapa; Ayuntamiento Constitucional de Xalapa de Enríquez, 2016.

Martínez, Emma Irene L. "Sumisión: Enseñanza mortal." In *¡Basta! Cien mujeres contra la violencia de género*, 50. Mexico City: Universidad Autónoma de México–Xochimilco; Coordinación de Extensión Universitaria, 2014.

Mbembe, Achille. "Necropolitics." Translated by Libby Meintjes. *Public Culture* 15, no. 1 (2003): 11–40.

McQueeney, Krista, and Alicia A. Girgenti-Malone, eds. *Girls, Aggression, and Intersectionality*. New York: Routledge, 2018.
Melchor, Fernanda. *Aquí no es Miami*. Rev. ed. Mexico City: Random House, 2018.
Melo Guzmán, Guillermo, ed. *Historias de niñas extraordinarias*. Xalapa, Mexico: Instituto Municipal de las Mujeres de Xalapa; Ayuntamiento Constitucional de Xalapa de Enríquez, 2016.
Menchaca Castellanos, Ludivina. "Fiscalía especial de delitos contra las mujeres." *Diario de los Debates: Órgano oficial de la Cámara de Diputados del Congreso de los Estados Unidos Mexicanos*. 60th Legislature, Year 1, 1st Period, Session 27, November 21, 2006, 43–46.
Menchaca, Cynthia. "Fibonacci." In *¡Basta! Cien mujeres contra la violencia de género*, 41. Mexico City: Universidad Autónoma de México–Xochimilco; Coordinación de Extensión Universitaria, 2014.
Menton, Seymour. *La nueva novela histórica de la América Latina, 1979–1992*. Mexico City: Fondo de Cultura Económica, 1993.
Meredith, Dana A., and Luis Alberto Rodríguez Cortés. "Feminicide: Expanding Outrage: Representations of Gendered Violence and Feminicide in Mexico." In *Modern Mexican Culture: Critical Foundations*, edited by Stuart A. Day, 237–258. Tucson: University of Arizona Press, 2017.
Merina, María Eugenia. "En la cocina." In *¡Basta! Cien mujeres contra la violencia de género*, 76. Mexico City: Universidad Autónoma de México–Xochimilco; Coordinación de Extensión Universitaria, 2014.
Miller, D. A. *The Novel and the Police*. Berkeley: University of California Press, 1988.
Molloy, Molly. "Homicide in Mexico 2007–March 2018: Continuing Epidemic of Militarized Hyper-Violence." *Small Wars Journal*, April 27, 2018. https://smallwarsjournal.com/jrnl/art/homicide-mexico-2007-march-2018-continuing-epidemic-militarized-hyper-violence.
Monárrez Fragoso, Julia, Pedro Díaz de la Vega García, and Patricia Morales Castro. *Sistema socioeconómico y geo-referencial sobre la violencia de género en Ciudad Juárez: Análisis de la violencia de género en Ciudad Juárez, Chihuahua: Propuestas para su prevención*. Ciudad Juárez, Mexico: Comisión para Prevenir y Erradicar la Violencia contra las Mujeres; El Colegio de la Frontera Norte, 2006.
Monárrez Fragoso, Julia. *Trama de una injusticia: Feminicidio sexual sistémico en Ciudad Juárez*. Mexico City: Porrúa; Ciudad Juárez: El Colegio de la Frontera Norte, 2009.
Monroy Nasr, Rebecca. "Presencia y ausencia." In *¡Basta! Cien mujeres contra la violencia de género*, 97. Mexico City: Universidad Autónoma de México–Xochimilco; Coordinación de Extensión Universitaria, 2014.
Morales Gasca, Fabiola. "Modelo." In *¡Basta! Cien mujeres contra la violencia de género*, 52. Mexico City: Universidad Autónoma de México–Xochimilco; Coordinación de Extensión Universitaria, 2014.

Morales Ríos, Gabriela. "Duelo eterno . . ." In *¡Basta! Cien mujeres contra la violencia de género*, 54. Mexico City: Universidad Autónoma de México–Xochimilco; Coordinación de Extensión Universitaria, 2014.

Morales Vega, Luisa Gabriela. "Categorías migratorias en México: Análisis a la Ley de Migración." *Anuario Mexicano de Derecho Internacional* 12 (2012): 929–958.

Moreno, Rosario. "SOS ¿Nos ayudamos?" In *¡Basta! Cien mujeres contra la violencia de género*, 103. Mexico City: Universidad Autónoma de México–Xochimilco; Coordinación de Extensión Universitaria, 2014.

Morrison, Toni. "Conversation: Toni Morrison." Interview by Elizabeth Farnsworth. *PBS NewsHour*, March 9, 1998. https://www.pbs.org/newshour/show/toni-morrison.

Mújica Valenzuela, Rodrigo. "Alto." Comisión Nacional de los Derechos Humanos-México, 2017. http://www.cndh.org.mx/sites/all/doc/programas/mujer/Material_difusion/poema-Alto.pdf.

Narváez Cadena, Natalia Shirel. "La niña de las manos mágicas." In *Historias de niñas extraordinarias*, edited by Guillermo Melo Guzmán, 52–55. Xalapa, Mexico: Instituto Municipal de las Mujeres de Xalapa; Ayuntamiento Constitucional de Xalapa de Enríquez, 2016.

Negrete Sandoval, Julia Érika. "Archivo, memoria y ficción en Nadie me verá llorar de Cristina Rivera Garza." *Literatura Mexicana* 24, no. 1 (2013): 91–110.

Nichols, William J. "A los márgenes: Hacia una definición de 'negra.'" *Revista Iberoamericana*, 76, no. 231 (2010): 295–303.

Nodelman, Perry. *The Hidden Adult: Defining Children's Literature*. Baltimore: Johns Hopkins University Press, 2008.

Nolen, Stephanie. "Southern Exposure: The Costly Border Plan Mexico Won't Discuss." *Globe and Mail*, January 5, 2017. https://www.theglobeandmail.com/news/world/the-costly-border-mexico-wont-discuss-migration/article30397720.

"Nombra Calderón subsecretarios en Segob." *El Universal*, January 2, 2008. https://archivo.eluniversal.com.mx/notas/477399.html.

Nozal, Carmen. "Ciudad Juárez." In *¡Basta! Cien mujeres contra la violencia de género*, 38. Mexico City: Universidad Autónoma de México–Xochimilco; Coordinación de Extensión Universitaria, 2014.

Ordaz, David. "Denise Maerker conducirá el noticiero estelar de Televisa; se va El mañanero." *Aristegui Noticias*, May 30, 2016. https://aristeguinoticias.com/3005/mexico/denise-maerker-conducira-el-noticiero-estelar-de-televisa-se-va-el-mananero.

Ordaz, Pablo. "Literatura para liberar la verdad." *El País*, March 26, 2018. https://elpais.com/cultura/2018/03/23/babelia/1521803125_386534.html.

"Orden del día." *Diario de los Debates: Órgano oficial de la Cámara de Diputados del Congreso de los Estados Unidos Mexicanos*. 60th Legislature, Year 1, 1st Recess, Session 4, January 17, 2007, 17–24.

"Orden del día." *Diario de los Debates: Órgano oficial de la Cámara de Diputados del Congreso de los Estados Unidos Mexicanos.* 60th Legislature, Year 1, 1st Recess, Session 5, January 24, 2007, 13–17.

Osorio Vélez, Diana Laura. "¡Ya no más!" In *Historias de niñas extraordinarias 2*, edited by Marisol Polanco Mendoza, 135–136. Xalapa, Mexico: Instituto Municipal de las Mujeres de Xalapa; Ayuntamiento Constitucional de Xalapa de Enríquez, 2017.

Padilla, Ignacio. "Crack Postmanifesto." In *The Mexican Crack Writers: History and Criticism*, edited by Héctor Jaimes, 199–201. New York: Palgrave Macmillan, 2017.

Paley, Dawn. *Drug War Capitalism*. Oakland, CA: AK Press, 2014.

———. "Legal Battles in Mexico." *Upside Down World,* December 12, 2011. http://upsidedownworld.org/archives/mexico/legal-battles-in-mexico.

Palou, Pedro Ángel. "The Poetics of Crack." In *The Mexican Crack Writers: History and Criticism*, edited by Héctor Jaimes. 197–199. New York: Palgrave Macmillan, 2017.

Palumbo-Liu, David. "Fragmented Forms and Shifting Contexts: How Can Social Media Work for Human Rights?" In *The Routledge Companion to Literature and Human Rights*, edited by Sophia A. McClennen and Alexandra Schultheis Moore, 233–242. New York: Routledge, 2015.

Pardo Cerecedo, Carmen. "La lluvia." In *Historias de niñas extraordinarias*, edited by Guillermo Melo Guzmán, 72–75. Xalapa, Mexico: Instituto Municipal de las Mujeres de Xalapa; Ayuntamiento Constitucional de Xalapa de Enríquez, 2016.

Pâtea, Viorica. "The Short Story: An Overview of the History and Evolution of the Genre." In *Short Story Theories: A Twenty-First Century Perspective*, edited by Viorica Pâtea, 1–24. New York: Rodopi, 2007.

Paul, Marcie. "The Search for Identity: The Return to Analytic Detective Fiction in Mexico." In *Hispanic and Luso-Brazilian Detective Fiction: Essays on the Género Negro Tradition*, edited by Renée W. Craig-Odders, Jackie Collins, and Glen S. Close, 180–203. New York: McFarland, 2006.

Pavlakis, Alyssa, and Rachel Roegman. "How Dress Codes Criminalize Males and Sexualize Females of Color." *Phi Delta Kappan* (2018): 54–58.

Pavón Castelán, Fabiana. "La increíble historia de Alondra y Darilé." In *Historias de niñas extraordinarias*, edited by Guillermo Melo Guzmán, 86–93. Xalapa, Mexico: Instituto Municipal de las Mujeres de Xalapa; Ayuntamiento Constitucional de Xalapa de Enríquez, 2016.

Paz Soldán, Edmundo. "Alejo Carpentier: Teoría y práctica de lo real maravilloso." *Anales de Literatura Hispanoamericana* 37 (2008): 35–42.

Pedroza, Liliana. *Historia secreta del cuento mexicano, 1910–2017.* Monterrey, Mexico: Universidad Autónoma de Nuevo León, 2018.

Peña Sánchez, Ángel. "Violencia contra las mujeres." *Diario de los Debates: Órgano oficial de la Cámara de Diputados del Congreso de los Estados Unidos Mexicanos.* 60th Legislature, Year 1, 1st Recess, Session 3, January 10, 2007, 39.

Pensado Ortega, Amy Lee. "Una buena niña." In *Historias de niñas extraordinarias*, edited by Guillermo Melo Guzmán, 120–121. Xalapa, Mexico: Instituto Municipal de las Mujeres de Xalapa; Ayuntamiento Constitucional de Xalapa de Enríquez, 2016.

Perales Garza, Claudia Yadira. "Ley de migración: 'Reforma a cuentagotas.'" *Boletín Mexicano de Derecho Comparado* 46, no. 137 (2013): 749–767.

Petersen, Amanda L., and Deborah Shaw. "Mexican Women Aren't Just Fighting for Equality—But Survival." *Globe Post*, March 25, 2020. https://theglobepost.com/2020/03/25/mexico-femicides.

Petersen, Amanda L. "Breaking Silences and Revealing Ghosts: Spectral Moments of Gender Violence in Mexico." *iMex: Interdisciplinary Mexico* 8, no. 2 (2019): 22–40.

Picatto, Pablo. *A History of Infamy: Crime, Truth, and Justice in Mexico*. Berkeley: University of California Press, 2017.

Pinal, Norma. "Palabras." In *¡Basta! Cien mujeres contra la violencia de género*, 89. Mexico City: Universidad Autónoma de México–Xochimilco; Coordinación de Extensión Universitaria, 2014.

Pohl, Burkhard. "'Ruptura y continuidad': Jorge Volpi, el 'Crack' y la herencia del 68." *Revista de Crítica Literaria Latinoamericana* 30.59 (2004): 53–70.

Polanco Mendoza, Marisol, ed. *Historias de niñas extraordinarias 2*. Xalapa, Mexico: Instituto Municipal de las Mujeres de Xalapa; Ayuntamiento Constitucional de Xalapa de Enríquez, 2017.

Polit Dueñas, Gabriela. *Unwanted Witnesses: Journalists and Conflict in Contemporary Latin America*. Pittsburgh, PA: University of Pittsburgh Press, 2019.

Pulido Navarro, Margarita. "Manipulación." In *¡Basta! Cien mujeres contra la violencia de género*, 74. Mexico City: Universidad Autónoma de México–Xochimilco; Coordinación de Extensión Universitaria, 2014.

Quemado-Díez, Diego, director. *La jaula de oro*. Mexico City: CONACULTA, Estudios Churubusco, and IMCINE, 2013.

Ramírez-Pimienta, Juan Carlos, and José Pablo Villalobos. "Detección pública/detección privada: El periodista como detective en la narrativa policíaca norfronteriza." *Revista Iberoamericana* 75.231 (2010): 377–391.

"Rebellion in the Village: NEW Adventure Novel." *Kids' Own Publishing Partnership*. Sligo, Ireland: Kids' Own, 2013.

Rebolledo Argueta, Karla Zoé. "Las salvadoras." In *Historias de niñas extraordinarias*, edited by Guillermo Melo Guzmán, 56–63. Xalapa, Mexico: Instituto Municipal de las Mujeres de Xalapa; Ayuntamiento Constitucional de Xalapa de Enríquez, 2016.

Regalado López, Tomás. "El Crack vs. la crítica: Encuentros, mediaciones, contrastes." In *McCrack: McOndo, el Crack y los destinos de la literatura latinoamericana*, edited by Pablo Brescia and Oswaldo Estrada, 87–101. Madrid: Albatrós, 2018.

———. "The Crack: Generational Strategies in Mexico at the Turn of the Century." In *The Mexican Crack Writers: History and Criticism*, edited by Héctor Jaimes, 13–38. New York: Palgrave Macmillan, 2017.

Renzetti, Claire M. *Violent Betrayal: Partner Abuse in Lesbian Relationships*. Newbury Park, CA: Sage, 1992.

Reveles, José. *El affair Cassez: La indignante invención de culpables en México*. Mexico City: Planeta, 2013.

Ribando Seelke, Clare. "Mexico: Evolution of the Mérida Initiative, 2007–2020." *Congressional Research Service: In Focus*. July 20, 2020. https://crsreports.congress.gov/product/pdf/IF/IF10578.

Rivera Garza, Cristina. *Había mucha neblina o humo o no sé qué: Caminar con Juan Rulfo*. Mexico City: Literatura Random House, 2016.

———. *Nadie me verá llorar*. Barcelona: Tusquets, 1999.

Rodríguez García, Arely Yamileth. "La lucha de Jovita." In *Historias de niñas extraordinarias 2*, edited by Marisol Polanco Mendoza, 127–130. Xalapa, Mexico: Instituto Municipal de las Mujeres de Xalapa; Ayuntamiento Constitucional de Xalapa de Enríquez, 2017.

Rodríguez, Ileana. *Gender Violence in Failed and Democratic States: Besieging Perverse Masculinities*. New York: Palgrave Macmillan, 2016.

Romero Chumacero, Leticia. "Despierta." In *¡Basta! Cien mujeres contra la violencia de género*, 69. Mexico City: Universidad Autónoma de México–Xochimilco; Coordinación de Extensión Universitaria, 2014.

Rosas Pineda, Hortensia. "Desde aquel día." In *¡Basta! Cien mujeres contra la violencia de género*, 61. Mexico City: Universidad Autónoma de México–Xochimilco; Coordinación de Extensión Universitaria, 2014.

Ruiz, Daniel, director. *Duda razonable*. Mexico City: Fluxus Comunicaciones, 2014.

Ruiz Carbonell, Ricardo. *Análisis jurídico de la nueva Ley general de los derechos de niñas, niños y adolescentes*. Mexico City: Comisión Ejecutiva de Atención a Víctimas, 2016. http://www.ceav.gob.mx/wp-content/uploads/2016/06/SERVICIO-DE-ASESORIA-EXTERNA-PARA-LA-REALIZACION-DE-UN-ESTUDIO-SOBRE-LA-VIOLENCIA-CONTRA-NI%C3%83%C2%91AS-4.pdf.

Ruiz, Miriam. "Aún no responde Fox a invitación para visitar Ciudad Juárez." *Cimac Noticias* 25 (2003). https://www.cimacnoticias.com.mx/node/29389.

Ruvalcaba Rodríguez, Teresa Isabel. "Más de tres motivos." In *¡Basta! Cien mujeres contra la violencia de género*, 111. Mexico City: Universidad Autónoma de México–Xochimilco; Coordinación de Extensión Universitaria, 2014.

Saavedra Hernández, Laura Edith. "¿Por qué las leyes son así?" In *¡Basta! Cien mujeres contra la violencia de género*, 67. Mexico City: Universidad Autónoma de México–Xochimilco; Coordinación de Extensión Universitaria, 2014.

Sadowski-Smith, Claudia. *Border Fictions: Globalization, Empire, and Writing at the Boundaries of the United States*. Charlottesville: University of Virginia Press, 2008.

Saunders, Candida Leigh. "Rape as 'One Person's Word against Another's': Challenging the Conventional Wisdom." *International Journal of Evidence and Proof* 22, no. 2 (2018): 161–181.

Segato, Rita Laura. *La guerra contra las mujeres*. Madrid: Traficantes de sueños, 2016.

"Seminario 'La Constitución: Análisis rumbo a su centenario.'" Senado de la República, April 15, 2015. https://www.senado.gob.mx/comisiones/puntos_constitucionales/docs/Seminario_Constitucion/SC_conclusiones.pdf.

Shine, Jacqui. "What Perry Mason Taught American Audiences about the Criminal Justice System." *Smithsonian Magazine*, June 19, 2020, https://www.smithsonianmag.com/arts-culture/moral-order-perry-masons-universe-180975140.

Shirk, David A. *Justice Reform in Mexico: Change and Challenges in the Judicial Sector*. Washington, DC: Woodrow Wilson International Center for Scholars, 2011. https://www.wilsoncenter.org/sites/default/files/media/documents/publication/Chapter%207-%20Justice%20Reform%20in%20Mexico%2C%20Change%20and%20Challenges%20in%20the%20Judicial%20Sector.pdf.

Shrader, Stuart. "Defund the Global Policeman." *n + 1* 38 (2020). https://nplusonemag.com/issue-38/politics/defund-the-global-policeman.

Slaughter, Joseph. *Human Rights, Inc.: The World Novel, Narrative Form and International Law*. New York: Fordham University Press, 2007.

Song, H. Rosi. "En torno al género negro: ¿La disolución de una conciencia ética o la recuperación de un nuevo compromiso político?" *Revista Iberoamericana* 76, no. 321 (2010): 459–475.

Staudt, Kathleen. *Violence and Activism at the Border: Gender, Fear, and Everyday Life in Ciudad Juárez*. Austin: University of Texas Press, 2008.

Steels, Emmanuelle. *El teatro del engaño: Buscando a los Zodiaco, la banda de secuestradores que nunca existió*. Mexico City: Grijalbo, 2015.

Székely, Alberto. "Democracy, Judicial Reform, the Rule of Law, and Environmental Justice in Mexico." *Houston Journal of International Law* 21, no. 3 (1999): 385–424.

"Teatro de marionetas." *Una novela criminal* (Podium Podcast), November 30, 2018, https://www.podiumpodcast.com/una-novela-criminal/temporada-1.

Torres Hernández, Darianny. "La muerte de la creatividad." In *Historias de niñas extraordinarias*, edited by Guillermo Melo Guzmán, 138–141. Xalapa, Mexico: Instituto Municipal de las Mujeres de Xalapa; Ayuntamiento Constitucional de Xalapa de Enríquez, 2016.

Trejo Delarbe, Raúl. "Bajo el imperio de la televisión." *Infoamérica* 6 (2011): 75–85.

"Tres preguntas sobre el incremento de la violencia en 2020." *México Evalúa*, July 19, 2020. https://www.mexicoevalua.org/tres-preguntas-sobre-el-incremento-de-la-violencia-en-2020.

Turner, Laura. "Redheads: A Personal History." *The Toast*, June 28, 2016. https://the-toast.net/2016/06/28/redheads-a-personal-history.

UN General Assembly. "Resolution Adopted by the General Assembly on 19 December 2011. 66/170. International Day of the Girl Child." March 30, 2012. http://undocs.org/A/RES/66/170.

"Una cuestión de poder." *Una novela criminal* (Podium Podcast), December 26, 2018. https://www.podiumpodcast.com/una-novela-criminal/temporada-1.

UNICEF México and Mauricio Ramos. "La agenda de la niñez y la adolescencia 2019–2024." *Fondo de las Naciones Unidas para la Infancia/UNICEF*. https://www.unicef.org/mexico/media/306/file/agenda%20de%20la%20infancia%20y%20la%20adolescencia%202019-2024.pdf.

Utrera Amaya, Divanni Xareli. "Una niña fuera de lo común." In *Historias de niñas extraordinarias 2*, edited by Marisol Polanco Mendoza, 73–74. Xalapa, Mexico: Instituto Municipal de las Mujeres de Xalapa; Ayuntamiento Constitucional de Xalapa de Enríquez, 2017.

Valderrábano Velasco, Shaden Jael. "Entrevista a las niñas extraordinarias." In *Historias de niñas extraordinarias 2*, edited by Marisol Polanco Mendoza, 25–30. Xalapa, Mexico: Instituto Municipal de las Mujeres de Xalapa; Ayuntamiento Constitucional de Xalapa de Enríquez, 2017.

Valencia, Sayak. *Capitalismo Gore*. Santa Cruz de Tenerife, Spain: Melusina, 2010.

———. "Psicopatía, *celebrity culture* y el régimen live en la era de Trump." *Norteamérica* 13, no. 2 (2018): 235–252. http://dx.doi.org/10.22201/cisan.24487228e.2018.2.348.

Varona, Rubén. "*No habrá final feliz*, de Paco Ignacio Taibo II: Una mirada a la (in)justicia del detective Héctor Belascoarán Shayne." *Chasqui: Revista de Literatura Latinoamericana* 49, no. 1 (2020): 18–30.

Vásquez Mejías, Ainhoa. "Un detective tras la pista de feminicidios: *El leve aliento de la verdad* de Ramón Díaz Eterovic." *Acta Literaria* 52 (2016): 33–57.

Vázquez Hernández, Paula Acic. "Yo soy niña." In *Historias de niñas extraordinarias*, edited by Guillermo Melo Guzmán, 76–79. Xalapa, Mexico: Instituto Municipal de las Mujeres de Xalapa; Ayuntamiento Constitucional de Xalapa de Enríquez, 2016.

"Verdades y mentiras." *Una novela criminal* (Podium Podcast), December 7, 2018, https://www.podiumpodcast.com/una-novela-criminal/temporada-1.

Vergara Sánchez, Patricia Karina. "Violación." In *¡Basta! Cien mujeres contra la violencia de género*, 93. Mexico City: Universidad Autónoma de México-Xochimilco; Coordinación de Extensión Universitaria, 2014.

Vigna, Anne, Alain Devalpo, and Jorge M. Mendoza Toraya. *Fábrica de culpables: Florence Cassez y otros casos de la injusticia mexicana*. Mexico City: Random House Mondadori, 2010.

Villafuerte, Nadia. *Barcos En Houston*. Tapachula: Gobierno del Estado de Chiapas, 2005.

———. "Blanco sobre blanco." Review of Ximena Sánchez Echenique's *El ombligo del dragón*. *Nexos* 29, no. 359 (2007): 97–98.

——. "Cosmo Girl." Translated by Julie Ann Ward. *World Literature Today* 91, no. 1 (2017). https://www.worldliteraturetoday.org/2017/january/cosmo-girl-nadia-villafuerte.

——. "Sacrificio de doncellas, sin doncellas." Review of Vicente Alfonso's *Partitura para mujer muerta*. *Nexos* 30, no. 360 (2008): 101–102.

——. *Ships in Houston*. Translated by Julie Ann Ward. Unpublished manuscript.

——. "Turn Around?" Translated by Julie Ann Ward. *Latin American Literature Today* 1, no. 1 (2017). http://www.latinamericanliteraturetoday.org/en/2017/january/turn-around-nadia-villafuerte.

Villalobos, Elizabeth. "Cartografías corporales: La violencia travestí como recodificación de la masculinidad en la frontera sur de México en '¿Te gusta el látex, cielo?' de Nadia Villafuerte." *Chasqui: Revista de Literatura Latinoamericana* 45, no. 2 (2019): 54–64.

Vital, Alberto. "La novela policíaca mexicana reciente, ¿propuesta de un nuevo realismo? Apropiación de realidad en *La bicicleta de Leonardo*, de Paco Ignacio Taibo II." *América: Cahiers du CRICCAL* 25, no. 2 (2000): 179–185. https://doi.org/10.3406/ameri.2000.1489.

Vivero, Elizabeth. "Más allá del vacío." In *¡Basta! Cien mujeres contra la violencia de género* 48. Mexico City: Universidad Autónoma de México–Xochimilco; Coordinación de Extensión Universitaria, 2014.

Vogt, Wendy A. "Crossing Mexico: Structural Violence and the Commodification of Undocumented Central American Migrants." *American Ethnologist* 40 (2013): 764–780.

Volpi, Jorge. *Una novela criminal*. Mexico City: Penguin Random House, 2018.

——. "Yo soy una novela." *Nexos,* March 1, 2011. https://www.nexos.com.mx/?p=14167.

Walker, Lenore. *The Battered Woman Syndrome*. 3rd ed. New York: Springer, 2007.

Ward, Julie. "An Interview with Nadia Villafuerte." *World Literature Today*, January 2017. https://www.worldliteraturetoday.org/2017/january/interview-nadia-villafuerte-julie-ann-ward.

——. "The Other Southern Border: Mexico's Forgotten Frontier in Nadia Villafuerte's *Barcos en Houston* (2005)." *Revista de Estudios Hispánicos* 53, no. 1 (2019): 59–75.

Washington Valdez, Diana. *The Killing Fields: Harvest of Women*. Los Angeles: Peace at the Border, 2006.

Waters Hood, Edward. Review of *Una novela criminal*. *World Literature in Review* 92, no. 4 (2018): 81–82.

Williams, Raymond. *Television: Technology and Cultural Form*. Edited by Ederyn Williams. New York: Taylor and Francis, 2005.

Worden, Daniel. *Neoliberal Nonfictions: The Documentary Aesthetic from Joan Didion to Jay-Z*. Charlottesville: University of Virginia Press, 2020.

Wright, Melissa W. "Public Women, Profit, and Femicide in Northern Mexico." *South Atlantic Quarterly* 105, no. 4 (2006): 681–698.

Zamudio, Angelina. "Muñeca." In ¡Basta! Cien mujeres contra la violencia de género, 24. Mexico City: Universidad Autónoma de México–Xochimilco; Coordinación de Extensión Universitaria, 2014.

Zavala, Lauro. *La minificción bajo el microscopio*. Mexico City: Universidad Nacional Autónoma de México, 2006.

———. "The Boundaries of Serial Narrative." In *Short Story Theories: A Twenty-First Century Perspective*, edited by Viorica Pâtea, 281–298. New York: Rodopi, 2007.

Zavala, Oswaldo. *Los carteles no existen: Narcotráfico y cultura en México*. Barcelona: Malpaso, 2018.

Zavala, Pablo. "La producción antifeminicidista mexicana: Autoría, representación y feminismo en la frontera juarense." *Chasqui* 45, no. 2 (2016): 57–68.

Žižek, Slavoj. *Violence: Six Sideways Reflections*. New York: Picador, 2008.

# Index

"Amor, miedo y costumbre" (González), 81, 83
*amparo*, 13, 62, 173n4
Archivo General de la Nación (AGN), 58–59, 73, 75–76, 106–7, 123, 130. *See also* letters to Mexican presidents; *peticiones presidenciales*
aspiration (for a better future), 9, 53, 100, 165, 168
Atención a la Ciudadanía program, 70–73, 76, 79, 108–10, 114–16, 131, 166, 183n48
   letter from Márquez Hernández and, 59, 62–63

*Barcos en Houston* (*Ships in Houston*, Villafuerte), 5, 12, 139, 149–52, 162–64
*¡Basta! Cien mujeres contra la violencia de género*, 5–7, 10–11, 58, 64–65, 79, 85–86, 88, 92–93
   murder of violent men and, 90, 167
   policing and, 80–81
   *porno-miseria* and, 67
   violence in children's lives and, 123
Boom literary movement, 26–27
Branley, Mary, 102, 104, 191n35
bullying, 101, 116–18, 121, 123, 126, 167, 194n106
bureaucracy, 42–43, 57, 59, 63–64, 70, 166, 183n48
   Atención a la Ciudadanía and, 115, 131
   austerity and, 77, 80
   child protection and, 100, 109
   Graeber on, 73
   murdered women in Ciudad Juárez and, 74, 76
   neglect and, 110
   violent status quo and, 61
   *See also* policing

Cabeza de Vaca, Daniel, 76–78
   in *novela criminal, Una*, 34, 36
Cabrera Santana, Adriana, 63, 70
Calderón, Felipe, 2–3, 13, 16–18, 44–45, 51–52, 55, 58, 183n46. See also *¡Basta! Cien mujeres contra la violencia de género*; drugs: war on; Ley General de Acceso de las Mujeres a una Vida Libre de Violencia
Calderón Ramos, Paulina, 88–89
Campos Villa, Guadalupe, 71–72
capitalism, 1, 4

Cárdena Palomino, Luis, 32, 45
Cárdenas, Lázaro, 58, 183n45
Carrera Lugo, Laura, 76–79
"cascarita por la igualdad, Una" (Gutiérrez Acosta and Trasancos Pérez), 116–17, 119
Cassez, Florence, 13–15, 32, 38, 41, 174n7. See also *novela criminal, Una*
Castillo, Irma, 130–31
Chamber of Deputies (Mexico), 5, 16, 51, 88
childhood, 96, 102, 106, 124–25
children, 1, 4, 12, 109, 118, 124, 126, 192n53
  abuse of, 129
  defense of, 8
  education and, 112–14, 122–23, 128, 168
  Ley de Migración and, 143–46, 148
  migration and, 140–41, 161
  protection of, 11, 97–100, 131, 138, 146
  See also *Historias de niñas extraordinarias*; letters to Mexican presidents: about children's experiences of violence; Ley General de los Derechos de Niñas, Niños y Adolescentes; sexual abuse
children's literature, 101–2, 104, 119, 126, 138
children's rights, 11, 97–100, 113, 129, 190n10
Ciudad Juárez, 70, 80
  murdered women in, 50, 61, 66, 71–75, 77–79, 90, 181n18
  portrayals of women who died in, 92
  women's experience of violence in, 67, 170n16
  See also femicide; feminicide
"Ciudad Juárez" (Nozal), 66–68
Colombia
  incarceration in, 41

  McOndo literary movement in, 176n65
  violence in, 33
colonialism, 8, 19
Comisión Nacional de los Derechos Humanos (CNDH), 100, 146, 191n23
Constitution (Mexican), 1–2, 14–15, 18–22, 25
  "Cascarita" (Villafuerte) and, 153
  children's rights and, 97, 112, 128
  educational structures and, 113
  Ley de Migración and, 148
  Ley General de Acceso de las Mujeres a una Vida Libre de Violencia and, 55
  Ley General de los Derechos de Niñas, Niños y Adolescentes and, 96, 98
  violence against women and, 54
constitutional reforms, 2, 5–6
  criminal justice system and, 11, 18, 22, 24
  Ley de Migración and, 162
  *novela criminal, Una*, and, 14–15, 45–46
Convergencia, 51, 53
Coordinadora de Organismos No Gubernamentales en Pro de la Mujer, 75–76
Cortázar, Julio, 26–27
Crack literary movement, 15, 25, 46, 176n75
  novels, 26–27
criminal justice system, 1, 5, 20–21, 23, 57, 62, 91–92, 143
  "Amor, miedo y costumbre" and, 83
  constitutional reforms of, 11, 18, 22, 24
  courtroom dramas and, 175n52
  *Historias de niñas extraordinarias* and, 108–10, 166
  misogyny and, 70

*novela criminal, Una,* and, 7, 14, 42, 167
"120 kilómetros por hora" (Villafuerte) and, 161
*crónica* (genre), 7, 38, 40, 172n36
Cruz Morfín, Angela
  "Bondad sobre ruedas," 116
  "princesa vengadora, La," 134, 136
"Curso de inglés" (Corna Meneses), 87–88

Deleuze, Gilles, 50, 147
description (of Mexican context), 9, 165
  aspirational as, 20
  in "Cascarita" (Villafuerte), 154–55
  in "Ciudad Juárez" (Nozal), 68
  in "Frente al destino" (Calderón Ramos), 89
  Ley de Migración and, 149, 163, 167
  Ley General de Acceso de las Mujeres a una Vida Libre de Violencia and, 53–55
  in "Lili la guerrera," 129
  in "Yo soy niña," 128
"Desde aquel día" (Rosas Pineda), 66, 68
detective fiction, 15, 25, 37–40, 46, 179n128
disability, 4, 105, 107, 109, 119
disorder, 8, 29, 41, 57, 97
  "Cascarita" (Villafuerte) and, 153
  forces of, 15, 58
  *novela criminal, Una,* and, 7, 30, 33
  status quo and, 44, 48, 87
  strategies of, 14–15, 32, 34
  of structural violence, 11
Driver, Alice, 50, 66–67, 126, 180n7. *See also* feminicide; *porno-miseria* (porno-misery)
drugs, 2, 16–17, 90
  antiretroviral, 140
  war on, 2–3, 17, 170n16
drug trafficking, 2, 14, 17

"Duelo eterno . . ." (Morales Ríos), 66, 69

education, 95–96, 99, 112–14, 116–20, 122–23, 140, 144, 167
  letters to Mexican presidents and, 109, 112
  level, 69, 92, 131
  "Lili la guerrera" and, 133
  right to, 22, 113, 128
  for victims of violence, 56
  about violence against women, 57
  "Yo soy niña" and, 132
"Entrevista a las niñas extraordinarias" (Valderrábano Velasco), 117, 121–22
"Escribiendo mi futuro" (Fernández Gercía), 106, 113, 116

femicide, 48, 58, 76
  machine, 50, 67, 75
  *See also* Ciudad Juárez; González Rodríguez, Sergio
feminicide, 67, 89, 180n7
  in Ciudad Juárez, 79
Fernández, Macedonio, 26–27
flash fiction, 9, 58, 183n47
flow, 11, 21–22, 29, 55, 105–6
forces of order, 10, 14–15
  "Amor, miedo y costumbre" and, 83
  in *Barcos en Houston,* 12, 152, 163
  *¡Basta!* and, 80, 82, 85, 93
  in "Cascarita" (Villafuerte), 156
  in "Chica cosmo" (Villafuerte), 157–58
  in "Darse la media vuelta" (Villafuerte), 160–61
  letters to Mexican presidents and, 59, 61–62, 80, 93, 108
  Ley de Migración and, 144, 146
  Ley General de Acceso de las Mujeres a una Vida Libre de Violencia and, 53, 57, 93

forces of order (*continued*)
    Ley General de los Derechos de Niñas, Niños y Adolescentes and, 100
    in "niña que logró su meta, La," 122
    in *novela criminal, Una*, 25, 29–30, 33, 41, 46
    in "120 kilómetros por hora" (Villafuerte), 162
    "salvadoras, Las" (Rebolledo Arguetas) and, 134
    *See also* disorder; violence: objective
form, 6–7, 9, 14–15, 19, 57, 138, 165–68
    *¡Basta!* and, 64
    "Cascarita" (Villafuerte) and, 154–55
    *Historias de niñas extraordinarias* and, 100
    Ley de Migración and, 149, 155
    Ley General de Acceso de las Mujeres a una Vida Libre de Violencia and, 53
    Ley General de los Derechos de Niñas, Niños y Adolescentes and, 99
    neoliberalism and, 38
Fox, Vicente, 16, 115, 183nn45–46
Franken Kurzen, Clemens, 38–39

García Luna, Genaro, 32, 44–45
Gaspar de Alba, Alicia, 50, 68, 76, 181n18
gender dynamics, 116, 117, 121
genre, 7, 19, 25, 37–38, 46, 138, 165–68. *See also specific genres*
girlhood, 104–5, 124
Goldin, Daniel, 101, 126, 194n106
González Quintos, Angélica, 114–15
González Rodríguez, Sergio, 50, 67, 75–76
    *Femicide Machine, The*, 181n14
Graeber, David, 42, 70, 73–74
Guatemala, 139–40

border with Mexico, 12, 87, 142, 147, 150–52, 154, 156, 161–62
Guattari, Félix, 50, 147
Gulick, Anne, 8, 19, 166

Habashi, Janette, 126, 135, 194n108
Hernández Hernández, Silvia, 114–15
Hidalgo González, Yadira, 101, 103
Hind, Emily, 101, 126
Hine-Ramsberger, William, 22, 24
*Historias de niñas extraordinarias* (*Stories of Extraordinary Girls*), 10, 12, 100–106, 110–11, 126–27, 130–38, 151, 164, 166–67, 191n25
    education and, 116, 119–20, 123
    *See also* "Entrevista a las niñas extraordinarias"; "lucha de Jovita, La"; "niña fuera de lo común, Una"; "niña que logró su meta, La"; "niñas merecemos respeto, Las"; "Sara"; "¡Ya No Más!"; "Yo soy niña"
historical novel, 25, 27, 31
Hood, Edward Waters, 14, 27
human rights, 1, 6, 8, 74, 93, 192n53
    abuses, 9, 142, 173n4 (see also *amparo*)
    bureaucracy and, 73
    Fox's professed interest in, 72
    girls' access to, 95–96, 99
    laws, 1–2, 153, 166
    Ley de Migración and, 144–45, 148–49, 153, 163
    Ley General de Acceso de las Mujeres a una Vida Libre de Violencia and, 48, 52–53
    Mexican constitution and, 15, 20, 22
    Mexican government and, 77–79
    security state and, 45
    violations of, 14
    *See also* Comisión Nacional de los Derechos Humanos (CNDH)

ideal family, 71–72, 79, 107
immigrants, 139–42, 148–49
immigration, 141
  authorities, 148, 158
  courts, 146
  detention, 149, 153
  law, 142–43
  officials, 140, 142
  status, 144
  undocumented, 5
incarceration, 25, 28, 40, 46
  in Colombia, 41
  Ley de Acceso General de las Mujeres a una Vida Libre de Violencia and, 56
  migration law and, 142
Instituto Nacional de Migración (INM), 145, 147–48, 163
Instituto Popular de la Mujer (Xalapa), 100–101, 103, 183n43. *See also* Hidalgo González, Yadira; *Historias de niñas extraordinarias*
intertextuality, 9, 167
  in *novela criminal, Una*, 15, 30–33, 46

Jameson, Fredric, 21–22, 29

kidnapping, 13–14, 31, 72, 81
  in *novela criminal, Una*, 2, 15, 28, 32, 38
Kornbluh, Anna, 6–7, 166

Lagarde, Marcela, 51, 182n24
Laiz García, Hannia
  "extraordinaria Hannia, La," 132, 134, 136–37
  "Triunfos logrados: La historia de la extraordinaria Hannia," 103–4, 134
legal reforms, 5, 22, 24, 53
legislators, 5, 51–52, 165
León Hernández, Gloria, 69–70, 93

letters to Mexican president, 1, 59–60, 63–64, 111–12, 116, 135, 137, 144, 165–66, 192n53
  about children's experiences of violence, 11, 94–96, 99, 106–7, 123, 129–31, 138
  about education, 112, 114, 122–23
  Mexican government's response to, 77–78, 80
  about sexualized violence, 110, 114–15, 123
  about women's experiences of violence, 11, 48, 57–58, 66–67, 69, 71, 74–75, 79–80, 85, 88, 92–93
  *See also* Atención a la Ciudadanía program; bureaucracy; Calderón, Felipe; Castillo, Irma; Fox, Vicente; González Quintos, Angélica; Hernández Hernández, Silvia; León Hernández, Gloria; Márquez Hernández, María Antonia; Peña Nieto, Enrique; *peticiones presidenciales*; Romo Fregoso, Adriana Laura
Levine, Caroline, 9–10, 19, 166
Ley de Migración (Migration Law), 5, 12, 139, 142–49, 153, 155, 162–64, 167. *See also* Instituto Nacional de Migración (INM)
Ley General de Acceso de las Mujeres a una Vida Libre de Violencia, 5, 10–11, 48, 51–57, 66, 86, 93, 98, 162, 166
Ley General de los Derechos de Niñas, Niños y Adolescentes (Children and Adolescents' Rights Law), 5, 11, 95–100, 112, 123, 137–38, 171n27
"libro mágico, El" (Martínez González), 132–34
"Lili la guerrera" (León García), 127–29, 132
literary nonfiction, 7, 15, 38, 40

literature, 6–10, 38, 40
  feminist activism and, 169n1
  light, 176n65
  Mexico's southern border in, 150
  truth and Latin American, 28
  See also children's literature
López Urbina, María, 73–74
"lucha de Jovita, La" (Rodríguez García), 118–20

Macario Hernández, Helena, 113
  "Mi vida y mi sueño," 112–13
Márquez Hernández, María Antonia, 59–64, 70, 72
Martínez, Emma Irene L., 66
  "Sumisión: Enseñanza mortal," 87–88, 91
"Más de tres motivos" (Ruvalcaba Rodríguez), 86–88
Mérida Initiative, 2–3, 14, 142
Michaus, Cristina, 75–76
migrants, 2, 4–5, 8, 140–52, 154–58, 161–64, 167, 196n2, 196n9
  Central American, 5–6, 12, 140, 147, 150–51
  female, 145, 160
  See also *Barcos en Houston*; immigrants; Ley de Migración
migration, 12, 139–43, 145, 149–55, 162, 164
  children and, 161
  women's experiences of, 158, 160
  See also *Barcos en Houston*; Ley de Migración
military, 3–4, 17, 40, 50, 142–43
minimum wage (Mexico), 50, 131
misogyny, 49–50, 58, 61, 70, 83–84, 131, 160, 180n7. See also femicide
"Modelo" (Morales Gasca), 86, 88
Monárrez Fragoso, Julia, 49, 82, 170n16
Morrison, Toni, 20, 132
"Muñeca" (Zamudio), 86–88, 129

murder, 1, 3, 70, 90–91
  "Amor, miedo y costumbre" and, 83
  of women, 47–49, 66, 75
  See also femicide; feminicide

narrative nonfiction, 19, 25, 37, 40, 46
neoliberalism, 7, 38, 40–41
"niña fuera de lo común, Una" (Utrera Amaya), 123–25
"niña que logró su meta, La" (Castilla Jiménez), 118, 122
"niñas merecemos respeto, Las" (Chávez Andrade), 117–18, 120
Nolen, Stephanie, 140, 147
*novela criminal, Una* (Volpi), 2, 7, 10–11, 13–18, 23, 25–46, 60, 154, 167, 174n7
  constitutional reforms and, 5
  See also Cabeza de Vaca, Daniel

organized crime, 2, 24, 42, 140, 177n91

Paley, Dawn, 16, 18, 33
Partido de Acción Nacional (PAN), 16, 38, 45
Partido de la Revolución Democrática (PRD), 16, 51–52
Partido Revolucionario Institucional (PRI), 16, 52
Peña Nieto, Enrique, 112, 183n46
Pérez Villavicencio, Lidia Salomé, 107–9
*peticiones presidenciales*, 58, 71, 106–7
police, 11–12, 17, 73, 95, 108–10, 163, 166, 187n120
  *Barcos en Houston* and, 149, 152–53, 155–56, 162
  ¡Basta! and, 80–84, 90, 92–93, 144
  constitutional reforms and, 24
  corruption, 70
  detective fiction and, 37
  femicide and, 50
  *Historias de niñas extraordinarias* and, 110–11, 120, 131, 144

Ley de Migración and, 148–49
Ley General de Acceso de las Mujeres a una Vida Libre de Violencia and, 57
migrants and, 140
militarization of, 3
military, 147
*novela criminal, Una,* and, 30, 32, 35, 38–40, 42–43, 143
voyeurism and, 48
policing, 46, 82–84, 114, 138, 184n50
letters to the Mexican president and, 62, 64, 71–72, 79–80, 108, 115
Ley General de Acceso de las Mujeres a una Vida Libre de Violencia and, 53, 56–57
Ley General de los Derechos de Niñas, Niños y Adolescentes and, 100
*novela criminal, Una,* and, 25, 28, 40
violence in children's lives and, 95
"¡Ya no más!" and, 110–11, 127
Polit Dueñas, Gabriela, 7, 38, 107, 192n50
*porno-miseria* (porno-misery), 66, 68, 72, 76, 126
poverty, 50, 125, 129
in film, 66
Mexican children and, 94, 96, 137
migration and, 139
See also *porno-miseria*
Procuraduría General de la República (PGR), 34–35, 73–74, 77
Puar, Jasbir K., 4, 147

rape, 47, 49, 108–9, 114–15, 130–31
in *¡Basta! Cien mujeres contra la violencia de género,* 68, 81–82, 84, 87
migration and, 140, 156, 160
Rebolledo Argueta, Karla Zoé, 136
"Las salvadoras," 105–6, 134
Rodarte de Lara, Miguel, 76, 78

Romo Fregoso, Adriana Laura, 70–74, 77

Saavedra Hernández, Laura Edith, 66
"¿Por qué las leyes son así?," 81–82
"Sara" (Aguilar Juárez), 123–25
Secretaria de Gobernación (SEGOB), 76–77, 147
security, 39, 42, 46, 76, 96
apparatus of, 10
border, 142
Calderón administration and, 16–17
Mexican people's, 14
national, 144
private, 3
rhetoric of, 17, 19
US government and, 18
See also Mérida Initiative
Segato, Rita Laura, 5, 67
Senate (Mexico), 5, 16, 51
Sepúlveda Iguíniz, Ricardo J., 76–78
sexism, 49, 126
sexual abuse, 94, 96, 115, 123
sex work, 49, 96
migrants and, 140, 157–58, 160, 163, 167
short story (genre), 7, 10, 26, 122, 150–51, 166
conventions of, 163
women writers of, 183n47
Sistema Nacional para el Desarrollo Integral de la Familia (DIF), 100, 146
sovereignty, 19–20, 54, 144
Staudt, Kathleen, 49, 80
suicide, 88–89

Televisa, 13, 31–35, 38, 45, 177n91
truthfulness, 14–15, 28–30
TV Azteca, 33, 45, 177n91

"Única" (Castro), 65, 123
utopia, 20, 26, 132

Valencia, Sayak, 4, 21, 29
Vallarta, Israel, 2, 13–15, 32, 38, 41, 45, 174n7. *See also* Cassez, Florence; *novela criminal, Una*
Villafuerte, Nadia, 149, 151
  "Cascarita," 153–56, 159, 164
  "Chica cosmo," 151–52, 156–58
  "Darse la media vuelta," 158–61, 163
  "120 kilómetros por hora," 152, 161–62, 164
  "Viernes," 150–51, 163
violence
  against Asian descendant Mexicans, 141
  against women, 11, 48–49, 51–54, 57, 66, 69, 71, 76, 79–80, 92, 129, 148
  bureaucratic, 63
  children and, 94–97, 101, 104, 106–7, 118, 123, 130, 168
  educational system and, 120
  gang-related, 139
  girls' experiences of, 110, 114, 116, 126, 129, 167
  intimate partner, 47, 49, 69, 80, 83–84, 87–88, 90, 111, 187n120
  intrafamiliar, 61, 96, 126–28, 134
  Mexican government's response to, 51, 56
  migrants and, 144–45, 148, 163, 167
  objective, 4, 14–15, 32, 165
  sexual, 10, 54, 130
  sexualized, 96, 114, 123, 130, 138, 140
  structural, 11, 15, 57, 143, 165
  subjective, 4, 47
  systemic, 1, 4, 49, 52, 69, 100, 122, 167
  women's experiences of, 47, 49–50, 52–53, 72, 80, 83, 85, 92, 118, 170n16
  in women's lives, 48–49, 51, 53–54, 56–58, 64–66, 68–69, 71, 75, 80, 82, 93, 110
  See also *¡Basta! Cien mujeres contra la violencia de género*; children's rights; Ciudad Juárez; femicide; feminicide; *Historias de niñas extraordinarias*; letters to Mexican presidents; Ley de Migración; Ley General de Acceso de la Mujer a una Vida Libre de la Violencia; Ley General de los Derechos de Niñas, Niños y Adolescentes; police; "¡Ya No Más!"
violent status quo, 15, 45, 57, 72, 95, 116–17, 123, 162
  *¡Basta!* and, 88
  Ley de Migración and, 146, 148–49
  Ley General de Acceso de las Mujeres a una Vida Libre de Violencia, 51
  Márquez Hernández's letter and, 61
  Mexican constitution and, 21
  *novela criminal, Una*, and, 29, 41
Volpi, Jorge, 1, 14, 26–27, 177n77
  *En busca de Klingsor* (*In Search of Klingsor*), 28, 30, 38
  See also *novela criminal, Una*
voyeurism, 48, 57, 69, 72, 76, 80
  literary, 64
  See also *porno-miseria* (porno-misery)

Williams, Raymond, 21, 29
women, 1, 4, 8, 47–53, 84–86, 90–95, 144, 192n50
  genocide of, 11, 180n7
  letters to Mexican presidents and, 61–67, 69–80, 165
  Ley de Migración and, 145, 148, 162
  men controlling, 194n108
  Mexican constitution and, 22
  Mexican government and, 71, 77–78
  migration and, 140–41, 143, 160–61, 167
  protection of, 5, 145
  short-story writers, 183n47

See also "Amor, miedo y costumbre"; *¡Basta!: Cien mujeres contra la violencia de género*; "Cascarita" (Villafuerte); Ciudad Juárez; "Ciudad Juárez"; "Curso de inglés"; "Desde aquel día"; "Entrevista a las niñas extraordinarias"; femicide; feminicide; *Historias de niñas extraordinarias*; Instituto Popular de la Mujer (Xalapa); Ley General de Acceso de las Mujeres a una Vida Libre de Violencia; "Lili la guerrera"; "Más de tres motivos"; "Modelo"; "Muñeca"; "niña fuera de lo común, Una"; "Yo soy niña"

women's rights, 10, 51, 58, 61, 129, 133

Worden, Daniel, 7, 38–41

Wright, Melissa W., 68, 81, 83

"¡Ya No Más!" (Osorio Vélez), 110–11, 127, 129

"Yo soy niña" (Vázquez Hernández), 127–29, 132–33

Zavala, Lauro, 64, 104, 151

Žižek, Slavoj, 4, 14, 32. *See also* violence: objective

www.ingramcontent.com/pod-product-compliance
Lightning Source LLC
Chambersburg PA
CBHW030647230426
43665CB00011B/991